French Impressions

THE INNOCENTS ABROAD. Passport photo: from left to right, Mary, John, Frank, and Stephen Littell. This was a "Head of Household" passport, which meant only Frank, the passport holder, could travel alone.

French Impressions

THE ADVENTURES OF AN AMERICAN FAMILY

John S. Littell

BASED ON WRITINGS BY
MARY W. LITTELL

NAL BOOKS

NAL Books
Published by New American Library, a division of
Penguin Putnam Inc., 375 Hudson Street,
New York, New York 10014, U.S.A.
Penguin Books Ltd, 27 Wrights Lane,
London W8 5TZ, England
Penguin Books Australia Ltd, Ringwood,
Victoria, Australia
Penguin Books Canada Ltd, 10 Alcorn Avenue,
Toronto, Ontario, Canada M4V 3B2
Penguin Books (N.Z.) Ltd, 182–190 Wairau Road,
Auckland 10, New Zealand

Penguin Books Ltd, Registered Offices:
Harmondsworth, Middlesex, England

First published by New American Library, a division of Penguin Putnam Inc.

First New American Library Printing, September 2000
10 9 8 7 6 5 4 3 2 1

🅝 REGISTERED TRADEMARK—MARCA REGISTRADA

LIBRARY OF CONGRESS CATALOGING-IN-PUBLICATION DATA:
Littell, John S.
French impressions: the adventures of an American family/by John S. Littell, based
on the writings by Mary W. Littell.
p. cm.
ISBN 0-451-20098-5 (alk. paper)
1. Americans—France—Attitudes. 2. Littell, Mary W.—Family—Homes and
haunts—France. 3. France—Social life and customs. I. Littell, Mary W. II. Title.

DC34.5.A44L57 2000
944'.00413—dc21
00-35481

Printed in the United States of America
Set in Sabon
Designed by Leonard Telesca

This book is printed on acid-free paper. ∞

MARY W. LITTELL as an intrepid Texas newspaper woman in the 1930s. Her stories, diaries, and memories form the soul of this book.

Contents

French Impressions

Introduction

Like millions of readers, I was enchanted by Peter Mayle's *A Year in Provence*. The thought of packing up and moving to a foreign country holds great romantic appeal to those of us who are stuck in the flypaper of modern life. But as much as I enjoyed the book and its sequel, *Toujours Provence,* I couldn't shake the feeling that some of the author's material was eerily familiar. Eccentric Frenchmen, insouciant plumbers, and a failure to communicate, of course, are to be expected, yet there was something about Mayle's deft impressions that reminded me of . . . what?

The mystery was solved when my sister and her family returned from a vacation in Europe. We were looking at snapshots and talking about the trip when Sue asked me a provocative question: Did Montpellier look the same as it had when I was there? That was it! That was what had been rattling around in the back of my mind—all the things my mother had written and said about the twelve months we spent in France way back in 1950.

In later years my parents would shake their heads sadly and wonder what they had been thinking when in 1950, without a care, a clue, or a *sou,* they dragged me, age four, and my fifteen-month-old brother across the Atlantic. No normal people, unless facing imminent arrest, would even contemplate such madness. But my parents, the original innocents, went abroad in the sure and certain knowledge that things would work out. Amazingly, things did work out, after a fashion, and therein lies the story.

As a frequent victim of the dreaded it-seemed-like-a-good-idea-at-the-time syndrome, I can sympathize with my parents' initial idea that moving to the south of France would not be unlike moving to the south of, say, New Jersey. Oh, it might be a bit more complicated, but all obstacles could be overcome by a combination of unbounded optimism and good old-fashioned American know-how. Or at least that was what they believed at the time.

Of course, it was all my father's fault. He had always wanted to live the Hemingwayesque life of an expatriate in Paris. He could see himself at the George V, sipping Pernod or something stronger, ogling the women, and dining in three-star restaurants. And since he had no desire to write novels, he figured he would have a lot more time to drink, ogle, and dine. He was ready to depart for Paris in 1940, but Hitler got there first, dashing his plans. Furious at his bad luck, my father joined the Army Air Force with a burning desire to evict the Germans from Paris and free up a table at Maxim's. This was personal.

War, however, accelerated the unexpected. In 1943 he found himself in Texas instructing Free French airmen in the intricacies of the B-17 bomber by day and courting my mother by night. Seven years later, he was married and the possessor of two kids, a master's degree, a teaching post, and still no reservations at the Tour d'Argent. It was time to go, now or never, do or die. Unfortunately, Dad had no money and huge expenses, so this trip had to be on the cheap with a minimum of dining and drinking. The ogling, however, was free.

Wangling a sabbatical and G.I. Bill money, he convinced my mother that the trip would be a good career move for him and an unforgettable experience for her. He would enroll at the University of Montpellier, which offered a one-year degree program, the equivalent of a master's, at a price he could almost afford. Living in the south, he knew, would cost half as much as living in Paris, and the weather was better. For a few francs my parents could pop up to the City of Lights anytime they felt like it and become regulars at the Ritz.

My mother was game for anything in those days and readily assented to this preposterous proposal, dismissing dire warnings from family and friends. Although she found it difficult enough to operate here in the U.S., Mom firmly believed that foreigners, like children and pets, could interpret your meaning if you spoke loudly and clearly in English. Secure in the knowledge that she could handle anything thrown at her, she sailed off into the sunset and right into the storm.

But by then she was used to storms. Mom was born and raised in St. Louis, where her father was an attorney who specialized in criminal law—until his partner was shot dead on the street. Then, sensibly, he switched to corporate law, won a term as a state senator, and represented the St. Louis transit authority. Sadly, he died when my mother was only thirteen, leaving no insurance and a pile of debts. My grandmother was forced to go to work as a schoolteacher to support the family. Yet she managed to send her two children to college. The low point of Mom's college career was being abandoned in a sleazy roadhouse by an Anheuser or a Busch—I forget which. Her crime? Not being "fast enough" for the millionaire beer baron. She never saw him again. Shortsighted of her, but upon graduation she secured a job interview with the Big Spring (Texas) *Herald*. The editor held up a copy of the paper and asked her if she could find anything wrong with the huge seventy-two-point headline that read: JAPAN INVADES JAPAN. My mother opined that perhaps it should be JAPAN INVADES CHINA, and she was hired on the spot.

Making the princely sum of fifteen dollars a week, she moved into the penthouse of the Settles Hotel with three other girls and made a life for herself. Eventually, she began broadcasting a gossip show on local radio for an additional ten bucks a week. She also received case after case of the sponsor's product, Wrigley's Spearmint Gum—a substance she learned to loathe.

In the 1950s Mom landed a part-time job with *Life* magazine. For a Missouri girl and Texas newspaperwoman this was big-time journalism and the epitome of glamour. She loved to regale us with tales about Henry Luce, Claire Boothe, the nutty writers, and the equally demented editors and photographers. She found it incredible that a photo editor, unhappy with a shot of Mount Everest, would dispatch a crew to Nepal just to snap three pictures of the mountain. Ah, the days before corporate accounting.

At the same time she developed a successful career writing for women's magazines such as *Parents* and *Woman's Day*. Her stories, mostly about children, were charming, fragile, and funny. She wrote on the train between New York City and the suburbs where we lived. In the morning, while most commuters played bridge, slept, or read newspapers, she would curl up in the seat, produce several pieces of paper, and begin writing. When the train pulled into Grand Central Station, she would cram the pages into her purse. Then on the way home after work, she would somehow pick up the thread and continue writing. She always swore that someday she would buy a train ticket to Los Angeles and write a novel. But she never did.

When she had collected enough handwritten pages, Mom would sit at her ancient Underwood portable typewriter—the one she had dragged around with her since the 1930s—and begin the final draft. Although she was proud of her commercial success, she downplayed her abilities. And because she didn't take herself seriously, we didn't either. Mom working on another story meant pizza for dinner, which was a welcome relief from the usual cobbled-together meals she served with airy indifference.

Food, especially its preparation and its digestion, played a large part in Mom's impressions of France. This was the first time she had encountered an entire country devoted to cuisine, and that devotion puzzled her. She didn't enjoy cooking and she wasn't shy about admitting it. In an age before Julia Child, Mom found it hilarious that anyone would make her own mayonnaise. As far as she was concerned, if it wasn't Hellmann's, it wasn't really mayonnaise.

Mom was, however, quick to make reservations, for she was an adventurous eater who delighted in sampling all sorts of international dishes. As long as she didn't have to make the meal herself or clean up afterward, Mom was generally in favor of food.

But Mom's anti–James Beard attitude was to bring her into conflict with the relentlessly working-class and bourgeois women of Montpellier—a conflict Mom won by simply ignoring the gossip and buying canned food whenever possible.

Another problem my parents faced on the trip was my brother, Stephen, and his incessant crying. He was only fifteen months old when we left, but he had a voice that could drown out an opera. He cried at night, he cried in the morning, he cried when he was hungry, he cried when he was full, he cried when he was happy, he cried when he was sad. He cried constantly until he was two and a half years old. Then he stopped, and to my knowledge he hasn't cried since. No one ever figured out what was wrong with him. Was he suffering from some undiagnosed ailment? Was he frustrated by his inability to make himself understood? Or was he just being perverse? Whatever it was, his crying accompanied us everywhere like Muzak from hell.

Yet despite the clash of cultures, mores, and values, my mother found humor in most situations. She realized the truth in the truism that people are pretty much the same all over the world—especially if you speak to them clearly and loudly in English.

She recorded her impressions in a diary, then mined that diary for years, producing scores of stories about our life in Montpellier. I have used her writings as a template and added a substantial amount of both published and unpublished material. The result, I think, is a chronicle of a vanished way of life—both French and American—and a record of those funny, frustrating, and finally fascinating twelve months in France.

I chose to write this book from my mother's point of view and in her voice because that was the only way the story made sense to me. I was only four years old at the time and hardly a keen observer of the passing scene. Potty jokes were more my style. But after reading all of Mom's diaries and other writings, and remembering the family tales of our adventures, I felt confident I could speak for her. After all, I had the privilege of knowing her for thirty years and knew how she viewed the world.

Whenever I think about France, in fact, it's Mom's voice I hear. So when I sat down to write, her voice came naturally.

The project would have been much easier to complete if Mom had been around to do the work herself. Alas, she died in 1975, followed by my father in 1978.

A Word about Montpellier

I was visiting the palace of Versailles when it suddenly dawned on me that the Indiana town of the same name is pronounced Ver-SAILS. So, for those of you living in the capital of Vermont—Mount-PEEL-yer—the French know their eighth largest city as *Mon-PELL-yay*.

But regardless of the pronunciation, Montpellier can best be described by what it is not rather than by what it is. Although it is only six miles from the sea, the city is not a port like Marseilles or a resort like Nice. Founded more than a thousand years ago, it is neither historic nor very old by French standards. When Montpellier was a dry, uninhabited plain, nearby Narbonne was the busiest port in Roman Gaul. Nobody really famous ever lived there for very long, and even the weather is not as good as it is in Cannes. The food is fine, but Provence boasts an international cuisine that blows poor Languedoc, and its capital, Montpellier, out of the culinary water. I am tempted to compare Montpellier to Cincinnati, a city that gets little recognition or respect.

At the time we lived there, Montpellier was a sleepy university town with fewer than a hundred thousand inhabitants. The city's charms left the *Guide Michelin* yawning with ennui, but what do editors from Paris know about the South anyway? For wide-eyed Americans like my parents, Montpellier seemed as exotic and mysterious as Istanbul or Marrakech.

Remember, all this took place in the dim days before television, jet travel, women's liberation, and the New Coke. Nineteen-fifty had more in common with 1940 than with the Eisenhower era. We didn't even get our giant twenty-one-inch Muntz TV until 1952. Ward, June, Wally, and the Beaver were still in the distant future.

France in 1950 was reeling from the effects of the war and the lengthy German occupation: Its economy was shattered, its people worn out and dispirited. The Korean conflict was just beginning, and many people believed the fighting heralded the start of World War III—a terrible global catastrophe that would see the massive use of nuclear weapons. My father faced the very real possibility that he would be recalled to active duty. Fortunately, his expertise was in the B-17, by then obsolete; many B-29 crews weren't as lucky.

Even in a backwater like Montpellier, there was a burgeoning antiwar movement and a strong Communist party. We lived in a heavily working-class district, where the local people had been whipped up into a frenzy of anti-American fervor. I think our neighbors were extremely disappointed when they discovered that the warmongering capitalist oppressors who moved in next door turned out to be a family that evoked more amusement than antagonism, more pity than proletarian outrage.

So I guess we did our bit for international relations. In one small part of France, at least, the locals figured that if all Americans were as incompetent and ineffectual as the Littells, perhaps America wasn't the worldwide scourge they had been led to believe. Besides, as my father pointed out, a French Communist was a Frenchman first, last, and always. According to him, a typical Frenchman hated everyone from the Russians to the Americans to the butcher down the street who had shortchanged his grandmother in 1908.

My own recent experience in Montpellier began on a hot, humid day in June 1996. As I pulled up to the hotel, the doorman winced visibly at my Paris license plates. He was probably expecting to be mistreated by a supercilious resident of a snooty arrondissement. His apprehension, however, soon turned to relief when he realized I was just another American tourist with a bad French accent. He allowed me to babble on incoherently for a minute, then mercifully broke into perfect English—a language everyone in France speaks, if prodded—instructing me where to park the car. The first place I visited was the Place de la Comédie, the heart and soul of Montpellier. This is an enormous piazza, lined with restaurants, bars, cafés, and even a McDonald's. Known locally as l'Oeuf (the Egg) because of its oval shape, the outdoor pedestrian mall is closed to traffic. It is open, however, to tourists and students lounging about, enjoying the hot sun and cold pints of English and Belgian beer. As pleasant and low-key as it was, I realized that my parents would have been shocked at how modern and vast Montpellier had become.

With a population approaching three hundred thousand, including fifty-five thousand university students, Montpellier has been on a building spree for the last twenty years. At one end of l'Oeuf is old Montpellier—the eighteenth-century fountain of the *Three Graces,* the opera house, and the intricate bourgeois buildings built in the 1800s. At the other end is a silly modern fountain with three nude bronze guys spastically emerging from the water and the enclosed glass-and-steel shopping mall called Polygone.

After maneuvering through the chic shops of Polygone, you exit to confront the postmodern, neo-Roman mixed residential and business complex called Antigone. Intended as a showcase for the vaunted European Union, Antigone was supposed to be a marvel of style and technology. But wandering its sterile, one-hundred-acre precincts, I noticed that the mammoth buildings, like the dream of European Union, were beginning to fray. The unintended effect was more like visiting Brasilia than arriving in the twenty-first century.

Despite the modernization, Montpellier's older districts are probably much the same as they were fifty or a hundred years ago. Armed with a fistful of old photographs. I ventured into the neighborhood where we had once lived. I looked at the photos. I looked at the street: Was I in the right town? What had been a fiercely petit bourgeois area, crammed with tiny businesses, was now a commercial area in an Arab *quartier.* Large, sparsely stocked warehouses sold exotic spices, clothing, pots and pans, and even live lambs—presumably for culinary and religious purposes. More redolent of the souk than of southern France, Faubourg Figuerolles, like Montpellier itself, had undergone a massive transformation.

I worked up the nerve to find our house, but I didn't have the guts to ring the bell. Convincing myself that my French—or Arabic—was inadequate to explain my visit, I slunk away and returned to l'Oeuf for a much needed dose of courage: a pint of John Courage.

I mention all this in case the IRS questions my deductions for the research on this book, and because I was curious to see the places I had heard about since childhood. I would like to report that I was suddenly struck by the thrill of recognition, but I wasn't.

As I sat in the sun nursing a few ales and ogling the women (an inherited trait), I realized that for me there will always be two Montpelliers. One is made of yellowing photographs and family stories. The other is the memory of a modern, vibrant city.

Frankly, I find it more fun to see the city through my mother's eyes, as she saw it so long ago. Mom's French impressions impress me still.

Chapter 1

HAVING A *VEENDAM* GOOD TIME. From left to right, Mary, John (standing), Stephen (with his famous leash), and Frank (always dapper in his two-toned shoes) aboard the Dutch ship *Veendam*.

Great Expectations

July 1950

Okay, this was the plan: We would rise early—not a difficult chore when you have two boys, one aged four, the other fifteen months. Then after a leisurely breakfast, I would don my new traveling outfit, and with the help of my husband, Frank, I would make a last-minute check of our luggage to make sure we had everything we would need for our year in France.

The limousine would arrive and we would be whisked effortlessly to Pier 51 in Manhattan, where our luxury liner would receive us at noon. The dozen relatives and friends we had invited to see us off would pop into our magnificent stateroom for a glass of champagne. We would make a teary-eyed toast, the ship's horn would sound, and all our guests would depart. Then Frank and I would stand at the rail, watching New York harbor slowly slip away while we engaged in a wonderful conversation about what we would see and do on our grand tour.

We had chosen a slow boat across the Atlantic: ten glorious days of rest, relaxation, gourmet meals, entertainment, and as the brochure promised, "days of idleness and activity." Give me that idleness. I was looking forward to lolling in a deck chair, languidly sipping bouillon, being waited on hand and foot, and trying to decide between the lobster and the steak. Now, that's my kind of travel.

Sounds great, doesn't it?

Okay, here's what really happened: We got up early, all right. In fact, we were up the entire night, trying to quiet our toddler, Stephen, who took it in his head to cry until sunup. The only thing that pacified him was to be carried up and down the living room. If you put him down, he howled like he was being murdered. I'd like to say that somehow he sensed that big changes were occurring, but screaming all night was pretty much routine for Stephen.

Along about two a.m., our older son, John, staggered out of the bedroom, hands clasped firmly on his ears, and demanded, "Why don't the gods come and take him away?" That's what you get for reading Greek mythology to your children. But the child had a point.

I had never imagined that two brothers could be so different. John was born blond like his father, but his hair soon turned dark like mine. Stephen was still a towhead, a fireplug of a child, with a voice that could be heard in five counties. John had been an easy baby to care for; Stephen was a difficult, restless baby. Their personalities had always been as different as night and day, but the analogy that springs to mind deals, not surprisingly, with firearms. Stephen is like a machine gun, rattling away constantly, demanding attention. John is more like a howitzer: He is silent most of the time, but when he goes off—look out.

Haggard and bleary-eyed, we greeted the misty morning sun with relief—until the temperature began to rise. By six a.m. it was already eighty-six degrees and the humidity must have been well over a hundred percent. You could chew the air, which was a good thing because, in my haste to leave a spotless house, I had thrown out all the food the night before—including the coffee.

Now, Frank and I disagree on many subjects, but coffee is not one of them. We both believe that several cups of hot, strong coffee in the morning are essential to life: no coffee, no point in getting out of bed.

Since we had sold our car to help finance the trip to France, Frank volunteered to make the long trek to the drugstore and bring us back some breakfast. I sneakily suggested that he take Stephen with him, but Frank, like the gods, was too smart for that one. By the time he returned, dripping with sweat, Stephen was wailing at full volume and John was banging on a pot with a wooden spoon—his version of a prison food riot.

"You know," Frank said, observing the chaos, "we could always cancel the trip."

What he really meant, I think, was that he would have liked to cancel me and the children. For as long as I'd known him, Frank had had one dream—to live in France. He had been on his way, tickets in hand, when the war broke out. Eleven years later, richly endowed with a wife and two children, he could do nothing but bring us along. A dream deferred is not a dream denied, but it never stacks up to the original. Poor soul.

After drinking two cups of coffee, I felt prepared to give him the news. In his absence the steamship company had called. We were no longer leaving from Manhattan. A longshoreman's strike had forced the *Veendam,* our ship, to dock at Hoboken, New Jersey. Bolstered as he was by his morning fix of java, Frank took this change of plans with aplomb. Now all I had to do was call the dozen or so people who were to meet us at Pier 51 and tell them they had to hie themselves to the wilds of New Jersey.

Fed and watered, the children settled down to chasing each other around the house and breaking things. I took advantage of the relative calm to nurse a big bottle of (I'd like to say gin) calamine lotion, for I had picked up a rousing case of poison ivy on my heel. It was so painful that I couldn't wear regular shoes and had been forced to cut the back out of an old tennis shoe. Shuffling around like a Chinese princess with bound feet, I made a sorry sight in my new dress and shabby footwear. And since our suitcases were already so filled that a hairpin would have exploded them, I stood on one foot complaining to my elegantly dressed husband.

"What will I do? I still can't get my shoe on."

"Wear one shoe and one sneaker," he said unsympathetically.

"But I just can't," I said. "It looks ridiculous."

"So? Be different," he muttered.

And different I was, hobbling out to the waiting limousine. Unwilling to leave my new shoes behind, I grabbed a clean diaper, which had been laid out for more conventional use, and wrapped my shoes in it. Then, limping slightly, I made it to the car. This odd bundle went unnoticed, though, because I was loaded down with teddy bears, coloring books, and crayons, as well as the hats and coats that the children had shed in the ninety-degree heat. All the travel writers warn you to travel light, but then they should have seen what we left behind.

The luxurious leather seats of the limo immediately grasped me like a wet hand, turning my crisp new dress into a damp rag. My only consolation was that it now matched my wretched, mismatched shoes. If I had run my purse through a mangler, I would have been totally coordinated, down to my formerly carefully permed hair, which was hanging in limp strings down my neck.

But at least we were off and traveling in style. Unfortunately, within minutes Stephen discovered the jump seats. He might have been short, but he was strong as an ox. So it was not difficult for him to slam the seat up and down with a child-satisfying bang that made us all edgy. John had to be restrained from thrusting his head out the window, a canine trait of some kind, for fear a passing truck would decapitate him. He finally sat back grumpily, claiming he'd rather be dead than hot. Again, the child had a point.

When we pulled up to the toll booth at the George Washington Bridge, Frank instructed the boys to give the toll taker a big "Howdy, pard!" As a New Yorker to the core, my husband always maintained that everyone living west of Manhattan was some kind of hayseed cowboy.

"Do you think he has a horse?" John asked as we slowed to a halt.

"Of course," said Frank. "And a six-shooter and a girlfriend named Miss Betty."

"Where does he keep his horse?"

"In a garage in Montclair, New Jersey," Frank said. "He uses it to commute to work on the bridge."

"Oh, I thought so," John said sagely.

Normally, I would have taken Frank to task for filling the kids' heads with such nonsense, but it was too darned hot to argue. It was also too hot to put up with Stephen's seat slamming any longer.

At the risk of a fatal heat stroke, I picked him up and put him in my lap. After a few minutes of blissful silence, the driver turned around to me and said, "Bless you, madam." The man should have given *me* a tip.

When we finally arrived at the designated pier in Hoboken, we had another delightful surprise awaiting us. Our ship wasn't there. We sat in the limo staring at the empty berth, wondering what to do next.

"Do you think they sailed without us?" I asked.

"Possibly," Frank said. "They might have heard about Stephen and fled in terror."

Instructing the driver to wait, Frank went to do some reconnaissance and returned with the intelligence that the ship had been rerouted to Staten Island.

"This is a sign," I sighed.

"From the gods?" John asked.

"No," Frank said to John. "From Holland-America Line."

"We're doomed," John said darkly.

Frank glared at me and said, "And stop reading him that crap. He's turning into a Cassandra. We'll follow the goddamned boat to Dover, Delaware, or Newfoundland or Los Angeles," Frank continued, his voice rising to new heights of indignation. "We'll follow the damned thing to the ends of the earth. Effing boat." After many years in the Air Corps, Frank had developed an array of curse words that had been known to make sailors blush.

The journey to Staten Island was unusually quiet, marred only by Stephen's attempt to hurl his bottle out the window. Frank made a sparkling catch, a tribute to his misspent youth on the baseball diamond. "Good arm," was all he said. Stephen smiled at the compliment and burrowed deeper into my lap. Children get affectionate at all the wrong times. They're all over you like a rash at the height of summer and ignore you completely in the depths of winter, when they might be useful.

Despite Frank's mutterings about striking longshoremen and the nincompoops (I paraphrase) at Holland-America Line, we eventually made it to Staten Island, where the *Veendam* was actually waiting for us.

"You take Dizzy Dean and the Greek chorus over to the terminal. I'll I find a porter," Frank said. "Also, look around for a rich old man."

"A rich old man?"

"Yes, so I can knock him on the head, steal his wallet, and pay for the damned limo." It had cost us three times what we had figured.

"Well, at least we didn't miss the boat," I said, trying to be cheery.

"That's what the last passengers aboard the *Titanic* said," Frank growled.

Grabbing the kids and our arsenal of toys and equipment, I limped toward the ramshackle building to get my first glimpse of our ship. We were almost there when Stephen bolted—if *bolted* is the right word for a toddler's lurching gait. Fearing he would throw himself into the water, I sent John legging after him. What I had in mind was for John to overtake him, turn him around, and head him in my direction. What I got was a bone-crunching tackle. Stephen went down like, well, twenty-five pounds of bricks. By the time I got there, John was standing over the poor child, a foot planted firmly on Stephen's back, looking for all the world like Tarzan lording it over a fallen enemy.

I picked Stephen up, dusted him off, and found to my surprise that he was laughing.

"Mo'," he said, indicating that he thought this was a great game.

"No mo,'" I said firmly in my best toddlerese. Then I lambasted John for his treatment of his little brother.

"You told me to stop him and I did," John said defiantly. "Besides, he likes it."

"Mo,'" said Stephen, grinning from ear to ear, straining to run away so he could be tackled again.

That settled it: I was about to do something that I really hated to do. I reached into my purse and produced the brown leather harness I had bought for the trip. It was humiliating, both for the child and for me. Humiliation, though, was better than losing Stephen over the side of the ship—where he was sure to wind up. You always read those stories about a mother who turns her back on her child for just a second, only to have him fall or drown or burn to death. I knew from experience that fifteen-month-olds are slier than foxes and quicker than lightning when they want to be and I was determined to get Stephen to France—alive. So I slipped the harness over him, telling him we were going to play doggie.

"Woof," he said. You couldn't fool Stephen when it came to animal noises.

Then without concern for his strange new restraints, he trundled off with me in tow. We made our way to the terminal, pausing for a moment to look at the ocean liner that would be our home for the next ten days.

"So that's the effing boat," John said in perfect imitation of his father.

"That's the *Veendam*," I said. "And don't say effing."

"Why not?"

"Because I said so. That's why." When dealing with children, it is important to explain to them slowly and patiently in minute detail, making sure they understand everything thoroughly. At least that's what all the books say, which is why I threw all the books away a long time ago.

Amazingly, eight of our twelve guests had defied the odds and made it to the bon-voyage party. Since our cabin, as the old-time vaudeville comedians used to say, was so small you had to go outside to change your mind, we invited everyone up on deck. Frank, still stinging from the limo bill, ordered some inexpensive champagne, which he later swore had been produced in Montana. It did have a sheep-y taste, but by the fifth bottle everyone was feeling better. The one sour note was that we had to endure a selection of dog tricks John had taught Stephen. Everyone was suitably aghast, especially when Frank said, "Here, boy. Shake." And Stephen dutifully shook his hand. Disgraceful behavior, from all three of them. It really made me feel worse about the darned leash.

We sailed out of Staten Island amid fond farewells, spiraling streamers, and a fog of cheap champagne. I was looking forward to a nice relaxing evening, but Stephen had other plans. Without any warning, we were off to the races. Leading me by his leash, he took me for a tour of the ship from stem to stern, up ladders, and down ladders, inspecting every nail head, crack, and spot. He just wouldn't be still for a second. After what must have been the hundredth circuit of the boat that first day, I tried to get him to sit. I begged, threatened, and pleaded, but like a caged animal, he had to be on the move. My left foot, the one crawling with poison ivy, was swollen and awful looking, but I didn't have a moment to rest.

We tried tying Stephen to his chair with his leash, but the howls of anguish he raised attracted so many black looks from the other passengers that we gave up and accompanied him on his endless rounds. He was just acquiring skill as a walker, so land or sea made little difference to him, but just limping after him was wearing me out.

John seemed determined to leave the ship. The place he liked best was the stern, where he hung halfway off the rail and stared hypnotically at the wake. Frank had thoughtfully, then sternly, and finally incoherently explained the dangers to him. But John continued to slip away from us to search the seas, precariously balanced over the rail until yanked back by the seat of his pants. Maybe I should have bought two leashes.

We spent the first night in a sort of fugue state, never quite asleep, yet never fully awake. Breakfast was served between eight and nine, a leisurely hour designed for adults on vacation. Stephen, of course, was raring to go by six a.m. and John soon after. With a couple of hours to kill before the dining room opened, we had to do something. Frank summoned the steward—a small, intense man named Wouter—and explained the situation to him, first in English, then in French, and finally in German. Wouter, however, spoke another language—cash. A fistful of bills produced sudden comprehension, along with a large order of toast and four glasses of orange juice to tide us over.

Then we were off to the dining room. John was an old hand at dining out. The first three years of his life had been spent in restaurants, coffee shops, cafés, and greasy spoons. He had learned to deal with waiters, ordering, and sitting still for, oh, minutes at a time. Stephen had just begun to feed himself, and at home we were quite proud of him. So we had no misgivings about taking him to the dining room.

After we installed him in the high chair furnished by the boat, Stephen banged away with his assortment of silverware. He was especially fond of a large knife, something he had never been allowed to hold before.

However, when no food appeared immediately as it did at home, he began wailing lustily for his breakfast. After some delay, we met our future nemesis, Geert, the waiter. A Hermann Goering look-alike, Geert was a fat man with beady eyes and an air of menace. He was a martinet who thought of the passengers as nuisances to be endured none too graciously. God help anyone who didn't sit quietly, gulp down his meal, and then depart quickly.

Geert scowled at us, but eventually brought us our breakfast, including a bowl of hot cereal for Stephen. Clearing the deck by tossing all his excess silverware on the floor, Stephen dug into the oatmeal with the giant dinner knife. I was afraid he'd cut himself to ribbons, so I ignored the stares of the other diners and began feeding him. Resentful of this reversal of fortune, he howled and brought his fist down with a thud in the gummy substance. It spread beautifully over my arm, down the side of my new blouse, and into the carefully trained curl over my ear. Everyone found this hilarious but me—and Geert.

Beating a hasty retreat, we were suddenly blocked by Geert. "*Madame, la serviette*. In the ring, please." This was his obsession. Captain Ahab had had his whale, and Geert had his napkins. He insisted that, after every meal, the passengers replace their napkins in their napkin rings. Those who failed to do so were scolded like children. Of all life's problems, napkin placement was way down on my list, but it was Geert's raison d'être. As a result, we dutifully did as he commanded before leaving.

John immediately headed for the stern, with Frank in hot pursuit, while I scrambled after Stephen on one of his incessant inspection tours. That's pretty much the way it went for the next nine days. If I was aft, Frank was fore. Occasionally, we got close enough to wave and shout words of encouragement to each other. But only occasionally.

One advantage of my aimless rambles with Stephen was that I became something of an expert on the ship. The *Veendam* was quite an old liner, launched in 1922, and not very big by modern standards. She was 519 feet long and carried 223 first-class and 363 tourist-class passengers. The company eliminated steerage class after the war, and that was a good thing for us, I suppose. Otherwise, on our budget, we would have been forced to squat in the scuppers or whatever it was that steerage passengers were required to do.

In 1940 the *Veendam* was captured by the Germans in Rotterdam and turned into a U-boat tender and recreation ship for submarine crews. Or at least that was what I was told. For the life of me, I couldn't picture U-boat commanders, hats turned backward, enjoying spirited games of shuffleboard—unless, of course, the ship was packed to the gunnels with girls.

After the war the *Veendam* was discovered in Hamburg by the Allies and towed back to its home port in Rotterdam, where it was refitted for the Atlantic run. My informant was the third mate, Erik, who was the only officer on the ship who admitted speaking English. A brave man, he was also the only officer who didn't run from real danger: talking to Stephen and me. Erik loved the ship and was delighted to show it off. He even took us to the boiler room, the only place on board that was louder than Stephen. Perhaps, I thought, we could install Stephen's crib down there. The oilers and engineers would never hear him crying amid the thundering crash of machinery.

With the sound of the engines still in our ears, Stephen and I headed for more rarefied and quieter territory. I had an appointment with the ship's doctor. I had to get over that darned poison ivy. It was driving me crazy.

We showed up on time at the infirmary and met Dr. Van Somethingorother. I never did get his name. He was a young man, just out of medical school, and he had never seen a case of poison ivy before. Dr. Van's inexperience wasn't to blame. Apparently, they don't have poison ivy in Holland. They wouldn't allow it, the doctor assured me. Still, the rash fascinated him and he called his colleagues together to see this remarkable malady. I felt like an experimental animal being viewed by an entire medical school.

As the days went by, more and more people would be on hand for my daily examination. Nurses, curious crew members, and even a chef made the morning rounds to view the damage. I gave lectures on the subject and they took endless notes. One evening we were treated to Poison Ivy Sorbet: raspberry ice, implanted with three sprigs of mint shaped in the telltale leaf formation. The chef had done his homework; I had become a minor celebrity—Typhoid Mary, according to my husband.

Fame, however, was fleeting. Despite the doctor's best efforts and an ocean of lotion, the rash eventually dried up and went away. So it was back to the ranks of the anonymous for me. Well, almost anonymous. I still had one more chance at unwanted notoriety—Stephen.

Lunch that first day began pleasantly enough. I ordered a lobster salad, which was delicious, and chopped steak for the boys. John wouldn't eat his until I told him it was a Dutchburger and Geert produced a bottle of ketchup, which he held between two fingers as if it were a dead skunk. Stephen attacked his meal with various eating implements and managed to get most of it in his hair. However, he was happy and mercifully quiet. Then he made his grand discovery. His high chair had obviously been designed by a bachelor manufacturer, a man who didn't have children and had probably never met any. A model of Dutch efficiency, the chair doubled as a toilet seat.

Fascinated, Stephen explored the chair until he found the ring that pulled the plug that held the seat together. It parted and he slid into the basin. Fancying himself stuck, he gave an indignant howl that echoed throughout the quiet dining room. Geert immediately waddled over, a dark look on his face, and tried to use the power of his thought waves to silence Stephen. I could have told him to forget it. Mental appeals for quiet never worked. Stephen beamed at him, then continued to howl.

As Geert retreated in defeat, I quickly replaced the part that held the seat together and tried various ways to divert Stephen's attention. But I knew in my heart the little villain had found a new game. And sure enough, in and out of the basin he slid, with me replacing the plug quietly but firmly just as all the baby books advise. His lunch was forgotten with this new way of annoying Mama.

When my patience was exhausted, I threatened him with a big, fat spanking if he continued to misbehave. This time his cherubic face grew thoughtful, as if he were mulling over his options, and peace descended. Eyeing me angelically, he extracted the plug and with a shriek, he hurled the inch-thick wooden peg as far as he could. Frank looked up and said, "Good arm."

Several people nearby choked on their apple strudel and one man gave a gasp of pain as the wooden plug glanced off his ankle. Our exit was not dignified, but it was fast. Even Geert, running after us at full waddle, shouting about the *serviettes*, couldn't stop us. Frank was all for turning around and telling Geert exactly what he could do with his effing *serviettes*, but I stopped him just in time. We still had nine days to go.

"Are we having a *Veendam* good time yet?" Frank wondered when we were safely out of range. "Stephen will get us all thrown in the brig."

"Send him to Hades," John suggested.

"Meh an' gogos," Stephen said. That's milk and cookies. *Now* he was hungry.

I put my face in his and said, "Stephen, why can't you behave?"

Stephen kissed me on the nose and laughed. He was having the wonderful time I was supposed to be having.

After several such dramas we did what we should have done in the first place—banished Stephen to the cabin for all his meals. As Frank pointed out, "These people are on a pleasure trip and listening to Stephen is no pleasure." So from then on I fed him in the cabin, which wasn't as easy as it sounds. He sat on a swaying stool and I sat on a swaying chair and the tray sat swaying on the bed. Proper coordination of all these movements took the remainder of the voyage to perfect.

When I was done feeding Stephen and putting him to bed for his nap or for the night, I rushed to the dining room to join the others, leaving a well-bribed steward lurking in the corridor to keep watch.

Geert, of course, took a dim view of my constant late arrivals and complained, "You miss sloup." Each time I explained to him that I had plenty to eat without "sloup," but he was never convinced. Frank had to threaten him with Stephen's reappearance to get him to leave me alone. But no amount of bullying would divert his attention from my napkin etiquette. "*Madame*, please, *la serviette*. In the ring," was his constant refrain. He scolded, pouted, pleaded, or growled it out, depending on his mood.

One evening after dinner, I was thinking about poor Stephen, who was coming down with a cold, and decided to look in on him. I pushed the chair away from the table and a chorus of "*Madame*, please, *la serviette*. In the ring," erupted from my husband, my son, and all the nearby tables. They were laughing uproariously, but Geert was seething and watching me like a hawk. It was unnerving. Sometimes I did remember, but I never once got a commendation for good napkin behavior.

"The problem with most waiters is that they've never been in a good restaurant to see how it's done," Frank said. "Wait until we get to Paris."

It wouldn't be long now, I consoled myself. Already Frank and I had fallen into a routine. After a full day of chasing the kids around, we put them to bed at the stroke of seven. Then with our young safely tucked in their bunks, we staggered and limped to the deck and looked for a place to sit. But we hadn't reckoned with the methodical Dutchman who was vice president in charge of putting away deck chairs. Ours, bought and paid for, were always on the bottom of a large stack. They might as well have been on the moon.

That left us the public rooms, where for an hour or so we just sat and rested our feet. We had the place pretty much to ourselves because after the hearty, heavy Dutch food, the hearty, heavy Dutch men and women shot from their chairs like plump gazelles to take their constitutionals. They walked with chins jutted out, chests expanded, and they bragged about the number of times they had circled the ship. Ha! Amateurs. Every night I pondered the injustice. A mere twenty minutes a day of following our children around would have turned them all into Olympic athletes.

By eight o'clock, feet rested, spirits lifted, we headed for the bar to lift some spirits of our own and mingle with our fellow passengers. One group was returning home to Rotterdam after spending a year in America. They sat together in the dining room and at the bar. The women were beefy and jolly and, with their husbands, consumed great quantities of Bols, aquavit, and Belgian beer. They had such a riotous time they made us feel like Quakers. One thing Frank noticed: They all paid for their own drinks. They were practitioners of the famous Dutch treat, he said.

Then there was the group of young would-be intellectuals. These American college students were going abroad for the summer to soak up a little culture. They all wore tortoiseshell glasses that they whipped off or on to emphasize a point in their conversation. The boys drank cup after cup of espresso and never smiled. The girls seemed to equate personal hygiene with bourgeois sentimentality, but I noted they all carried expensive alligator handbags—stuffed full of Daddy's hard-earned money, no doubt.

These college kids spoke to no one but each other, and no one dared to speak to them. The girls insisted on paying for their share of everything (which they could afford), and there was obviously *no* flirting. They attended the nightly dances en masse, got ringside tables, then either read or played cards. Apparently they thought dancing was for feebler intellects—like ours.

I began to feel sorry for them and their false sophistication. They should have been having the time of their lives, not glowering at each other and grumping around. A few hours with Stephen would have made them appreciate being young, rich, and unattached. Maybe we should have rented him out to further their educations.

Frank, as usual, took a dimmer view. He claimed that it would take years to restore good relations with Europe after the natives got a look at those kids. I think he wished he were one of them.

By the seventh day, however, most of the other passengers had lost their inhibitions. Cookies appeared from nowhere and were suddenly clutched in Stephen's greedy little hands. John was constantly smeared with good Dutch chocolate, and we were shown snapshots of families back home.

An American girl, one of the students, tried to get me into a conversation about the Korean situation. Her view was that the United States was an evil, imperialistic empire that wanted to annex Korea. I suggested that perhaps we should conquer Canada first—it was closer and most of the people spoke the language. She looked at me closely, decided I was making fun of her, and stomped off indignantly. Is that why we spent four years fighting the bloodiest war in history? So these kids could have the freedom to hate their own country? Irony, thy name is Marx. And I'm not talking Groucho.

But Korea was no joke. Frank wondered constantly if we would get to spend the entire year abroad, and he was worried that he would be recalled to active duty. He had spent five years in the U.S. Army Air Force, and he felt he had done his duty. War was a game for young men, he said, pointing to a knot of students arguing politics and sipping espresso.

Between my war with Geert and my war with Stephen, I really didn't have the time to worry about the war in Korea. Some of the other passengers, however, had begun to shake us up a bit. We were besieged by people who said incredulously, "You're not taking those little children abroad for a year!" They invariably followed up with a barrage of "what'll you do if's." This list include sickness, death, bad food, bad climate, bad schools, bad housing, and language difficulties. Since we had no ready answers for these as yet unencountered problems, we smiled thinly and changed the subject quickly.

By the evening of the ninth day, I found it hard to believe the trip was almost over. We were to dock at Southampton early in the morning and at Le Havre in the afternoon. As much as I enjoyed the ship, I was more than ready for the feel of solid land under my feet. We went to bed early that last night, tingling with expectation.

It must have been the sound of engines slowing that awoke me. I yelled at one and all to get dressed and threw clothes on the baby and myself. Then dashed down the corridor.

"England awaits!" I called to my slowpoke family, urging them on.

And there was England, shimmering in the morning sun. It was love at first sight for me. Southampton in the distance looked like all the picture postcards I had ever seen of England.

"If we could only get off here, Frank. It's so beautiful," I murmured.

"If we can survive a year in France, I'll be satisfied," he said. I noted his voice was beginning to get tense. The "what'll you do if" people had begun to shake his confidence.

Right after breakfast a fine misty rain began to fall, and the sage travelers nodded happily and announced, "It always rains in England."

Rain or no rain, England had won my heart.

Reluctantly, I left Frank and the boys on deck and raced down to our cabin to pack. Waiting for me was the day's collection of baby clothes. They were dirty, of course, and took up twice as much room as clean clothes. There were also jars of baby food, can openers, and an enormous box of disposable diapers, which had made the trip possible. There were books, coloring books, crayons, balls, trucks, teddy bears, games, and assorted toys. Anyone who has children knows that traveling with them is like a medieval progress: You need a baggage train to haul your possessions from place to place. Unfortunately, I didn't have hundreds of lackeys, knaves, and varlets to help me out. Oxcarts, too, were at a premium. So I was forced to toss out all but the essential matériel.

By pushing, shoving, sitting, and permanently springing the lids of our four once-smart suitcases, I got everything packed. I put the flotsam into a giant shopping bag and explained to Wouter that he was to dispose of everything not crammed into a suitcase. Then I rushed back up to the deck.

In a fit of idleness, I contacted the vice president in charge of putting out deck chairs. Then for the first time I got a hint of what the other passengers had enjoyed all along. I even ordered a cup of bouillon and sat and watched the rain.

I hated to admit to myself that this long voyage wasn't exactly the dream vacation I had imagined. Every time I got into the swing of shipboard life, I suddenly came crashing back to reality. Dirty diapers and dyspeptic waiters will do that to you. Still, we were almost in France and the boys were alive and kicking—a victory of sorts. But I wondered if living abroad was going to be all I expected. Based on my experience so far, life was going to be beyond my wildest imagination: Whether good or bad, I didn't know.

I was just enjoying my contemplative mood when John came charging up to me and demanded to know if there were any graveyards on the ship.

"I don't think so," I said, startled by the question. "Stephen and I have scoured every square inch of this ship and we have failed to discover a single graveyard."

"How about convicts?" he asked.

"Well, our waiter Geert is probably a war criminal," I said. "But there are no proper convicts that I know of."

"I'm bored," he said. "Can we go home now?"

"Tell me more about the graveyards and the convicts," I said, mystified.

"Daddy read me *Great 'Spectations* by Charles Dickinson," he said. "I'm playing Pip, but we got no graveyards."

That explained it, I thought. Frank had been reading him Dickens—so much for Greek mythology.

"Why don't you color me a picture?" I said, seeking to divert him.

"Can't. Don't have any blue crayons," John said.

"Why not?"

"I threw them in the water," he said sadly.

"Why on earth—"

"The sea is supposed to be blue, right?" he said. "This morning it was gray, so I made it blue again."

"John, I thought we told you why the sea is blue," I began. But he grabbed me by the arm and led me to the rail.

He pointed at the water and said, "See? It worked."

Well, the child had a point. The sun had come out and the water was a deep blue—as blue as a crayon.

Sometimes great expectations require great faith.

Chapter 2

GETTING AN EIFFEL. Frank, Stephen, and John about to embark on a soggy tour of the Tour Eiffel.

Getting an Eiffel

"We seem to be incontinent on the Continent," Frank said, removing a dripping Stephen from his shoulder.

"I just changed him," I said with a sigh.

"Then it must be his allergy," Frank said, dabbing ineffectually at his suit coat with a handkerchief.

"What allergy?" That was a new one on me.

"His allergy to clean clothes of any kind. He would never wet an old shirt. He saves it up for new suits," Frank said, holding Stephen at arm's length. "Welcome to France."

In our usual lucky manner, we had been the last ones to get through with the boat officials, and we were now on our way down the gangway. I was carrying a suspiciously familiar-looking shopping bag that Wouter had told me contained box lunches for our trip to Paris on the boat train.

We stopped for a moment at the bottom of the gangway, and I got my first good look at the port. I was shocked by its condition. Le Havre had been bombed mercilessly during the war and still showed the scars. Several terminal buildings looked as if Allied bombers had just made a lightning raid. But after ten days at sea we were about to step on French soil, and even a wet Stephen and a damp Frank couldn't spoil the moment for me. *Vive la France!*

"Just put Stephen down and let him walk," I said. "Then you can carry this bag. I don't know what's in it, but it weighs a ton."

So Stephen was unleashed and he broke into a sailor's trot

across the rough cobblestones of the quay. He got about five yards, stumbled, then fell to the ground. His head hit the stones with the sound of a ripe melon being thumped. He was unhurt, but I winced.

A mighty "aah" rolled out from the ship, and we looked behind us in surprise. Lining the rails of the *Veendam* were hundreds of passengers bound for Rotterdam. They had been watching our progress and had seen Stephen fall. We gave them a wave, and Frank held Stephen up for them to see he was all right; then we hurried off for customs.

"I'll bet not many people get a send-off like that," I said.

"They probably think we'll be dead in a week," Frank muttered. "And they're probably right."

We made it unscathed to customs and stood under L to be inspected. I thought our woman inspector was going to be really thorough—she looked very broody.

She began with the overflowing shopping bag first. I was interested, too, in discovering what it contained. Besides our lunches there was a large ball, a teddy bear, four children's books, two toy trucks, and all the other items I had instructed Wouter to throw out. The pièces de résistance were two soiled disposable diapers, whose odor threw the inquisitive inspector's head back with an involuntary jerk. She started next on our suitcases, but by then Stephen was bored and began howling. So she let us go with a dark look and a hasty stamp of approval. Stephen could have found gainful employment as a smuggler's assistant.

The last train to Paris was waiting for us impatiently as we hurled ourselves on board.

Now, some people crave cars, some dote on boats, and still others are plane crazy. I admit it: I love trains. Any kind of train: diesel, electric, or steam; commuter or long-distance trains; even cable cars and trolleys. There is something exhilarating about a train that appeals to me. I like to be on the go.

As much as I enjoy riding on trains, I hate sleeping on them. Pullman bunks make me nervous. I always feel as if I've been interred. On one memorable journey from Texas, where I was working as a newspaper reporter, to St. Louis to visit my mother, I was stuffed in an upper berth, and I felt uncomfortably like the victim in Poe's "Cask of Amontillado." The only relief I got was sticking one foot out of the curtains. That assured me I wasn't terminally immured. Finally, I thought, I could get some sleep on that long, long journey.

Boy, was I wrong. The train was loaded with servicemen, who thought it was hilarious to shake my bare foot as they went by.

"How do you do, ma'am?" they would say and laugh.

Pretty soon there was a line of these guys, shaking my foot, tickling my foot, and playing "This little piggy went to market."

No amount of pleading would get them to stop, so I finally gave up and returned to my seat. I spent the night sitting up, spitting mad, and very much awake.

Fortunately, the journey from Le Havre to Paris was only three hours, but with two restless children it was beginning to feel like three days. Frank suggested opening the lunches, since chewing on a sandwich might act as a sedative for Stephen. That didn't work, of course, because he was too busy running up and down the aisle, yelling at the top of his lungs. The rest of us tried to eat daintily and admire the scenery that was just a blur of buildings and greenery.

On one of his brief visits, Stephen spotted a clutch of hard-boiled eggs in the box lunch and immediately began whining for an "aig." I offered to peel it for him, but he wanted the whole thing so I handed it over to him. Then, thinking he had a pretty good idea, I cracked two eggs together with some force.

Maybe we didn't tip enough; maybe dissatisfaction lurked in the *Veendam*'s kitchen; or maybe this was Geert's revenge for my breach of napkin etiquette. Who knew? But our eggs were raw. In seconds we were well egged up on our faces, skirt, knees, and trousers. Stephen took this opportunity to hurl his egg at John, hitting the poor child on the forehead. The egg poured down John's face as, with a roar, he launched himself at Stephen, intent on throttling his brother.

Torn between remarking, "Good arm," and saving his youngest son from murder, Frank did the right thing. He grabbed John and restrained him. I just sat there looking at my lap, where two bright egg yolks stared back at me—sunny-side up. *Geert,* I thought. *It must have been Geert.* The Napkin Nazi had struck back! But I quickly recovered my composure, and with a little spit and a towel, I soon had everyone cleaned up to minimum standards.

The excitement over, Stephen resumed his primordial screaming and John sat fuming, planning his revenge. Frank pretended he didn't know any of us, and I couldn't blame him.

"Why don't I go to the dining car and see if I can liberate a couple of stiffeners?" Frank suggested.

"Coward," I said.

"No," Frank said. "If I were a coward, I'd *stay* in the dining car. I'm offering to return, so that makes me merely pusillanimous."

"Daddy, can I go with you?" John asked.

"No, you smell like an underdone omelette," Frank said truthfully, but unkindly. John retreated into his funk, Stephen screamed lustily, and I could feel a migraine coming on.

By the time we pulled into the Gare St.-Lazare, we were eggy, dirty, tired, and harassed. But it didn't matter. We were in Paris!

"Get rid of that damned shopping bag," Frank said. "You look like an immigrant." He always claimed that no matter how much regular luggage I had, I always carried a shopping bag filled with old tennis shoes, used Kleenex, and God knew what else. To him, I looked like a recent arrival at Ellis Island. I probably did.

Happily, I shoved the bag down between the floor and the seat. I'm sure they had to retire the entire car for a good cleaning after our departure, but I could feel pinpricks of anticipation. Our year of adventure had begun.

Frank's first step after the approval of his sabbatical had been to write to his old cronies. During World War II, when the Free French were training in the United States, he had instructed the Frenchmen in the fine art of bombardiering. Some of his students had become close friends, and two of them were waiting for us at the station. Paul and André were brothers who had escaped the Nazis in 1940 and made their way over the Pyrenees to Spain—

where they were immediately arrested. Knocking a guard on the head, they had escaped from prison and eventually wound up in England. There, André volunteered for the air force and was shipped to Texas, where he learned all about the Norden bombsight from Frank. His brother, Paul, had slipped back into France and joined the French Resistance. He spent years blowing up buildings, trains, and trucks. Then, on the run from the Nazis, he joined his brother in Texas.

Frank shouldered Stephen, and I held on to John as we stumbled off the train to a royal welcome.

"How the holy hell are ya—ya effing SOB!" André yelled at Frank and embraced him. "May-ree! Kiss my ass and call me stupid! How the effing hell are ya?" André shouted and grabbed me in a bear hug.

"Mom, he said 'effing,'" John advised me.

André, unfortunately, had learned his English in Texas, on an air base. He spoke like a cowboy with a case of beer under his belt. His vocabulary would have melted tar.

"Effing," Stephen mimicked André carefully. How cute. He was learning a new word.

"André, please," Frank said, explaining to him in French that the barracks language they had used at the airfield was not appropriate for women and children.

Red-faced with embarrassment, poor André told us that he had practiced the greeting for a week, wanting to get it just right.

"That's okay," Frank said. "We'll speak French. I need to practice."

We walked through the Gare St.-Lazare, with Frank translating as we went. Like all big-city train stations in July, this one was hot, noisy, and depressing at nine p.m. But with André and Paul overwhelming us with love and affection, we soon began to feel like the first division of American soldiers in Paris.

First, they insisted we must have a drink. André ushered us to a table and spoke authoritatively to the waiter, who then produced Coca-Colas all around. When we expressed surprise, André dismissed our wonder with a wave of his hand. Subsequently, we found Coca-Cola was served all over France, although in the grape-growing areas it was kept under the counter and you had to know someone named Josef to get one.

We finished our American drinks, and André whisked us out to his tiny blue Renault. We became used to diminutive cars in time, but that evening the little Renault added to the unreality of the occasion. The stream of cars looked like children's toys, and I had to restrain myself from laughing when I saw those three grown men tuck themselves into the Renault. I wondered if we would all fit, but we did, and I later grew to respect the French cars and their drivers' ability to rush at one another, then stop just before colliding.

The first night's ride I'll always remember as one of the peaks of our trip. We drove from the station down the Champs-Élysées, and happily it was a night when everything was illuminated.

Even holding a weepy baby in my lap and a sleepy four-year-old at my side could neither dim the sights nor spoil the view. It was like a ride through a lighted fairyland, which we took as slowly as the French traffic would allow. The Arc de Triomphe, sheltering its tiny flame for the war dead, the fountains sending their spray into the lights, the formal gardens on every side, and the wide, wide boulevards where all Paris and its visitors gather on warm evenings at the sidewalk cafés—it all seemed unbelievable to me. At the end of the Champs-Élysées, I looked back to see the Arc de Triomphe in the distance—a truly thrilling sight.

As in a dream, I heard Frank and André telling me which buildings were which and showing me the sights made familiar by postcards, movies, and newsreels of the two-thousand-year-old city. Who could see such glamour and not be moved?

André drove us to the Hotel d'Avignon on the Left Bank. It was a small place, not fashionable, but located just off the Boulevard St.-Michel in the Latin Quarter. There, too, the nightlife was in full swing and the streets were crowded with young people eating, drinking, and laughing. The sweet night air was punctuated by the acrid smoke of a thousand Gauloises cigarettes, the French national brand, which makes American cigarettes smell like Chanel No. 5. But it didn't matter to me. I was entranced.

André told us that the hotel wasn't the Ritz, but it was famed among Sorbonne students as cheap and clean. He had booked us two rooms on the second floor—one for the children and one for Frank and me.

"Put the children to bed and we'll take you on a real tour," André said. "It's only eleven o'clock."

It pained me to turn him down, but I insisted that Frank go with them. What trouble could three good-looking men get into in Paris, after all? By the time I had thought that one through, they were gone. Rather too quickly, if you ask me. But I really was exhausted. So I undressed my sleepy children, put them to bed, and then returned to my room at the end of the hall.

I opened the long windows and stepped out on the balcony to inhale the atmosphere of Paris. Music, muted and melodious, made me romantic; the smell of good cooking made me ravenous; and the laughter from below made me envious. With all these conflicting thoughts, I lay down on the bed and closed my eyes.

In what seemed like only seconds, Frank appeared at the door. It was two a.m.

"I've got a couple of boys here with me. They want to see you," he said.

"Frank! I'm not dressed," I cried.

"I don't think they'll mind," he said, opening the door wide.

Covering myself with a sheet, I watched in amazement as John and Stephen, pajama clad, trooped into the room.

"I found them at the bar," Frank said, "knocking back a couple of Oranginas."

"What on earth were they doing there?" I sputtered.

"I don't know, but they had dates," Frank said.

"What?"

"A couple of American girls found them wandering around the lobby and bought them drinks. André, Paul, and I should have been so lucky," he said, rather too wistfully.

"Hi, Mama," Stephen said cheerfully, crawling into bed with me. John followed.

I scolded them for leaving their room without asking me, but by the time I finished my lecture, they were both asleep.

"Ah, married life," Frank said, looking at the crowded bed. "So romantic."

The next morning we were up early. We had complete instructions about where to catch a bus, and André had even provided us with tickets so that, with a minimum of trouble, we could enjoy our first bus ride around the city. But a crowd of other people were interested in getting on the same bus, and not wanting to be pushy, we held back. In France, as in New York, that was a mistake.

John spotted a break in the crowd and dashed ahead of us and onto the bus. The dictator who ruled over the back platform suddenly decided that enough people were aboard and locked a chain across the platform. He tinged a bell and before we could catch on to the procedure, the bus was off and away—with John on board. I screamed in English to the conductor, who shook his head and turned away. Frank retreated to the sidewalk with Stephen on his shoulder, but I was a mother aroused.

Yelling and loping down the streets of Paris, dodging cars, bicycles, and motorcycles, I pursued the bus, waving my arms wildly in what I thought should be an international signal to stop. About three blocks away, the bus finally stopped, and in the distance I could see the weeping dot that I knew was John being helped off the bus.

He saw me and raced toward me as I sped on toward him, and we continued to foul up all traffic until we were reunited. Interested spectators cheered and laughed. My husband, who will go to any lengths not to be noticed in public, loitered a block away, whistling tunelessly and staring intently at the sky, trying to look as if he didn't know us. We got together again and went back to our original post. The second time we made the bus—together.

The subway was our choice after that. Frank, being a native New Yorker, found them easy to navigate, and we went willy-nilly wherever we wished without incident. As a family, we eyed the Paris buses with a certain distrust. The pushing, shoving mob that rode them made our five-o'clock subway crowds seem tame by comparison.

After a full day of touring the city, we decided to go to bed early that second night in Paris. Frank was still down in the bar nursing a nightcap when I heard a commotion in the hall.

"Mama!" I recognized John's voice and flung open the door. There stood the concierge, whom I later found to be a convivial sort, but who at the moment looked terrifying. She was holding John by the arm and going at him in a torrent of French that neither he nor I understood. I rescued him from her clutches, mumbled my thanks, and closed the door. Then she knocked again. This time she had Stephen. The two, it developed, had sneaked out of their rooms again. They were on their way to the bar, I suppose, to cadge some more free drinks. This time, however, they were caught by the concierge and returned to me. She really shook them up.

So that was the end of their private sleeping arrangements. Although we continued to pay for the second bedroom for the rest of our stay, the room was never slept in again. Neither John nor Stephen wanted to be snared by the intimidating concierge, or parted from his parents. We roomed *en famille* for the rest of our stay.

Sleeping with children in your bed puts the damper on thoughts of romance. In fact, *damp* was the appropriate word. All was peaceful and quiet until about midnight, when nature's unrelenting call woke up John. I knew there was a WC out in the hall but the long black corridor discouraged both of us. In one corner of our room, behind a screen, I had seen a bowl-shaped object with hot and cold running water, and wondered what it was. Now I thought I knew and marveled at the ingenuity of the French.

My husband informed me the next morning that the bowl was a bidet, the French solution to feminine hygiene. We later found that most French people think the U.S. a rather primitive nation because we have no such plumbing installation.

Several afternoons a week I took John and Stephen to the Luxembourg Gardens near the hotel. There the French children, guarded by women at least 105 years old, played happily with tin cans and rocks. I had hoped that the boys, armed with a sackful of toys, would make some friends, but I was wrong. They couldn't talk to anyone except themselves and us, and they specialized in fighting with each other. We drew the scornful looks of the old crones who never raised their derrieres or their voices from their rented chairs, yet seemed to control the kids in their charge by osmosis. The Parisian children were obedient, quiet, and well behaved, not like the wild Indians belonging to me.

In the center of the Luxembourg Gardens was an ornate fountain surrounded by a large shallow pool of water. Frank rented a two-foot sailboat that John immediately loved. He put it in the pool with the other boats and was soon on his way to becoming a first-class skipper. Armed with a long stick to prod the little boat in the direction he wanted it to go, John spent hours watching its progress. However, one day it got caught up with another boat in the center of the pool, and desperate measures were called for. John waded into the water and immediately drew the censure of a park policeman, who yelled at him much as the concierge had done. Shaken, John did what any sensible four-year-old would do. He took it out on his brother. Stephen had been sitting idly on the side of the fountain, minding his own business, when from the corner of my eye, I saw John casually tip him into the water.

Now, the water was only a foot deep, but from Stephen's howls, you would have thought he had just been dumped into the North Atlantic—in winter. I raced over to rescue him and dry him off, while John stood innocently shaking his head.

"You're not 'apposed to go into the water," he said disapprovingly.

"I saw that," I said menacingly. "And you'll get yours when we get back to the hotel."

"That's for the 'aig,'" John said, revealing his true motives. His evil little mind has been harboring evil little thoughts of revenge ever since the train ride to Paris. Like a pint-size Bourbon, John forgot nothing, learned nothing. I took the miscreant and his sopping victim back to the hotel to read them the riot act.

We fared better touring the rest of Paris. Sacré Coeur, the tomb of Napoleon, the Louvre, and the palace of Versailles—we saw them all with André as our guide, our interpreter, and our learned friend. He was a living history and guidebook, and if he did take a dim view of our two little ones, he soon learned to take them in stride. I told him it was good training for when he decided to settle down and marry. Then he could take a dim view of his own children.

In the middle of our whirl of sightseeing, Stephen awoke one morning with a temperature and a cough. By afternoon John was as red cheeked and glittering of eye. They sounded like consumptive twins. Fearing they had contracted some dread foreign disease, I had Frank call a doctor. That was something I would never have done at home, at least not until their symptoms became more specific. But I keep thinking back to those well-meaning doomsayers on the boat. The answer to their nagging question was suddenly quite clear: I'd panic.

The doctor, who must have received his training during the Franco-Prussian War, tottered into the room, glanced at the boys, and informed us that they had colds and that they should be kept in bed and given pills. Deep down I had known that, and I felt like an idiot when the doctor gave Frank a prescription and me a look of pity. His fee was three dollars—reassurance money, really.

The kids' illness really put a crimp in our tourist activities from then on. If one of us went out, the other had to stay with the children. Maybe you can guess who was the goer and who was the stayer.

Thoughts of taking the next boat back home crossed our minds often during the next few days. Torn between sympathy for the boys and irritation at their conduct, we listened to them whoop and cough and quarrel and cry. Their attitude was "You got us into this. Now get us out."

"Let's face it," Frank said a few days later. "Paris in August is not much more exciting than Hobbs, New Mexico."

Everyone has a place he considers the absolutely worst spot on earth. For Frank, Hobbs, New Mexico, was that place. We had driven through the town during the war, and from the moment a tumbleweed got caught under the car until we escaped from a hostile mob at the local saloon, Frank had always thought of that little burg as the essence of a hick town—a place of utter desolation.

I thought Hobbs was rather quaint, but I knew what he meant. Paris closes down in August. Anyone with two francs to rub together goes on vacation, abandoning the city to the paupers, the pigeons, and the tourists from Pittsburgh.

We had planned to spend the entire month in town before traveling to Montpellier in time for Frank to enroll for the fall semester. Now, after much soul-searching, we decided that the boys' health would improve in the sunny south. So Frank reserved a compartment on the night train from Paris to Montpellier.

Before we left, I insisted that we visit the Eiffel Tower. Leaving Paris without seeing this monument would have been like going to New York and missing the Statue of Liberty. The Tour Eiffel was absolutely magnificent when it was all lit up at night and truly imposing in the daytime. I couldn't wait to see Paris from the very top.

Navigating the Métro with the practiced skill of the natives, we dragged our half-sick, fully unhappy children to see the internationally recognized symbol of the French nation.

André had told us that the best time to visit the Eiffel Tower was early in the morning, before the tour buses arrived. So we were first on line at the ticket booth, and the first to board the elevator.

We made it as far as the second level when Stephen, no doubt overcome by the magnificent view, deposited a surprise package in his diaper. The smell was intense, even within the breezy confines of the tower.

"I believe the iron is melting," Frank said, swaying like a drunk. "The entire structure is about to collapse."

The smell was pretty bad, I had to admit. I looked around for a place to change him, but of course there was none.

"What did you feed him last night?" Frank asked. "Artichokes, anchovies, and absinthe?"

"Alliteration won't help you," I said. "Please take him down and change him for me. Please?"

I hadn't come all this way to miss scaling the Eiffel Tower. Most men would have refused this disagreeable chore, but I looked so forlorn, Frank took pity on me. I wondered if it was his good nature or his seldom admitted dislike of heights. He had no problem flying a plane, but with no roof over his head, he tended to turn a bit green at high altitudes.

John and I peered over the side, looking at the École Militaire on the Champ-de-Mars and at all of Paris laid out below us.

We were waiting for the elevator up to the next level when John said, "Mom, can I tell you something?"

"Sure."

"I gotta go to the bathroom," he said with some urgency.

"Didn't I tell you to go before we left?"

"Yes, but I didn't," he said contritely.

"Can't you wait?" I asked.

"No."

"All right, we'll find a rest room," I said.

"No time," he said, clutching himself. "Now!"

If necessity is the mother of invention, mothers have to be inventive. So I led him to a quiet corner of the tower and told him to go over the side.

"Really?" he asked.

"Really. And hurry up before you attract a crowd," I said, turning my back on him to shield him from casual view.

He did his business from some hundred feet in the air.

"That was fun," John said when he was done.

"Fun for you, maybe," I said. "But embarrassing for your poor old mother."

When I told Frank about John's watering the tourists from on high, he laughed.

"At least anyone looking up certainly got an Eiffel," he said.

Incapable of holding our water, we knew it was time to leave Paris—before they threw us out.

Chapter 3

PEACE IN PALAVAS. John standing in front of a triangular concrete block planted by the Germans. They were originally mined and set at the water's edge to prevent Allied landings.

Spirits—High and Low

August 1950

Humber Wilson had returned and I was a nervous wreck. He had disappeared for almost two years, but now John could talk of nothing other than his imaginary friend. What was cute when he was three was not so funny now that he was going on five.

"Before you call the men in white coats," Frank said, "give him a little time to adjust."

Sound advice, no doubt, but I was really worried about the poor child. He had gone absolutely berserk, refusing or unable to learn French, refusing or unable to make friends. At home, he was part of a gang of kids that roamed the neighborhood from dawn to dusk, inventing their own games, running wild through the woods, and generally having a great time. It was next to impossible to get him to come inside even for meals. Winter or summer, the kids were constantly on the go, doing what kids are supposed to do—play.

But since we had left America, John was in mourning for his friends back home. Keeping him here seemed cruel, but we had little choice. Perhaps we had pushed him too far, forcing him to retreat into a world of his own—a world inhabited by Humber Wilson.

When I quizzed John about his phantoms, he got suddenly shy. All I knew was that Humber was "old"—at least twenty, I was told. He lived with his wife.

"What's her name?" I asked.

"Mrs. Humber Wilson," he said.

Silly me.

John spent hours deep in conversation with this specter. It was creepy and unnerving. My concern for our son's mental health was ruining a perfectly pleasant stay in Palavas-les-Flots, a fishing village about ten kilometers from Montpellier. How we wound up there was a story in itself—if not a ghost story, a spooky one nevertheless.

After our watery tour of the Tour, we went back to the hotel to pack. In my desire not to look like a refugee, I forsook my usual shopping bag and inadvertently left behind everyone's favorite toy. Frank was upset because he was now without his straw boater, the only one in all of France, he claimed, except for Maurice Chevalier's. Stephen was disconsolate at the loss of his stuffed rabbit, a toy he had paid scant attention to previously, and John was depressed because I had forgotten to pack *Great Expectations*. Apparently he was skeptical about Frank's ability to recite the story from memory.

So with this grumpy crew in tow, we boarded the night train to Montpellier. Trains, as I have said, are a passion of mine. And this one was fabulous. We were riding second-class, but we had the entire car to ourselves. What luxury! We couldn't imagine who would ever go first-class, except maybe the president of France, when second-class was so posh.

Stephen immediately conked out, much to my relief, and John settled down to coloring a picture for me and looking out the window at the night sky hurtling past.

With the domestic situation under control, Frank and I flipped a coin to see who would eat in the dining car. Good old heads. I won.

"Two out of three?" Frank asked ungraciously.

But I knew when not to press my luck, and I was on my way before he could talk me into twenty-three out of twenty-four or something.

The dining car was a deluxe mobile bistro, complete with starched white linens, gleaming silver, and sparkling crystal. It seemed like years since I had eaten alone and I reveled in the solitude.

Like the rest of the train, the dining car was practically empty, so the waiter hovered around me like an officious butterfly, replacing utensils and filling glasses with such fervor that I figured he was expecting a huge tip. Or perhaps he was just bored by the absence of customers. Whatever the reason, he made a refreshing change from the outrageous Geert. And he spoke perfect English. If I had been forced to order in French, I might have ended up with eel eyeballs on toast or some such dish.

I began with the escargot, tender snails awash in butter and garlic. By the time I was done, my breath could have removed paint, but I had a feeling I would be sleeping alone that night, so I didn't care.

Then I chose one of the specials, *bœuf à la bourguignonne,* which elevated plain old beef stew to an ethereal level. A glass or two of a good Burgundy went superbly with the meal. I followed the appetizer and main course with a selection of cheeses that were unfamiliar to me, but delicious. Then I ordered the *tarte tatin,* which was wonderfully crisp and apple-y. Coffee and little chocolates completed a meal that took two hours to eat and added two inches to my waistline.

Completely satisfied, I returned to our compartment. Stephen, unaccountably, was still asleep, but Frank was telling John his own version of *Great Expectations.*

"Why did Miss Havisham have that white dress?" John asked as I came in.

"It was her wedding dress from a long time ago, and it was crawling with mice and spiders—like her big wedding cake in the corner," Frank said.

"Mice?" John asked. He liked mice.

"Yeah, and rats and bats and things," Frank said. "Miss Havisham wasn't a fashion plate in the best of times, but today she was a total wreck."

Frank looked up, saw me, and said to John, "Do you know why Miss Havisham was left at the altar?"

"No," John said.

"Her future husband, uh, Mr. Fezziwig, couldn't get a bite to eat on his way to the wedding. 'Oh, I'm soooo hungry,' he said, 'I could eat a donkey, Janet. But no one will feed me.'"

Somehow the story had shifted from *Great Expectations* to *A Christmas Carol*, with a dash of *David Copperfield*. The bit about starving to death was for my benefit.

"Suddenly a ghost appeared," Frank said.

"A ghost?" I asked.

"When in doubt, go with ghosts," Frank said.

"Who was the ghost?" John asked, as confused as I.

"It was a Ghost of Christmas Weddings Past," Frank said. "And he looked just like Miss Havisham, only better groomed. Mistaking the ghost for Miss Havisham herself, Mr. Marley said, 'Oh please, Miss H., I'll have a blot of mustard, a crumb of cheese, and a fragment of underdone potato. Anything will do.'

"Then the ghost said, 'Booooo!' And Marley said, 'There's more of the gravy than of the grave about you!'

"I thought his name was Fuzzywig," John said, alert to the internal continuity, or the lack of it.

"And so it was—Marley Fezziwig," Frank said, recovering nicely. "Anyway, old Marley was starving to death, so he left the country."

"Where did he go?" John asked.

"Why, Hungary, of course," Frank said. "Leaving mean old Miss H. at the altar, hoping she'd choke on her delicious wedding cake."

"Where did the ghost go?"

"To the dining car for a wonderful dinner," he said. "Everybody in this story gets fed, except me. I mean, Mr. Fezziwig."

"I don't like this story anymore," John said. "It's not real. You're making it up." If a story didn't come directly from a book, John didn't consider it real.

"Well, we'll read something else tomorrow," Frank said, tucking John into his berth. "Assuming I don't succumb to malnutrition and waste away to nothingness."

As a peace offering, I produced a couple of rolls I had taken from the dining car and gave them to Frank. But it was the last time I ever got to eat alone in a dining car, although Frank did many times and in grand style. When I objected, he always pointed out, "Remember, you ate in the dining car coming down from Paris." For my sins, I, like Miss Havisham, got left, if not at the altar, then at least behind with the kids.

The train arrived in Montpellier at seven a.m. I was expecting a sophisticated resort city like Nice or Cannes, filled with chic restaurants and even chic-er residents. But Montpellier made Cleveland look like Paris. The rain beat down on the crumbling roof of the empty station; outside, what I could see looked foreign, old, stony, and completely unfriendly. I later learned that this wasn't true, but first impressions are unnerving. We finally got a taxi and, by paying enough to buy one of our own, got driven to the place that was to be our home for the next year, the Pension Louis.

I was looking forward to a relaxing year of no cooking, no cleaning, and no bed making. We had insisted that the pension give us a modified American plan for our stay. That meant we didn't get charged for meals we didn't take there, enabling us to sample freely the cuisine of the South.

We screeched to a stop in front of the pension and got out.

"My God," Frank said, standing in the rain looking at the Pension Louis. "I've seen this place before."

"You have? Where?"

"In a Charles Addams cartoon," he said. "This dump must have been his inspiration."

The Pension Louis was a nightmare of a building, cobbled together over the centuries from whatever materials were at hand. Part of it was made of brick, part of the local stone, and the rest of wood, painted olive drab. A cold wind whipped across me, sending droplets of water down my neck. Thunder crashed melodramatically. I expected Frankenstein's monster to open the front door.

"Well, let's get in out of the rain. It can't be as bad inside as it is out here," Frank said.

He was wrong. The temperature inside the pension was at least ten degrees colder, and it was so dark that the stormy skies outside seemed bright and friendly by comparison.

"I'm leaving," John said. "Miss Havisham is in here."

I had to collar him and drag him back, although my heart wasn't really in it. The child had a point.

"Hello?" Frank called out, his voice echoing eerily in the vast silence of the lobby.

The interior was decorated in the same haphazard manner as the outside of the building. Gigantic chairs and sofas were cheek by jowl with what looked like patio furniture. As my eyes adjusted to the stygian blackness, I saw ghostly shapes scattered about the lobby.

"It's a retirement home for the veterans of Napoleon's *Grande Armée,*" Frank whispered to me. "They've been here since 1815."

An ancient gentleman ensconced in a dusty wing chair let out a phlegmy cough.

Stephen, cowed by the menacing surroundings, hunkered down in my arms; John was hiding behind his father, trying to remain inconspicuous. We were too stunned to move.

Finally, the Madame appeared. Her wrinkled face fell when she saw the children. We had written and told her their ages, but apparently she didn't think they would be so little. Shaking her head sadly, she led us through the silent halls to our quarters on the third floor. The rooms were as dark and damp as a mausoleum. I had to turn on the light to see what a miserable place it was: two cramped rooms with peeling wallpaper and fly specked ceilings. The ancient beds squealed when you sat on them; dust was everywhere.

"Turn off the light," Frank said. "It looks better in the dark."

The chill in the room made its way to our hearts. Frank and I both knew that this wasn't going to be a happy affair. And it wasn't.

At noon we entered the dining room, where we were suddenly surrounded by ancient relics slurping soup and watching our every move.

"It looks as if these people were thrown out of the old folks' home for being too old," Frank said, surveying the depressing scene. "If anyone here is under eighty, I'd be surprised—and delighted."

"Maybe it won't be so bad," I said, not believing a word of it.

The children nibbled warily at the strange foods, turned away, then specialized in spilling. The Madame shuttled between the kitchen and the dining room, keeping a critical eye on us. Stephen took his plate and dumped it on the floor while John was busy creating a face from the food in front of him. With green beans for hair, olives for eyes, and a tomato slice for a nose, it was quite a work of art. However, when he borrowed the bony skeleton of a small fish from my plate and curved it into a ghastly grin, I told him to cut it out.

"It's Humber Wilson," he said, eyeing the portrait of his imaginary friend.

"So he has black eyes," Frank said unhelpfully. "Now eat your unimaginary lunch."

John picked at his creation, just as Stephen picked up a bowl of soup and placed it on top of his head like a hat. Madame's French sense of thrift finally overcame her, and she rushed over to rescue her crockery and consommé. Then with a burst of ill-conceived consideration, she insisted on feeding Stephen. He was charmed for about two minutes, and then he became not only sulky but antagonistic.

Shaken, we returned to our chilly rooms to decide what to do.

"This pension should be in Hobbs, New Mexico, not Montpellier," Frank said, invoking his highest level of disdain.

"We just can't stay here," I agreed.

"Suppose—"

He never finished his sentence, for just then we heard a clatter in the hall and a high-pitched voice raving about something. Two seconds later, John and Stephen came tearing in, with an old, old man in semi-hot pursuit.

The boys disappeared into the other room, while Frank went to confront their pursuer. The elderly gentleman came huffing and sputtering to the door, brandishing his cane. A burst of rapid-fire French led to a truce, and the old man crept off.

"What was that all about?" I asked.

"That, my dear," Frank said, "was the last straw—as if we needed one."

It turned out that old codger was being driven to distraction by the boys. The only fun they had in the pension was to challenge the universal French energy-saving device. In many hotels and pensions, the owners had installed timers on the hall lights. Before you went up or down the stairs, you turned on the lights, then ran to the next level before the timer plunged you into darkness. The boys found this a fascinating game, but their footraces were never successful. Stephen usually got caught in mid-flight and John would have to rescue him. But they kept trying to beat the clock. The old gentleman was properly appalled. The boys could make enough noise to wake the dead—or even the retired.

"Why don't you take the kids to the park?" Frank said. "I'm going to find us an apartment."

That sounded good to me, so I got the boys ready and we headed for the Promenade du Peyrou. I was anxious to see the park because it was mentioned in Henry James's *A Little Tour in France.* Highbrow stuff for me, but Frank had insisted I read it. James wrote that if Le Peyrou were in Shrewsbury, England, or Buffalo, New York, "we should have never ceased to hear about it." Unfortunately, it was tucked away in Montpellier, so no one had ever heard about it.

There was a fine mist in the air as the children and I started out. The mist became less and less fine the farther we walked, but at least it was warmer outside than it was inside the Pension Louis. On our right was the Hotel de Ville, which sounded like a cross between a Hilton and a Cadillac, but was really the city hall. Straight ahead, we passed triumphantly through the Arc de Triomphe, a pocket-sized version of the one in Paris. Who or what the citizens of Montpellier had triumphed over—the Germans? the English? the weather?—remained a mystery to me. But the arc provided a spectacular gateway to Le Peyrou.

Guarding the entrance was a giant equestrian statue of the Sun King, Louis XIV. It's a replica of the original smashed to bits during the Revolution, according to James. Obviously, the replacement wasn't doing its job. There was no sun, king or otherwise, in Montpellier that day.

We were practically the only ones braving the weather, although we found a knot of children playing happily and noisily at the far end of the park. I was delighted to note that the kids here in the provinces cried occasionally and squabbled over toys. The cardboard children of Paris had left a permanent scar on me. They were so quiet, so perfect, such well-behaved miniature adults, that they made our children seem frightful. These southern children weren't such ladies and gentlemen. I actually enjoyed watching one little girl get her bottom smacked. Maybe John's and Stephen's behavior wouldn't be so noticeable in the southern latitudes.

I sat on a bench and cursed the rain. Then Stephen rushed up to me, howling. John wouldn't share his trucks.

"That's all right," I said. "You can play with Mama."

That increased the volume of his screams, making me feel like a fifth-rate playmate. Thanks a lot.

With a sigh, I went over to John, who was talking to the air.

"Can't you let Stephen play with you?" I asked him.

"No. Humber Wilson and I are playing trucks," he said.

"You've got two trucks. Why don't you let Stephen play with one?" I said reasonably.

"No. One for me, one for Humber," he said.

"But he's only imaginary," I said. "He's not real."

"He still needs a truck," John insisted.

"Can't he use an imaginary truck?" I said. *Gotcha!*

"Here," he said, handing me both trucks. "You've ruined the whole game."

He got up and wandered off sulkily, leaving Stephen playing happily with the trucks and me to worry about the future. The rain continued to fall.

At dinnertime we returned to the pension for another strenuous meal. The Madame was determined that this time our children weren't going to waste her cooking. She tried mightily, but she lost this round, too. The boys spent the dinner hour trying to entice a large gray cat to come and be petted. The cat didn't like us either.

So we slunk out of the dining room in disgrace, a burst of conversation echoing in our ears. Whatever was being said about us sounded uncomplimentary, but since Frank wasn't there to interpret, I was gratefully left in the dark.

We all raced the electric light up the stairs to our gloomy rooms for a rest, three miserable, cowed, and hungry people.

I put Stephen down so he could wail in a horizontal rather than a vertical position. Then I pondered the folly of our trip. How were we going to survive another eleven months? We had no place to live and nobody to talk to except each other. We were lost in a totally alien land.

John interrupted these dark thoughts by appearing in his bathing suit.

"We're going to the beach," he said.

Thinking he was referring to himself and Humber Wilson, I smiled wanly.

"Get ready, Mama," he insisted.

"I didn't know there was a beach in Montpellier," I said. There wasn't, of course. It was all in his imagination.

"Humber Wilson said so," he said.

"That's nice," I said wearily. Not only were we stuck here, but John would soon be seeing six-foot-tall imaginary rabbits named Harvey.

He sat on the dusty green carpet and pretended to build a sandcastle, much as he was building sandcastles in his mind. It broke my heart. Stephen must have agreed with me because he howled even louder.

Just then Frank burst in the drab room like a ray of sunshine.

"I've got us an apartment," he crowed triumphantly.

"Wonderful," I said without hesitation. "Can we leave tonight?"

"Tomorrow morning," he said. "I've squared it with the Madame. She is as anxious for us to leave as we are to go."

"Great," I said. "Where is it?"

"In Palavas-les-Flots."

"And where is that?"

"About six miles from here, right on the Mediterranean," he said.

"The beach?" I asked incredulously.

"Half a block away," he said. "Are you surprised?"

"No. Humber Wilson warned me," I said.

Frank looked at me strangely, then said, "And the best part is the train you have to ride to get there. It's a regular Toonerville Trolley. You could walk as fast as it goes, but it is fun."

As if I needed to be convinced! I did, however, want Frank to convince me that the Pension Louis wasn't haunted. I explained John's spooky prediction to him.

"Don't you go loony on me, too," Frank said.

"How did John know we were going to the beach?" I asked.

"Simple," Frank said. "He was having a lousy time, and he loves the shore, so he pretended to go to the beach. Besides, the guests here are too old to be active ghosts. You might call them superannuated, but not supernatural."

I accepted his calm, rational explanations, but I still had my doubts. Perhaps it was reading Henry James, but suddenly I felt we were all characters in "The Turn of the Screw."

We left the next morning with no regrets. I was expecting a cheer from the aged residents, but they just didn't have the strength. In a way I felt sorry that we had interrupted their peace and quiet.

"Don't worry about it," Frank said. "It's the most excitement they've had since the Battle of Verdun."

We caught a taxi and found the station. And there it was! The cutest little train I had ever seen. It looked like the pictures in a children's book. John confirmed my theory by launching into a chorus of "I think I can, I think I can, I think I can."

I really enjoyed the ride, but all the way there Frank kept worrying.

"I'm afraid you won't like it," he said. "You've never seen a place like this before. But it was the best I could do on short notice."

Smiling bravely, I kept reassuring him, "I'll love it. I know I will. What could he nicer than an apartment right on the Mediterranean? Don't worry so. I'm not hard to please, and it will be perfect for the children."

Brave talk, but by the time we bumped to a stop and Frank led the way across a bridge over a canal, I was a bundle of nerves. What was wrong with it anyway?

The sun was shining brightly, the sky was cornflower blue, and the air was wonderfully tinged with salt. After the pension, this was perfect. I hoped.

We turned a corner and Frank pointed dramatically to an apartment building, two stories high, with screened porches front and back. Relieved, I clutched his arm.

"Why, Frank, this is going to be lovely."

"Now, don't get too enthusiastic," he warned. "You haven't seen it yet."

He introduced me to the landlady, Mme. Neros. She was totally square, not in the way jazz musicians might mean, but at four feet tall and four feet wide, she really was square. A rusty black dress, a foghorn voice, and a luxurious mustache completed the picture.

Mme. Neros ushered us through a second-floor apartment. When I saw the screened-in porches, the two large, high-ceilinged bedrooms, and the good-size kitchen, I looked at Frank, baffled by his attitude. Compared to the Pension Louis, this was the palace of Louis XIV.

Frank explained that Mme. Neros was even going to include blankets, dishes, and glasses since we didn't have any housekeeping equipment.

"I think this is perfect," I said.

Frank looked at me miserably. "Don't you want to see the bathroom?"

"Oh, yes, the bathroom, of course," I said. "Where is it?"

Mme. Neros and Frank led us across the back porch and the adjoining porch. "We share it," Frank muttered.

"That's all right. I don't mind." I smiled to assure him every-thing was fine.

The Madame opened the door to the little room and, in a voice that could have alerted all the ships at sea, cried, *"Voilà."*

I peered in. "Where's the seat?" I hissed at Frank.

"There's no seat," he hissed back.

"What happened to it?" I asked, still hissing.

"Nothing. It's made that way. They're very common here," he said knowingly.

"One good thing," he said. "They turn the water off at ten-thirty."

"That's good?"

"Yeah, then you have to use a chamber pot."

"That's not so good," I said.

"Speak up," he said. "If you don't like it, we can always go back to the Mausoleum."

That did it. Seat or no seat, I couldn't stand the thought of re-turning to that gloomy, cheerless place.

"If the natives have gotten the hang of this, we'll go native," I said. "Let's take it."

The usually undemonstrative Frank gave me a big kiss, sending Mme. Neros into gales of laughter. She sounded like a mule with a chest cold.

We moved in that night. Our bedroom was painted a bright periwinkle blue and contained a large old-fashioned bed with a white wicker headboard. Even better, the bed was outfitted with a feather mattress, and although it leaked, coating us with stray feathers, it was comfort itself.

The rest of the apartment was furnished in the eclectic (meaning cheap) French style. The combined living room/dining room area between the front and back porches was littered with *objets*. I gath-ered all the junk together and artfully shoved it into one corner. This opened up a sunny, breezy space that ran the length of the apartment. I loved it: the perfect beach house.

Less perfect was that my dreams of a year's vacation from cook-ing and cleaning went up in the cloud of dust that I raised getting the place habitable. Pension living, in the right pension, would have been my choice.

The first thing I did the next day was shop for a bathing suit. It was another beautiful day as we walked along the quay, watching the seabirds diving and calling. The fishing boats were long gone on their expeditions and wouldn't return with their catches until four in the afternoon. Stove-in wrecks and old bits of netting lined the shore, but the beach used by the tourists was sparkling clean. Blue, green, yellow, and red umbrellas sprouted like mushrooms from the sand.

One jarring note: Part of the beach was lined with triangular concrete blocks planted by the Germans to prevent Allied landings. They were originally mined and set at the water's edge. At the end of the war, they had been pulled back to the quay, but they were a grim reminder that the fighting had been over for little more than five years. The conflict in Korea was going well, and I hoped that, too, would soon be only a memory.

"I told you we were going to the beach," John said as we wandered into a little shop.

"Yes, you did," I said. The day was too fine and bright to dwell on darker thoughts.

The shop was filled with the usual tacky beach resort items, but it also featured bathing suits galore.

"How about this one?" Frank said, holding up a tiny bikini.

"There was more material in one of Geert's napkins than in that," I said, shocked.

Palavas was the home of the bikini: tiny little panties and a bra that would have been banned in a burlesque show. I don't know if the frugal French manufacturers were saving money on cloth or not, but their suits weren't suits at all. They were more like lingerie, which I didn't feel comfortable wearing on the beach.

"Well, they must have a grandmother's section," Frank said sourly.

Dismissing his snide remark, I discovered a (relatively) discreet number: It was a white one-piece with little blue dots. Unfortunately, it had virtually no back and it plunged alarmingly toward the part of my anatomy that I sat on. Still, it was as conservative a suit as I ever saw in Palavas, though it made me feel like a hoochie-koochie dancer for the rest of the summer.

The French girls, of course, made me look like Mother Hubbard. They were as cute as all the rumors would have them to be, and Frank's eyes kept roving in all directions. But as for the men, I must say my heart kept beating normally. In Palavas-les-Flots, which everyone shortened to Palavas, the native male population, mostly fishermen, wore unromantic costumes. During the week they appeared in heavy gray wool pants, dark wool caps, and dark blue sleeveless undershirts. On Sundays, however, they dressed to the nines by switching to white undershirts. They only concerned themselves with fishing and drinking; personal hygiene ran a distant third.

Frank told me the village got its name from nineteenth-century tourists who deemed the locals *"pas lava"* or *"pas lavé,"* French for *unwashed.* That seemed cruel to me because I took to Palavas right away. I even liked the way its name was pronounced in French. "Palavas-les-Flots" in print looked as if it had something to do with flotsam, as in flotsam and jetsam. However, when you said it, it came out as Pala-volley-flow, a much more euphonious appellation, as W. C. Fields might say.

The children and I hit the beach that morning, pale, ghostlike creatures, but by that afternoon, we were well on our way to glorious tans. John, with his pail and shovel, seemed determined to dig up the entire beach. Stephen, clad in a diaper, continually ran at the water, got his feet wet, then raced back to safety. I was glad he was on the beach because he had been falling a lot in recent months. He usually fell with his hands at his sides, so his head would smash directly into the floor or the pavement, as he had done on the dock at Le Havre. Perhaps on the beach he would survive without permanent brain damage until he got his balance.

At Stephen's age, John was still crawling. He was a first-rate crawler who saw no reason to totter around risking life and limb when he could crawl with speed and assurance. It was only when we settled in New York and he met other kids that he became interested in walking. By then he was old enough to make the transition smoothly. Stephen, faced with three mobile people at home, started toddling at thirteen months. And as with a dog walking on two legs, it was not that he did it well, but that he did it at all that was amazing.

Even more amazing, I made friends with a young woman who lived in the apartment below us. Madeleine Le Page had two virtues that made her my ideal companion. First, she lived with her elderly aunt, who was very deaf, so Madeleine was accustomed to speaking loudly, clearly, and slowly—with a minimum of words—the perfect way to speak French to me. Second, she was laid up temporarily with a broken leg and couldn't swim or run about the beach. What else could she do but sit and talk to me? I had a captive companion.

My English-French dictionary in hand, I would hobble to the beach with Madeleine and the kids. As best I could gather with my fractured French, Madeleine was a widow, although she was only twenty-four. Her husband had died during the war, in combat, I think, but I was never really sure. Her late husband and her aunt were from Montpellier, but Madeleine was Swiss and had a contempt for all things French. Or at least that was what I surmised, because sometimes it would take me all afternoon just to get across one thought.

Madeleine introduced me to many people on the beach, but they weren't incapacitated enough to suffer through my fumbling, dictionary-aided attempts to communicate. John and Stephen had the same problem. Other children would come up to them, begin speaking, then wander off as ours just stared at them uncomprehendingly. It was sad, but I didn't know what to do about it.

One thing I noticed was that, from tiny little girls to old, old women, every female, as far as the eye could see, was knitting up a storm. I found it difficult to explain that I didn't know how to knit. Nobody really believed my excuse, because apparently it put me in the same category as the feebleminded. But the more I insisted it was true, the less they believed me. Madeleine made a halfhearted attempt to teach me, but as with French itself, my grasp of knits and purls was minimal. Sometimes I wondered if I shouldn't buy a ball of yarn and stick two needles in it, as a sort of protective prop. If the ladies on the beach ever discovered what a lousy cook I was, I suppose I would have been declared an outlaw, hunted down, and shot. Fortunately, I had my hands full with my dictionary.

I also had my hands full getting into the social whirl of Palavas. *Whirl* is perhaps too strong a word. Social eddy was more like it. One great thing was that the fanciest place in town, the Casino, employed a town crier. He would ride his bicycle up and down the village, honking the horn and telling all who would listen what was happening that night. Not to be outdone, the other businesses in town financed a sandwich-board man who walked about advertising movies, special entertainments, and other events of note.

Frank and I were determined to enjoy the nightlife. The first place we went, of course, was the Casino. Any place that employed a town crier deserved our trade.

The Casino was a sprawling wooden building that offered drinks, dinner, musical acts, and roulette wheels. Although Frank disparaged the cuisine, I thought the food was wonderful, and with a $1.85 prix-fixe menu, including wine, it was my kind of place. I loved the food, the accordion player, the singer, and the dance acts. Frank preferred the wine, commenting that he was disappointed that vaudeville wasn't dead after all. But sitting there, breathing in the warm scent of the sea, sure beat slinging hash at home. This was a romantic setting, darn it, and I was going to enjoy it to the hilt.

With Madeleine to baby-sit, we made many forays about town, trying tiny restaurants and sitting in all the sidewalk cafés. Palavas was a honky-tonk kind of place, but that gave it a charm that enchanted me. Frank, always a man to stand drinks for the house, even got appointed to judge a beauty contest. I suppose I should have been jealous, but when you've been married for seven years, you learn to take these things in stride. Mostly.

Other things weren't so easy to swallow. It was on the evening of the great beauty pageant, while I was home alone with the kids, that John totally broke down. The boys had just finished their omelettes when my older son announced that he was going out.

"But it's almost dark," I said. "Where are you going?"

"To see Bobo," he said.

"Who's Bobo?"

"My friend. He only comes out after the sun goes down," John said.

Visions of Bram Stoker's *Dracula* raced through my mind. Had Frank been reading that awful horror story to John?

"Is he a vampire?" I asked.

"No," said John. "What's that?"

"Never mind," I said. "Can't you see him tomorrow?"

"No. Only after dinner," he said.

"Is he another imaginary friend?" I asked.

"No. He's real," John said.

Sure, I thought. The child was on the cusp of suffering a nervous breakdown. Was it better to go along with his delusions or to knock them out of his head? I really didn't know.

"Where is this Bobo?" I asked.

"Just down the street. I'll be back soon," he said, running for the door.

Before I could stop him, he was gone. I watched from the balcony and saw him run down to the beach, scoot across the sand, and duck into a green-and-white cabana. I wasn't afraid for his safety, because Palavas abounded with grandmothers, concierges, uncles, aunts, and busybodies of all descriptions. If he got up to no good, they would soon set him straight and send him home. No, it wasn't his physical safety that worried me. It was his seeming inability to grasp reality. Bobo, indeed. Where did he get that stuff?

After putting Stephen to sleep, I sat on the porch looking at the riot of stars shining overhead and keeping an eye on the cabana. I made up my mind to wait exactly one hour; then I was going to round him up and confine him to barracks.

I was just about to go after him when he arrived home, as happy as I had ever seen him. He spun an incredible yarn about how he and Bobo had played cowboys and Indians and had had a great time. Then he said he was going to bed and he did. This last bit of obedience took the wind out of my sails. Whatever Bobo was, he seemed to be a good influence on John. His going to bed without a fuss was a new experience for both of us. Perhaps Bobo wouldn't be so bad, after all.

I was still pondering what to do about John when Frank returned home from his parade of pulchritude.

"Do you want a drink?" he asked.

"Something weak to match the way I feel," I said.

The moon had risen and cast a silver streak across the dark water, but the cool breeze seemed more clammy than refreshing.

"I brought some extra glasses," Frank said, producing a cold bottle of the local white wine.

"Are you expecting company?" I asked.

"Just Humber and the lovely Mrs. Wilson," he said.

"That's not funny," I said heatedly.

"You're making too much out of this," Frank said, pouring two large glasses of wine. At forty cents a bottle, there was no need to stint.

"Really? Well, now he's invented a new one. Somebody called Bobo," I said.

"Bobo, eh? That *is* worrisome," Frank said.

"See?" I felt vindicated.

"Yeah, he's losing his creative ability. Humber Wilson is a much more believable character. Bobo sounds like a third-rate carnival clown. Maybe he's finding it more and more difficult to invent these creatures."

"Do you think so?" I was willing to believe anything.

"Maybe. Anyway, what's the harm? If he's happy with these silly characters, who are we to ruin it for him? Just leave him alone. He'll be fine. Besides, Einstein had imaginary friends," he said.

"Really?"

"Yep. Of course, so did Jack the Ripper. But the point is, children are inscrutable. Their brains don't work like ours; they don't live in the same world we live in. If he still has imaginary friends when he's seventeen, I suppose we'd be right to worry. At four, how important can it be?"

Mollified but not convinced, I went to bed. Still, I didn't sleep at all well despite the feather mattress.

Giving in to Frank's tolerant views, I allowed John out every night after dinner to play with his imaginary friend, Bobo. I had to admit he was a changed child—happier and more cooperative than he had been since we had left home. That both cheered and worried me. How could a kid live entirely in his own mind? It boggled mine.

Part of our daily ritual was to watch the fishermen unload their catch. We would stand with a crowd of tourists and goggle at the incredible diversity of seafood unloaded before our eyes. Stephen especially like this part of the day. He would poke the still quivering fish and laugh. Pointing at a red fish, he would pipe up with *"Rouge!"* He was learning his French. Of course, it was easy for him to replace his hundred-word English vocabulary with one hundred French words.

John still refused to utter a word unless it was in English. He was either dim-witted or stubborn. I opted for the latter explanation.

On that particular day, I had received a double dose of Bobo. On the beach John had told me that on Saturday there would be a great celebration, a festival. That was news to me, so I asked him how he knew.

"Bobo told me," he said.

Naturally, I thought. But when the Casino's town crier came by on his bicycle, announcing the celebration, I had to admit that Bobo was better informed about Palavas than I. That was galling enough, but as we were watching the fishermen, John darted off. I spotted him down the street talking to a stunning redhead wearing a shocking pink bikini and a large straw garden hat. They chatted for a few minutes; then he came racing back to help Stephen poke the fish.

"Who were you were talking to?" I asked him.

"Bobo's mommy," he said. "She's nice."

I let it go, but that evening I lectured Frank about the two incidents.

"Are you still going on about all this?" he said, exasperated. "Everybody in town knows about the Saint's Day. It's like the Fourth of July in America. You're the only person within a hundred miles who hasn't heard about Saturday's activities. Every kid on the beach knows."

"But what about that woman?" I asked.

"The redhead in the pink bikini? If that's Bobo's mother, I'd sure like to get to know the family," he said with a leer, tapping an imaginary ash from an imaginary cigar.

No sympathy there. Too many bathing beauties had addled Frank's brain. It was up to me. So the next day I laid down the law to John. He was forbidden to go out after supper to visit Bobo.

"But he's my only friend," John said piteously. His lip quivered.

"There are lots of kids on the beach. Why don't you make friends with them?"

"Bobo's the only one who understands me," John said, and burst into tears.

Someone who felt an inch tall would have towered over me at that moment. I desperately sought a compromise.

"All right," I said. "You can talk to Bobo. But only here in the apartment or on the beach."

John wiped away his tears and gave me a big hug, making me feel like the heel I was. It was for his own good, I convinced myself.

The next day, I left the boys with Madeleine while I went to buy some cigarettes, wine, and toilet paper. You know, the staples. When I returned, Madeleine was in the kitchen drinking a cup of coffee. Stephen was in her lap. When I asked her where John was she said, *"Avec Bobo."* With Bobo! *Good Lord*, I thought, *now he's got Madeleine caught up in his fantasies.*

I put down the bag and marched out to the back porch, where two chairs faced the garden behind the apartment. John was sitting in one chair, talking animatedly to what looked like a pile of towels on the other chair.

"Who are you talking to?" I demanded.

"Bobo," he said.

"I thought he only came out at night," I said, determined to break this evil spell.

Suddenly, the pile of towels moved, and a small head peeked out.

"Mummy said I could." The clipped British voice was coming from a little redheaded boy about John's age. He had a terrible sunburn and was swaddled in towels to protect his inflamed skin. That explained his vampire like existence, poor thing.

"This is Bobo," John said casually.

The pile of towels stood up. "How do you do? I am Beaumont Standish Johnston," he said, bowing slightly from the waist. Someone had obviously spent years pounding exquisite manners into him.

"I'm four," he said, holding up three fingers.

"Well, how do you do? I'm Mrs. Littell and I'm considerably older than four."

He looked up at me critically. "You certainly are," he said.

Some manners, of course, take more pounding than others.

"I can't tell you how glad I am to meet you," I said. That was the only time I ever used that phrase with absolute honesty. My son was not going off the deep end, though perhaps I had.

"Come on, Bobo," John said. "Let's play trucks." They rushed off together, leaving behind a few towels in their wake.

Okay, I'll admit it. I was acting like an out-of-control mother. It turned out that the beautiful redheaded woman *was* Bobo's mommy, Vera Johnston. Frank and I got chummy with her and her husband, Beau, who had just graduated from medical school in Montpellier. They were taking the summer off before returning to London. "Bobo," the child's first attempt at saying Beaumont, had struck the Johnstons as veddy amusing; so they continued to call him that long past the time when it was funny.

John had been a godsend, according to Vera. He had come over every night to play with Bobo, who was so sunburned he wasn't allowed out during the day. "Cabin fever and all that, what?" she said.

I was doubly grateful for the Johnstons. Vera gave me an opportunity to talk with someone without using a dictionary. And little Bobo became John's best pal. For a while the only loser was Stephen. Although he had been John's punching bag all summer, I think he missed the attention once his brother had a new playmate. However, he soon discovered that if he interrupted their games, both John and Bobo would chase him around and rough him up. Shrieking in mock terror, he would flee from his pursuers until they grabbed him and tossed him into the sea. Pretending outrage, he would come crying to me. But if the boys neglected him for too long, he would make sure they chased him again.

Frank, bless him, kept his I-told-you-so's to a minimum. Perhaps being in a foreign country had made me temporarily unable to distinguish between friends, real and imaginary; between states, natural and supernatural; and between spirits, high and low.

Chapter 4

LEARNING THE LINGUA FRANK-A. Frank's ability to speak French saved the family from certain doom. Even John, here hitching a ride with Frank, finally managed to grasp the language and became Mary's interpreter.

Learning the Lingua Frank-a

"*Là,*" I said, pointing.

The clerk nodded and produced a bar of Lux soap.

"Oh, and *là,*" I said.

The clerk put a package of Gillette razor blades on the counter.

"*Là,*" I continued.

A tube of Colgate toothpaste joined my growing pile of supplies, but you can see the trouble I had shopping for anything. Pointing and "*là*-ing" was the best I could do. I daresay, if I had broken my arm, I would have been unable to buy anything at all.

Frank was completely unsympathetic. He had a vexing ability to learn foreign languages quickly and completely. His was a skill not unlike being able to hit a baseball into the stands. Some can do it; some can't. I struck out consistently, while Frank hit home runs at a Babe Ruth clip.

"It's really not difficult," Frank told me. "Although speaking French takes a bit of practice, once you've mastered a few words, you can even speak Spanish by adding an 'o' to the end of the French words. Then, if you want to speak Italian, all you have to do is wave your arms around a lot."

That, according to my husband, was how simple it was to learn any Romance language. But the lingua according to Frank-a escaped me completely. To say that I had trouble with French would be like saying General Eisenhower had a bit of trouble with the

Germans on the way to Berlin. Nuts was all I could say to the whole business, and even that was in English.

I found the entire idea of speaking a foreign language, well, foreign. Worse, I had trouble controlling a hysterical giggle every time I used a French word. It took a long while before it dawned on me that speaking French was a normal experience for the French. Each time I said *entrez* I had to laugh and fight the urge to say, "Look, Ma, I'm speaking French!" Everyone must have thought me an idiot, but I just couldn't help myself.

I think that my eccentric habit of laughing out loud irritated Frank more than all my other faults put together. But even with trying, it took me months to suppress the nervous giggles.

I had to admit that my pronunciation of French words was—how do I put this gently?—lousy. Americans can speak rapidly and understandably without ever moving their lips. The French, however, cannot say *oui* without contorting their faces in eleven different directions. My self-consciousness, combined with an American reticence to make funny faces in public, made my rendition of French words totally incomprehensible. Some, like my husband, would have said bizarre.

My comprehension, of course, was anything but comprehensive. In Paris, they speak clearly, if quickly, and that gave me an opportunity to understand some of their words. In the south, however, the natives rattle on twice as fast as the Parisians, and they don't have the good grace to pronounce the words as God—and the textbooks—intended them to be spoken. It appeared the hotter the sun, the stranger the accent. Anyone who has lived in the American South can confirm this.

And then there were those pesky idioms. If you tell a Frenchman you were held up in traffic, he'll wonder who stole your money while you were sitting in your car. Likewise, if a Frenchman demands, *une blonde,* don't worry. It's not a scandalous affair. He just wants a light beer. Even Frank admitted to having trouble with these idiosyncratic expressions.

"My French is so formal and academic," Frank would say. "I can make small children cry."

As you can imagine, nouns made me nervous, diphthongs made me dippy, and tenses made me real tense. John, too, was still struggling. Or more accurately, he had stopped struggling since he had Bobo to play with. But trouble was on the horizon. Both Frank and I dreaded the Johnstons' impending return to England. We had tried to prep John with the bad news, but he remained unconcerned. I didn't know if he grasped the concept or not, but he seemed resigned to losing Bobo as a playmate.

On the morning of August 25, we awoke with a sense of foreboding. The men of the 101st Airborne could not have been more nervous on D day than we were on what we called "Bobo Removal Day," a date which would live in infamy.

"I've got good idea," Frank said. "Let's just stay in bed until tomorrow."

"Sounds reasonable," I said, closing my eyes and hoping everything would go away.

I was just dozing off when Stephen landed on my stomach like a cannonball.

"Meh-lay," he said, shaking me. It sounded like melee, but it was his new word for milk: a strange combination of *meh,* his baby word for cow juice, and *lait,* the French word for milk.

"Meh-lay it is," I said wearily.

I stumbled groggily into the kitchen and rustled up a glass of milk for Stephen, then looked around for something to feed him for breakfast.

Idly I asked him, "Where's John?"

"Bye-bye," Stephen said, vigorously wiping away a milk mustache with his arm.

"Bye-bye? Where?"

"Bobo."

Good grief, it was only six a.m. That was all Vera Johnston needed: putting up with John while she was trying to pack.

"Side," Stephen said, holding out his glass.

"I'm sorry, sweetie. I don't have any apple juice," I said. *Side* was Stephen's word for cider, his favorite drink. "I've got to go out and retrieve John."

"*Allez* bye-bye?" he asked.

"I'll be right back."

Throwing on my clothes, I left the house. It was going to be another hot day, judging from the angry sun just beginning to rise.

The Johnstons lived in a small rented bungalow, which was painted yellow. It was only four blocks away, but by the time I got there, I was, as my mother would have said, glowing. Glowing like a pig. I should have been asleep instead of tracking down a wayward child.

Getting testier by the minute, I turned the corner to confront the bleakest sight I had ever seen. John was sitting forlornly on the porch of the Johnstons' house, his suitcase by his side.

"John, what on earth are you doing here?" I asked, sitting down next to him.

"I didn't want to be late," he said.

"Late for what?"

"I'm going to London with Bobo," John said. "I'm all packed."

"Sweetie, you can't go to London," I said, understanding at last why he had been so unconcerned by Bobo's departure.

"Why not?" he asked.

"Because what would your father, Stephen, and I do without you?" I said.

"Bobo said I could," he insisted.

"I don't care. You can't go to London," I said, wiping a trickle of glow from my forehead. Boy, it was hot.

"I'm going," he said, setting his chin.

"This is ridiculous. You're coming home with me. This instant!" I said.

"No!"

I picked up the suitcase in one hand and grabbed John's arm with the other and began to drag him off the porch.

"No!" He resisted furiously.

By sheer bulk, if not conviction, I was winning the tug-of-war when a new player entered the fray. Bobo, dressed in his pajamas, came shooting out of the house and grasped John's free arm. John looked like a wishbone being pulled apart.

"He's going with me!" Bobo shouted.

"See?" John said, his arms about to be ripped from their sockets.

I couldn't help it. I had to laugh. It wasn't funny, but I couldn't help myself. I released John's arm and he collided with Bobo. They collapsed together in a heap on the porch.

"Mary?"

Beau Johnston, Bobo's father, appeared in the doorway, wearing a red silk dressing gown. The sight of that elegant affectation only served to increase my laughter. I must have looked like a madwoman.

"A bit early, what?" Beau Johnston said in a masterpiece of British understatement.

When I had finally got control of myself, I said, "Sorry to disturb you, Beau. I was just saying good-bye to John. I understand he's going with you to London today."

Beau's look was a priceless mixture of incredulity and horror.

"Well, so long," I said to John, putting his suitcase on the porch.

"I say, Mary," Beau began.

I knew if he added, "Old thing," I was going to lose it.

"Yes?" I turned.

"He's coming with us, Father," Bobo said, putting his arm around John's shoulder for solidarity. The two of them had obviously cooked up this plot.

"I say, but—" Beau began again. The man hadn't had his coffee yet. Come to think of it, neither had I.

"Have fun," I said, waving merrily.

"You can come, too, Mama," John called out to me.

"But, John—" Beau was totally flummoxed.

"It's okay, isn't it, Mr. Johnston," John said, seeking confirmation, not asking a question.

"Of course, you are more than welcome to visit us in London," Beau said, always the gentleman. "But I do not believe that today would be convenient."

"But, Father—" Bobo said.

"Beaumont Standish Johnston, get in the house at once and put on some clothes," Beau said to his son, finally gaining control of the situation. "You cannot lie about on the veranda looking like some sort of street Arab."

Bobo, recognizing his father's tone of voice, scurried into the house.

"What's a street Arab?" John asked.

"It is what you'll turn into if you do not return home immediately," Beau said forcefully. Coffee or no coffee, the man had his wits about him.

"But what about London?" John asked, a look of anguish on his face.

"Come on, John," I said, holding out my hand.

John watched Beau retreat into the house; then having no other choice, he picked up his suitcase and took my hand. His face was practically on the ground as we walked slowly back to the apartment.

We saw the Johnstons off that afternoon. I had to beg, bribe, and berate John to attend the festivities, but eventually he agreed to say a last good-bye to Bobo. Both boys looked miserable, but there are certain social conventions that must be observed, especially when dealing with the very formal British. Perhaps it was John's association with Bobo that saw him through the day. But his formerly stiff upper lip quivered alarmingly as soon as his friend was gone.

For the next week John's behavior made me wish I had secreted him away in Beau's luggage. Between bouts of tears and bursts of anger, John let us know he had lost his best friend and that his family was a poor substitute for Bobo.

Sulking, if not in his tent, in his room, John refused to go to the beach or do much of anything. He stalked around the house muttering to himself, a scowl permanently plastered on his face. Stephen couldn't get within ten feet of him without risking life and limb, and avoided his brother as much as possible. Mercifully, Humber Wilson was similarly intimidated and refused to reappear.

"Well, at least he's not hallucinating anymore," Frank said. "He's just antisocial."

"His behavior is deplorable," I said. "You should spank him into good behavior."

"Sure, make me the bad guy," he said. "You're right about the way he's acting, but spanking him won't help."

"Is flogging outlawed in France?" I asked.

"That might make you feel better, but I doubt it would do him much good," he said. "Just let him be. Maybe a new Bobo will appear."

"Or a new Humber Wilson," I said.

"Let me think about this," Frank said. "I've got the glimmering of an idea, something to bring him out of his funk."

Just then we heard Stephen howl and went to rescue him from John's clutches. Frank's glimmer had better blossom into a full-blown idea, I thought, and soon.

That afternoon we had company. On one of his forays to the university, Frank had met Peter Lord and Molly McGurr. They were to be fellow students at the Institut des Étudiants Étrangers. You might think that meant the Institute for Strange Students, and you might be right, based on Peter and Molly.

They came roaring up our street in Peter's MG, accompanied by a crowd of kids running along behind. Even John was shaken out of his torpor. Like every child in Palavas, he had to get a close look at the red MG with the fancy tan leather seats. When Peter let him sit in the car and pretend to drive, my son was as happy as he had been since Bobo's departure. John took Stephen for long, imaginary jaunts to Paris, London, and "Califormia." At least they were occupied and out from underfoot while we entertained.

Peter Lord was from Boston, single, and enjoying himself immensely. He had been involved with some type of secret work during the war, and was prohibited from talking about it—still. Whatever it was, I gathered it was not something that involved sitting behind a desk.

With his dark hair, black eyes, and handsome face, Peter was usually surrounded by a fluttering corps of women. On this occasion he was with Molly McGurr, a girl from Australia. With her eye for the absurd and cynical sense of humor, she kept us all laughing that day on the beach. Sporting platinum-blond hair and a permanent grin, Molly was what Frank's mother would have called "quite a biscuit." Whatever that means.

That evening, after a few rounds of the local white wine, the party really started to roll.

"You know," Molly said, quaffing a quick glass of wine. "This stuff better be cheap, because it's really, truly terrible. And I'm not talking *pipi de chat.*"

"I didn't notice that you've let up any," Peter said.

"I didn't mean I wouldn't drink it," she said. "You know me. I'll drink anything. More's the pity. In fact, that reminds me of the time I was leaving Sydney. I went out with the lads for a truly tremendous bon-voyage party. The boat was to leave at ten o'clock—sharp. But it had been one hell of a bash, and I found walking to be a chore, making it difficult for me to find the door, let alone a cab. Then I spotted a taxi across the street from the pub and staggered toward it.

"When I came to the curb, I stopped and looked down. It felt as if I were standing on a cliff looking into your Grand Canyon. How was I ever going to get to cross the street?" she said, pausing to refill her glass.

"Drunks, of course, are inventive," she continued. "I figured that if I couldn't walk across the street to the cab, perhaps I could roll. So I lay down in the gutter and proceeded to roll myself across the street, caught the cab, and made the boat. And here I am, darling. Aren't you glad?"

Molly was always the life of the party, and even in an animated group such as ours, she dominated the conversation with her quick wit and 'Strain accent. Apparently, there was nowhere she hadn't been and nothing she hadn't done. I could see why Peter liked to be with her. Life for her was hilarious and she wanted to share it—and herself—with everyone.

"What do you think about Montpellier?" Peter asked me late that evening.

"Old and cold," I said, thinking of the Pension Louis moldering in the rain.

"Precisely," he said as precisely as he could after several bottles of wine. "I knew you were not just beautiful but intelligent and intuitive as well."

You can see why I liked him immediately.

"Montpellier is not even a has-been. It's a never-was," he continued. "Rabelais hung around here for a while, and the medical school was a big deal in 1392. But other than that, this is strictly a bush-league town."

"Paris is too expensive for us," Frank said, anticipating the suggestion that we return to the capital.

"I wasn't thinking of Paris," Peter said. "How about Grenoble?"

"Ohh, I love to ski," Molly said.

"The university there is first-rate," Peter continued. "And the town is smaller and prettier than Montpellier. It's an Alpine village, really, with good food."

"Grenoble, eh?" Frank said. "That sounds great. Mary hates Montpellier. Besides, we wouldn't have to deal with M. Dufin."

A shudder passed through the three of them. M. Dufin was the ferocious dean of the Institut des Étudiants Étrangers. The mere mention of his name made foreign students tremble. Frank had told me M. Dufin was just plain nasty, upset because he had been shunted off to the foreign students by the solidly pro-Communist administration. Instead of making the best of it, the conservative M. Dufin took out his frustrations on the students assigned to him.

"Oh, I don't know," Molly said. "I think he's kind of cute—in a gruesome sort of way."

"Cute like a cobra," Frank said. "When they were auditioning for the part of the führer, M. Dufin finished second to Herr Hitler. But it was damn close."

They spent an hour extolling the virtues of Grenoble, never once mentioning what was obvious to me. How was Frank going to switch schools and still receive his G.I. benefits? The original paperwork had practically required a battery of lawyers and accountants to complete. I could imagine the bureaucratic chaos we would create by making a last-minute change in plans. The fall semester started in two weeks.

Their enthusiasm for the new venture built on itself. By the end of the evening they had convinced themselves that Grenoble was Eden and Montpellier was the place down below. With one final toast to Grenoble, Molly and Peter stood up to leave.

Then they sat down to rest a bit.

Then Frank fell asleep in his chair, and soon all three of them were snoring away.

I went to check on the boys. Stephen was asleep and John was— missing!

Not again, I thought. *I really must nail the front door shut to prevent his frequent escapes.*

I raced back into the living room, which now resembled a barracks filled with sleeping people.

"Frank, wake up," I said, shaking him.

His eyes opened. Then he smiled, nodded, and went back to sleep.

"Frank!"

"What?" he said finally.

"John's gone."

"Probably hitchhiking to London," he said, then returned to blissful slumber. No help there.

I charged out the door and into the night. There was no moon and I could hear distant thunder. Resigning myself to a long, wet search, I decided to go in the direction of Bobo's former abode in the hope that John had gone there. I hadn't taken more than a few steps when I spotted him. John was asleep at the wheel of Peter's MG. Rather him than Peter, I thought, dragging John out of the car.

"La MG, elle est très jolie," John said sleepily.

That was the first time I had ever heard him utter a sentence in French. Of course, he had to be half asleep to do it, but perhaps he wasn't dim-witted after all. I put him back to bed and made a mental note to buy a hammer and nails for the door.

The day after our bacchanal with Peter and Molly, I told Frank about John's comment on the MG.

"And I thought he had inherited your linguistic abilities," was all Frank said.

Ignoring his sarcasm, I pressed my husband for his reputed "glimmering of an idea" about helping John.

"The key is language," Frank said. "Or more precisely, John's lack of it. There must be a way of teaching him French, and I think it must have to do with one of his favorite activities."

"Okay?" I said. I hated it when he did his college professor routine.

"I think I can get through to him," Frank said.

I was doubtful.

"You've probably driven him half mad with all those scary stories you tell him," I said. "Miss Havisham exploding in flames and all."

"Nonsense," Frank said. "He's old enough for real books, not that awful crap they publish for children."

"Can't you read him *Peter Rabbit* or *Winnie-the-Pooh?*" I said, knowing Frank hated those charming tales.

Frank made a gagging sound. He was an enthusiastic supporter of Dorothy Parker's assessment of *Winnie-the-Pooh:* "It made me frow up." And I once had to lie to John about the meaning of hasenpfeffer after Frank had told him that was how Peter and his rabbit family had ended up.

"I refuse to believe that Dickens, Robert Louis Stevenson, Jules Verne, or even Shakespeare can be harmful to children," Frank continued, getting warmed up. "Hell, I'll bet John would even enjoy *Hamlet.*"

"Oh, Frank," I said. "He couldn't possibly like that."

"What's not to like?" Frank said. "It's got ghosts, graveyards, skulls, sword fights, and dead girls floating down rivers. All great stuff."

I thought his analysis was a load of hasenpfeffer, but I had no alternative to offer.

"What's that stupid story about the train?" he asked disingenuously. "You know, 'I think I can, I think I can' and all that. The one he parrots endlessly?"

I hunted up the book in John's room. "Here, Mr. Smarty-pants," I said. "This is a lovely story about a little engine that could."

"When I get through with it, you'll see I'm right. Lurk in the doorway tonight and I'll show you pedagogical brilliance in action," he said, looking at the slim volume. "Despite the inferiority of the teaching materials."

That afternoon I cajoled John into accompanying us to watch the fishermen repair their nets. As August had waned, the summer crowd had drifted off, abandoning the village to its real residents—the fisherfolk. They had hidden out during the high summer, but returned when most of the tourists had departed.

All resort towns have a bittersweet season when the weather is still magnificent, but there are fewer people around to enjoy it. Palavas was no exception. I wondered if we should spend the winter there or move to Montpellier. Frank was still talking about Grenoble, but that was a pipe dream as far as I was concerned.

When we arrived in greater downtown Palavas, we found that the fishermen had stretched their long nets along the sidewalk and tied them to trees. The nets were so large that they covered almost an entire block. Then the old men and women came out to repair them and tie on new floats. The nets spilled all over the sidewalks, and although passersby had to detour out into the street to get past them, no one seemed to mind. As you can gather, greater downtown Palavas wasn't exactly the Champs-Élyseés.

Stephen took the opportunity to hurl himself at a stretched net, bounce off, and crash to the pavement. Dirty and bruised, he found his game satisfying and didn't cry once. John, ignoring the nets, was intent on getting ice cream. We sat at a café and watched the deft fishermen work steadily, all the while stuffing ourselves with ice cream. It was a pleasant yet sad kind of day. Summer was almost over.

That evening Frank sprang his great experiment on John with me lurking dutifully in the background.

"I'm going to tell you a new story," Frank said. "It's called *The Little Engine That Couldn't.*"

"No," John said. "It's *The Little Engine That Could.*" He knew the book by heart.

"This one's different," Frank said.

"Is it a real story or a made-up story?" John asked suspiciously.

"This is a made-up story, based on a real story, from an idea developed by the story department of Warner Brothers, the movie people," Frank said.

"It's a movie?" John asked.

"A Franco-American coproduction," Frank said. "And you have to listen carefully."

John nodded.

"Once upon a time there was a little engine named N. Gene, N. Gene Number Nine, but people just called him N. Gene. He was bright red, with shiny brass fittings and a silver bell. He was born in Bethlehem—"

"Like Jesus?" John asked.

"No, N. Gene was born in Pennsylvania, home of Bethlehem Steel," Frank said, an air of authority in his voice. "Anyway, N. Gene was given the job of hauling freight between New York City and Philadelphia—great big loads of bricks and cement and mortar."

"What's mortar?"

"It's used to make hats for college graduates," Frank said with a straight face. "You've heard of mortarboards, haven't you?"

Unsure, John nodded tentatively.

"Every day N. Gene huffed and puffed—"

"And blew the house down?" John asked.

"Wrong story," Frank said, unperturbed. "One day as N. Gene was chugging through Neptune, New Jersey, he was waved to a stop by a special mail train named Post.

" 'I've got a letter for you,' Post the mail train said.

" 'Thanks,' said N. Gene. 'I'll read it later.'

" 'You'd better read it now. It looks important,' Post said.

"So N. Gene opened the letter up and—"

"How did he open a letter if he's got no arms?" John asked.

"He steamed it open, of course. N. Gene was a steam engine, after all," Frank said with his usual faux logic.

"Now pay attention. The letter was from the president of France and it read: '*Mon cher* N. Gene, *Il est très important que tu viennes en France.* We have *beaucoup de briques, du ciment, et des chapeaux* for you to haul. *Viens à toute vitesse.* Come quick.'

"But *malheureusement,* N. Gene *ne parlait pas français.* He couldn't *compris* a word of the letter. Can you *l'aider?*"

"Help him?" John said. "*Bien sûr.* N. Gene, *va en France et* help the president haul hats."

"Don't forget *le ciment et les briques,*" Frank said. "Now, what was the *meilleur moyen pour* N. Gene to get to France? Walk?"

"No!"

"Fly, *par avion?*"

"No!"

"*Par bateau?*"

"*Oui. Bien sûr,*" John said.

"Right. So N. Gene bought a ticket on the *Veendam* and sailed all the way to Paris. *Tu te rappelles de Paris?*" Frank said.

"Yes. *C'est très jolie,*" John said.

"N. Gene thought so, too," Frank said. "He toured all around and he even *a fait pipi du deuxième étage de la Tour Eiffel!*"

"*Vraiment?*" John asked, wide-eyed.

"*Oui, vraiment,*" Frank said. "Then he went to *la gare* to go to work."

"The station?" John asked.

"*Oui.* But *quand il arriva à la gare,* he was very confused. Instead of saying 'woo-woo' *comme les locomotives américaines, les locomotives françaises* said, '*Le toot, Le toot.*'"

"*Le toot?*" John looked dubious.

"Girl engines said, '*La toote, La toote,*'" Frank added.

"Oh."

"But there was no time for N. Gene to feel *très triste.* There was a big emergency, *une urgence grave.* Palavas had run out of *cha-*

peaux! There wasn't *un seul* hat *dans toute la ville . . . plus rien.* None.

"So N. Gene volunteered to carry *les chapeaux à Palavas. Mais,* which way should he go? Should he *aller au sud ou au nord?*"

John thought that over for a minute, then said, "*Va au sud!*"

"Right!" Frank said. "But should he go south *par la mer en bateau? Ou par voie ferrée*—by rail?"

"By rail," John said.

"Right. So N. Gene took off like a bat out of *l'enfer* and headed *au sud.* Then he came to a great big mountain, *une grande montagne,* and he got scared," Frank said.

"Why?"

"It was a very high mountain, and N. Gene was afraid he would fall off. But he was *très brave,* and started up the mountain, saying, '*Je pense* I can, *je pense* I can, *je pense que j'y arriverai,*'" Frank said.

"I think I can, I think I can, I think I can," John repeated enthusiastically.

"After that mountain, the rest of the trip was a piece of *gâteau,*" Frank said. "And who do you think was waiting at *la gare de Palavas?*"

"*Je ne sais pas,*" John said, caught up in the story.

"Mama!" Frank said. "She needed *un chapeau pour porter avec* her new bikini," Frank said.

"She has a beret," John said.

"But she needed a mortarboard to be *à la mode,*" Frank said.

"There was ice cream on her hat?" John knew all about pie à la mode.

"Strawberry, I think," Frank said, without missing a beat. "She was so happy with her new hat that she gave N. Gene a big kiss and a handful of coal."

"Was he bad?" John asked. Coal in the Christmas stocking was his bête noire.

"No, *la petite locomotive mange* coal like you eat food," Frank said. "He was *très content. Pourquoi?*"

"He brought Mama *un chapeau* and ate coal," John said.

"*Bien sûr,*" Frank said. "And *où allez N. Gene quand il quitta Paris?*"

"Palavas!" John said.

"*Oui. Tu vois,* you see, *tu parles français,*" Frank said.

"*Non, je parle américain,*" John said stubbornly, not realizing he was speaking French.

"*Non, ce n'est pas vrai. Tu parles comme un petit garçon français.*"

"*C'est vrai?*" John asked, wide-eyed.

"*Oui, c'est vrai,*" Frank said. "It's true."

And it *was* true. After that John really began learning French. Eventually, he could carry on a conversation with anyone, switching back and forth between English and French with an ease that made me envious. His brain was like a sponge, absorbing it all. My brain was like a sponge, too: a dry sponge, brittle and unable to soak up anything.

We never heard from Humber Wilson again, thankfully, because John could now talk with real kids. Frank had been right: All John had needed was a little confidence. He just had to think he could, think he could, think he could.

Chapter 5

CHARIOTEER. Stephen's French-built stroller caused great excitement in Montpellier.

A Plunge in the Market

September 1950

Alone and abandoned! That was how I felt when Frank and Peter Lord took off for Grenoble in the MG. John, left behind, was in high dudgeon. Stephen, however, surprised me. Instead of throwing a monumental fit, he walked around the house clutching one of Frank's shoes and sighing piteously.

"I remember Daddy so well," John said mournfully.

"For goodness' sake," I told him. "Your father's not dead. He'll be back in four days."

My protests had little effect on the funereal atmosphere. If you listened closely, you could almost hear the lugubrious strains of Handel's "Dead March" in the background.

Of course, if I had known Frank was serious about moving to Grenoble, I would have quashed the whole idea from the beginning. But I had dismissed all the talk as just that—talk. I should have known that with Frank you could expect the unexpected. Even after seven years of marriage, I needed an interpreter to determine if he was joking or not.

"You'll love Grenoble," Frank had said before he left. "The skiing is fantastic."

The fact that I had never been on a pair of skis in my life bothered him not a whit.

"Then it's about time you learned," was all he had said.

"But I'll be lost without you to translate for me."

"Then it's about time you learned," he repeated, his sangfroid showing.

"Well, don't blame me if you return to find three decaying skeletons."

"I'll hire professional mourners to wail and rend their garments," he had said. "See you Wednesday."

"But—"

Then he and Peter were off—and I was on my own.

Oh, and by the way, we had just moved to Montpellier, rented an apartment, and I was in the process of getting organized. We had been at Number 18, rue de Claret for exactly seventy-two hours.

We had whiled away the last days of August trying to decide whether to stay in Palavas, move to Montpellier or relocate to Grenoble. The thought of moving to a new neighborhood, plunging in with my terrible French, and waiting for people to stop being amused had filled me with apprehension. I would have liked to stay on in Palavas for the rest of our year because I was old hat for the locals and no longer a one-woman sideshow when I ordered groceries.

I tried to imagine what Palavas would be like in winter without the pleasures of the sun and beach. It was not a pretty picture. But what finally made up our minds was that the Toonerville Trolley would soon revert to its fall schedule—one train to Montpellier each morning and one back each evening. Without a car we would be stranded. Worse, half the businesses shut their doors for the colder months, and those that remained open severely curtailed their hours.

The only sensible thing to do, we agreed, was to move to Montpellier. Of course, if we were really sensible, we would have never left New York. In this light, I guess Frank's Grenoble adventure was only relatively senseless.

We packed up, hired a van for our poor possessions, and said effusive good-byes to Mme. Neros. She threw her heart into the farewells by crying her eyes out. So it was with her foghorn sobs still in our ears that we boarded the Toonerville Trolley and once more made an attempt to survive in Montpellier.

"This is it—Number 18, rue de Claret," Frank had said as we looked at the big stone house with the massive front door. After he counted heads and baggage to be sure that we were all together, he rang the bell. The door opened a crack, then was flung back, and we were welcomed by a torrent of French from Mme. Sauson, a large, volatile woman. She cooed, gooed, and baby-talked to our children as she swept us in.

Mme. Sauson gave the children cookies and chocolate squares; then she escorted us, with much huffing and puffing, to the top floor, which we expected to be our home for the next nine months. Mme. Sauson rolled her dark eyes and lifted her hands to thank the good Lord as she told us that the workmen had just that moment finished putting the apartment in order and that she hoped we would like it.

Proudly, she showed us the two big bedrooms, a real bathroom, the living room, and the kitchen. The rooms were spick-and-span and pleased me at once. We followed her around, admiring everything from the new furniture and fresh paper on the walls to the stone floors painted a dark red. Balconies opened off every room, and all the windows were equipped with screens. We all said with verve that the apartment was *"très joli."*

But I kept straying back to peek into the bathroom again. What a change from Palavas: The toilet actually had a seat! The walls were tiled in green and white, and the fixtures were standard. The pièce de résistance, however, was the bathtub. Big enough to have been William Howard Taft's, it stood high off the floor on gilded claw-footed legs.

Mme. Sauson approved of the bathroom, too, but what she really wanted us to appreciate was the fact that the house had central heating. The proud way in which she announced this made me imagine the heat in cold weather gushing out from every silvered radiator.

96   John S. Littell

When we had admired everything sufficiently, we were invited downstairs to meet her husband. The way in which she referred to him conjured up an image of Louis XIV impatiently awaiting us.

We hurried to the living room, a spot I never saw opened again except to be cleaned each week, and met M. Sauson. A sensitive-faced, slender man who barely reached his wife's shoulder, he wore the tight, standard French blue suit and, except for the lack of a mustache, could have been a model for the Timid Soul.

But they obviously adored each other. They sat together holding hands, and despite her bulk, she gave the impression of being ready to leap to do his bidding. She outranked him in size, and certainly in volume, but she knew the technique of making him feel he was the head of the house.

We sat and sipped a tiny glass of wine while Mme. Sauson raced on from one topic to another, quivering all over in her effort to please. Frank translated for me as she rattled on. The monsieur was quiet but smiled from time to time, punctuating his wife's remarks with a lifted eyebrow or a sage nod of his head.

Ignoring a wifely frown, M. Sauson explained that we were his first tenants. The house had stood empty for many years, but when he had retired, he had purchased it and created an apartment on the top floor. With the rent from the apartment, he hoped to supplement his pension.

After a good two hours, the boys were getting fidgety and Frank had nearly lost his voice translating Mme. Sauson's deluge of words. We finally pried ourselves away from their hospitality and went upstairs to collapse in our new apartment.

Now I was alone with two grieving children and the prospect of starving to death before my husband returned. I had to decide whether to take the boys out to eat and risk Stephen starting a riot, or go shopping and risk creating a riot myself. I looked up in time to see my younger son fling a full glass of milk to the red stone floor. *Shopping it is*, I thought with a shudder.

At home I shopped at Gristede's, a small chain of grocery stores that featured sawdust on the floor, a good meat department, and a relaxed—sometimes too relaxed—staff. Gristede's was more expensive than the big supermarkets, but I was and am a loyal customer for at least two reasons.

First, Gristede's saved our lives. It was during the Blizzard of '47, a massive snowstorm that swept through the Northeast, that Gristede's came to the rescue. I had gotten up the day after Christmas and looked out the window. All I could see was white. The snowdrifts were ten feet high, parked cars had disappeared, and there wasn't a soul to be seen. Frank was sick in bed, the right side of his face swollen to the size of a football. That was the result of his having been administered a new wonder drug called sulfa. It did wonders for him, all right, knocking him out for the duration. We had skipped Christmas entirely. Fortunately, John was too young to know what he was missing. Then the blizzard. Could a plague of locusts have been far behind?

I went to the kitchen to make an inventory: a few slices of bread, a couple of cans of vegetables, coffee, cigarettes, and two bottles of beer. A veritable feast. What was missing, besides any real food, was John's formula. I had planned to go shopping that day, but my plans had been snowed out.

"Hmmmbnnnn," Frank said, sitting up in bed and peering out the window. His mouth was pulled back into a grotesque grin.

"Okay, it does look like Hobbs, New Mexico, out there," I agreed. "But what are we going to do?"

Valiantly he tried to get up from the bed, but I pushed him down, my hand on his burning forehead. His temperature must have been 103 degrees. He wasn't going anywhere.

He mumbled something, pointing at the phone book under the nightstand.

"That's a thought," I said. "A long shot, but maybe some poor fool will brave the storm."

I took the phone book and thumbed through the grocery store section. There were five listed in our town. I called the A&P. No answer. Then I rang the others. No deal. Finally, I called Gristede's, a store I had never been to because I had heard it was expensive. They answered on the first ring.

"Uh, I was wondering. You see, I have an infant who doesn't have any formula. Could you, uh . . . ?"

"Certainly," the voice said. "We'll be delivering shortly. Hank's hooked up the snowplow to the truck. What do you need?"

I gave him my list, then added with an inward cringe, "Will you take a check? I'm afraid I haven't had a chance to get to the bank because of the storm and—"

"No."

"No?" My heart sank.

"No need for that," the voice said. "We'll open an account for you."

Two hours later, Hank the driver waded through hip-high snow carrying our box of supplies. He apologized for being late and refused a tip; from that moment on, I was hooked. What service!

The second reason I am a Gristede's fan is that you can order by phone—even when it's not snowing—eliminating the need to physically go to the store. What bliss! As much as I loved the guys at Gristede's, I was perfectly willing to forgo a personal relationship in favor of one conducted over the phone.

Once, in a fit of frugality, Frank insisted that I shop at a cheaper store—like normal people. He thought we would save a bundle. But after I trudged to the A&P for thirty days, our bill was about a hundred dollars more than it had been.

What my budget-conscious husband had forgotten in his calculations was my penchant for buying on impulse. Twenty-five pounds of paprika on sale? What a deal! Two kinds of pie? Why not a cake, too? If the rib roast looked wonderful, I'd forget about the hamburger.

After that month Frank had been forced to surrender. "Go back to Gristede's," he said, defeated. "If you can't see it, you won't buy it."

And I did go back to Gristede's. Like a shot. Who cared if the peas were eight cents a can more than at Safeway? I didn't. What we saved by my not being in the store more than made up for luxuriously priced legumes.

Shopping for me, as you can see, had always been an incidental part of my day, a five-minute affair conducted over the phone. In southern France, however, shopping was an art, with definite and unbreakable rules and regulations.

Rule Number 1: Thou shalt not go to the market unless all the housework is done.

If you looked up and down our street at eight a.m., you would have thought you were in the midst of a sandstorm. Scores of mops sent up clouds of dust from every house. Wash was strung up in long rows and excess water tossed into the street. Once the beds were made and the breakfast dishes washed, the French housewife was at last free to enjoy the fullest, gayest part of her day—her social hour at the store.

Rule Number 2: Thou shalt not be an early bird.

I quickly learned that no one rushes to get her grocery shopping done. (See Rule Number 1.) There was a good reason for this: The early bird got yesterday's worm. Most of the crates of fresh fruits and vegetables went on display at ten a.m. If you tried to beat the system, you got brown lettuce and limp carrots. The bakery would sell you stale bread and the dairy the curdled remains of yesterday's milk. There was a time for everything in France, and for grocery shopping that time was ten o'clock in the morning.

Rule Number 3: Thou shalt examine every item and criticize it.

The wives of poorer, working-class Frenchmen had almost no money to spend, and they had to get the most produce for the smallest amount of money possible. That required a great amount of squeezing, comparing, and seeking of alternatives. If the turnips were *trop cher,* then the beets would have to do. If those capers looked old, maybe they could be had for half price? Surely this bread is damaged and you have the nerve to sell it at full price? Frenchwomen never headed for the store with a list to fill. They made it up as they went along.

Rule Number 4: Thou shalt spend as much time as possible gossiping.

Going home meant going back to work for the French housewife. She had more cleaning, sewing, gardening, mending, and squabbling with in-laws to do. The longer she stayed at the store, the better she liked it. The storekeeper was just as interested as his or her patrons in hearing what had happened since the day before. He, or usually she, for France was a country of widows, was not at all loath to spend twenty minutes selling twenty-five cents' worth of goods in return for a good story, a tale of romance, or a description of the latest funeral.

There are approximately three hundred fifty-four more rules, I discovered later, but I was still a novice on the shopping circuit. I knew the basics from Palavas, so it was with at least a minimum of confidence that I set out that day to do the dreaded marketing.

Frank had provided me with a list of food phonetically spelled. By pronouncing the words as they sounded, I had a sporting chance of being understood. He had also given me directions to a brand-new shopping district not far from the house.

I installed Stephen in his stroller, grabbed John's hand for moral support, and marched out the door at precisely 9:45. By some quirk of fate, I went left instead of right, and it was not until later that I found out "nobody" on our block ventured into "that" neighborhood.

Blissfully unaware I was invading a poverty-stricken, working-class enclave, I hauled the stroller over sidewalks that got progressively narrower and more cracked. Stephen, thinking he was on an amusement ride, whooped with laughter at every jolt. John complained, "Slow down, Mama. My legs are out of breath."

But I soldiered on with grim determination until I spied a butcher shop, La Boucherie d'Or. The Golden Butcher. That sounded like a high-class place. I envisioned a glittering emporium neatly dispensing neatly wrapped viands.

I stood patiently in line, dreading my turn, and trying to remember the word for ham. Stephen, bored because he was not being bounced around, struggled out of the stroller. For some reason he was drawn to a severed pig's head set on a table, staring at us. Hanging above the butcher were the ghastly remains of various farm animals, so different from the sanitized, plastic-wrapped meat at home.

"Cochon!" Stephen said triumphantly, sticking two fingers up the pig's snout.

Meat on the hoof, or on the cranium, was not one of my favorite sights, but I had learned in Palavas to expect grisly displays in butcher shops. The French housewife wanted to see where her next meal was coming from. I'd rather not, thank you all the same.

"Stephen," I whispered. "Come back here."

"Le nez!" he shouted, sticking an additional finger in the pig's nose. A few of the customers in line smiled, but the majority of them frowned at his antics. Had I been a good French mother, I would have clouted him on the head, but being the permissive American mother, I rushed over, grabbed him, and plunked him back in the stroller. His howls of protest made me wish I were a good French mother.

I also wiped his hands to rid him of whatever swine germs he had acquired. A galloping case of trichinosis was not the way to begin our stay in Montpellier.

Before I knew it, I was next in line. With my heart beating at a stepped-up pace and an insane desire to let out a laugh, I asked for . . . "Ham bone."

"Ambon?" the butcher asked, perplexed.

"No, that's not it," I said in English, consulting my list encrypted in phonetic French. There it was.

"Jam-bone," I said confidently.

The butcher, who was wearing a bloody white apron, considered this request, then held up an end of ham and shrugged. I gathered that portion was no good.

Okay, on to Plan B. I asked for veal. Frank hadn't written it on the list, but I dimly remembered it was similar to English.

The butcher nodded sympathetically, went away, and waited on a few other people. Then, seeing me still standing there, he came back to confront me.

"Veal, please," I repeated, and again he showed me the ham and explained that it was only the end and no good. Again I agreed and again I asked for the veal. We went through this several times until he lost patience and began shouting at me. With flaming cheeks I held my ground.

In desperation he took my list and looked it over, even passing it around to the rest of his customers. All of them shook their heads at the phonetic spelling. They were dumbfounded; I just felt dumb.

Finally, I remembered another word, a word that had always worked in Palavas.

"Beef!" I shouted, on the theory that a whisper would have been ignored.

"Ah, *le bœuf!*" said the woman holding my list.

"*Le bœuf!*" confirmed another lady.

"*Le bœuf!*" the crowd shouted in happy unison, urging the relieved butcher to get on with filling my order. I received my package and hurried out onto the sun-blasted street, my hands shaking and my mouth dry. Once we were well away from the butcher shop, Stephen began chanting, "*Bœuf! Bœuf! Bœuf!*"

"Where were you when I needed you?" I said to him as we wheeled down the rue de Figuerolles. The Golden Butcher had left my confidence tarnished.

"Veal is *le veau,* Mama," John said a few more steps away, crushing any remaining courage I possessed.

"Then why the heck didn't you say anything?" I asked my son.

"You didn't ask."

Silly me.

Relying on a four-year-old to translate for you was an iffy business at best. If everything had been on display, I could have fallen back on my tried-and-true "*là*" method.

I hoped I would have better luck at the bakery. And I did. No problem there. A terse "*là*" and we were the proud possessors of a baguette, the long loaf of crusty French bread. Then it was on to the vegetable seller. The profusion of produce was astounding: tomatoes, potatoes, cucumbers, cauliflower, cabbage, eggplants, lettuce, mushrooms, garlic, asparagus, olives, and peppers. And those were just the items I could identify. Many of the vegetables were strange to me. I had never seen such abundance. And this was only a local market. The central market in Montpellier, I learned later, covered entire blocks.

Even if I couldn't identify the majority of the vegetables, I had no idea how to cook them anyway, so I settled on a few tomatoes, lettuce, and cucumbers. Not very exotic fare, but salads were about the limit of my culinary abilities. The *"là's,"* flying fast and furiously, made the young girl waiting on me hop around filling my order. It was nice to be in charge again. Then with a misplaced point, I was suddenly the owner of a large leafy thing. Not wanting to start a row for a few cents, I had it wrapped and put it in Stephen's lap, wondering what on earth it was. After I was satisfied that the scurvy had been averted by the purchase of fresh vegetables, the children and I wandered around the neighborhood at a leisurely pace, taking in the sights. Now, I'm not an architect, but all the buildings in this district looked as if they had been around since Charlemagne was Stephen's age. They leaned and careened into each other with the familiarity of old married couples. Around us, shoppers were shopping, hawkers were hawking, and skinny old horses were clip-clopping past, dragging overloaded wagons. We were witnessing a street scene that hadn't been enjoyed in America since the turn of the century. I liked it because the neighborhood made me feel nostalgic for a time I had never known in America. I did wonder, however, what Frank would consider old, if this was his idea of a new shopping district.

Suddenly we were surrounded by a gang of ragged kids. They were laughing and shouting and pointing at Stephen's stroller. They thought that it was the most hilarious thing they had ever seen. It was odd-looking, I admit. You had to pull it like a wagon, but since I had bought it in Paris, I didn't feel their laughter was warranted. I took smug pride in the fact that they were mocking solid French workmanship, not some American absurdity.

I tried to shoo them away by shouting something foreign and menacing, but all that came out was *"Vamoose!"* That was a good word for dispersing crowds in Texas, but it had no effect in Montpellier.

Stephen enjoyed being the center of attention for a minute or two; then he had had enough.

"*Non! Non! Non!*" he yelled at the kids and heaved the leafy thing at them. They laughed all the harder, scooped up the mysterious vegetable, and took off.

"Good arm," I said. At least Stephen had saved me the trouble of figuring out how to cook the darned thing.

Plodding onward, I thought ruefully that my prediction had come true: We were a sensation. The children and I couldn't have attracted more attention if we had driven a four-horse chariot through Times Square at noon. Okay, we looked a bit different from the locals and we certainly couldn't communicate very well, but I was always amazed that we were such a big deal.

"They're looking at us, Mama," John said uncomfortably.

"That's because they have never seen a fine American family," I explained.

The eyes of Montpellier were upon us, but I knew from my experience in Palavas that it would take only a few weeks for the locals to grow bored with us. Illicit romances, death, diseases, and violence would soon regain the power to entrance them, knocking the crazy foreigners down a peg to the merely weird.

"Let's go in here," I said, spotting a large, seemingly deserted store.

We walked into the dark interior, and for a moment I couldn't see a thing. Then my eyes adjusted to the gloom. Two old women wearing identical black dresses, the sign of widowhood in France, watched me with anticipation.

"*Bonjour,*" I said bravely.

That set off a chorus of *bonjours,* and the younger of the ladies rushed forward to press chocolates on the boys, exclaiming all the while what beautiful children they were. Or at least that was what I imagined she was saying.

I looked around what you might call a general store in rural parts of the U.S. One long shelf held canned goods, rusty-topped and dusty. Something I understood at last! Since each can was illustrated with its contents, I could select my own beans, peas, milk, and pineapple. No Frenchwoman worth her salt would be caught dead opening a can, so I imagined I was the only customer for these relics. From the width of Madame's smile when I selected several, I was sure of it.

Placed around the store were barrels of rice, dried beans, pasta, flour, and sugar. Those items were bought by the kilo, about two pounds, and placed in cornucopias of wrapping paper. I watched a few customers juggling these heavy packages and decided to postpone buying bulk items until I secured one of my infamous shopping bags. I could see me leaving a trail of tea, pepper, and flour from store to home, attended, no doubt, by a pack of wild dogs and a caravan of curious cats.

In the corner near the door was the icebox, filled with twenty-five pounds of chopped ice to keep the butter from melting. I created instant chaos by requesting a hundred grams, a fifth of a pound. I knew from Palavas that this was the largest amount of butter a storekeeper could bear to part with at any one time. Ordering a pound of butter here was like ordering a ton of the stuff back home.

"O-la-la," the older lady exclaimed.

Then, in case I missed it, she again said, "O-la-la!"

What an extravagant person I felt. I think I shocked them both by not asking how much each item cost. They made up a bill for me, written on a scrap of paper, and I paid the amount without arguing. Very un-French of me.

"Oh, one last thing," I said. *"L'oeuf?"*

The older lady nodded and produced a single egg from behind the counter.

Here we go again, I thought. *What was the word for a dozen?*

"A douzy?" I guessed wildly.

"Eh douzy?" The Madame was scratching her thin white hair. *That wasn't it.*

"John, what's twelve?" I asked in desperation.

"I don't know," he said. "I can only count to ten."

"Okay, what's ten?" I asked, momentarily blanking out the simple number.

Slowly, painfully he counted out each number on a finger; then he held up two hands and announced proudly, *"Dix."*

"Deece," I said determinedly.

"O-la-la!" both ladies cried at my extravagance.

I felt unfairly maligned. It was Frank who had grown tired of coffee and a roll in the morning, the traditional Continental breakfast, and demanded eggs, toast, and bacon. Eggs, although not expensive, except in winter, were bought in ones and twos here. I had watched the French ladies as they tucked eggs in a pocket, or held them in their hands, or carried them carefully in their straw shopping baskets.

But there I was, causing another sensation by ordering ten eggs at a clip. Worse, I had no place to put them.

The old, old lady handed me the eggs one at a time, and I put them in my pockets, my purse, and Stephen's stroller.

Then with a hearty farewell, juggling five-sixths of a dozen eggs, we trudged gingerly back out into the fierce sunlight. Most people would have been humiliated and shaken, but by my standards, we had enjoyed a successful shopping trip. At least we would eat that night.

So after a strenuous morning of making a fool of myself, I wheeled a now screaming Stephen and a less than jolly John to a shabby little café with two rickety tables out front. We sat there for a few minutes, and frankly I would have been delighted if no waiter had ever appeared. My feet needed a rest. But suddenly, a tall, thin man with a two-day growth of beard was looming over me. Screwing up my courage, I said, "Coca-Cola?" in a wee small voice.

The waiter shook his head.

"Café?"

A nod—a success!

Emboldened, I asked for cream with my coffee.

A frown—this time a failure.

"I can't believe they don't have cream for my coffee," I said aloud.

"I'll get it for you, Mama," John said. Then he turned to the waiter and said, *"Café crème pour Maman, s'il vous plaît."*

The waiter made a note. I made a note, too: John had repeated exactly what I had said. I had been undone by a four-year-old and a deliberately obtuse waiter.

"John, what do you want?" I asked.

"*Vin rouge,*" he said.

The waiter wrote that down.

"No red wine for you," I said sternly.

The waiter crossed it out. This time, of course, he had understood me, although I was speaking English. Or perhaps it was the tone of my voice. I disapproved of the French custom of starting their kids out drinking alcohol at an incredibly early age. Little children like John would be given a tablespoon of wine in their mineral water so they could join the party. I found this unconscionable. No alcohol for children, ever.

"How about a *menthe?*" I suggested.

John nodded and said to the waiter, "*Menthe à l'eau, s'il vous plaît.*"

Menthe is a French soft drink. When you order it, you get a glass of thick green syrup and a glass of water on the side, *à l'eau.* The idea was to mix the two and make your own drink. To me it tasted like menthol cough syrup, but John liked it.

Unfortunately, Stephen hated it.

"Stephen, do you want some milk?" I asked him.

"No! No! No meh-lay!" he screamed. Then he began to cry real tears. You would have thought I was trying to poison him.

I was glad we were sitting outside, where his screams were moderated by the noise of the traffic. He could compete with the whine of small French cars, but even Stephen couldn't overpower the overpowering sound of huge trucks rumbling and coughing down the cobblestone street.

Looking around desperately for something to quiet him, my eye caught a small sign in the window of the café. It advertised, *Le cidre. Perfect*, I thought. Stephen loved apple cider.

I pointed at the sign and said, "*Là.*" The waiter nodded and disappeared inside the café.

Wiping away Stephen's copious tears, I tried to calm him down, but he was throwing a tantrum for some reason. His face turned purple; his volume increased. I figured he couldn't keep going at this rate for very long, but he had fooled me before.

Passersby began giving us disapproving looks and shaking their heads, figuring me to be a deranged child beater. I smiled wanly at them and gave them what I hoped was a Gallic shrug, as if to say, "Kids! What are you going to do?" By the scowls I received in return, I don't think it worked.

The waiter finally brought our drinks. Like a mad scientist, John began mixing the *menthe* and water to the desired proportions, taking small sips, then adding more water until it met his standards. I tried my coffee. Cold. Ah, well. Then I turned my attention to my violet-faced baby.

"Look, Stephen. Apple juice," I cooed. "You know, apple cider? You love apple cider."

He stopped crying for a moment, his face returning to a lovely shade of scarlet.

"Here, take a taste," I said, holding the glass for him.

He took a sip, squished it around in his mouth, then swallowed it. "Mo' side," he said.

Thank goodness! "Side" was a hit. He grabbed the glass with both hands and went to work on it with obvious relish.

"You know, Mama," John said. "I think this is the first time he's been quiet all morning."

Stephen put the glass down, then let out a burp. He smiled and began to laugh.

Not to be outdone, John let loose a good burp, too.

"Manners, boys, manners," I warned. But it was too late. A belching contest had, you'll pardon the expression, erupted.

Stephen found the whole business remarkably funny. He laughed as hard as he had cried earlier—until he turned blue in the face. But at least I no longer looked like a child abuser.

All the way home, Stephen belted out his version of "Twinkle, Twinkle, Little Star," which sounded something like "Trinkle, Trinkle, Li'l Stir." How I wondered why he was in such a good mood, but I knew enough not to inquire too closely. He might change his tune and start crying again.

Gratefully, the three of us collapsed in our beds. It took us all afternoon to recover.

That evening, after an overdone omelette and a salad of incredible averageness, I wondered briefly if a letter-writing campaign might induce the Gristede brothers to open a store in Montpellier. That would have solved a lot of problems. But somehow I couldn't see our driver, Hank, abandoning his beloved truck, complete with snowplow, for a horse-drawn cart. Alone and abandoned! By both Frank and Gristede's—what a thought. I really had to learn to become a typical French housewife.

As an atypical American housewife, I had taken a plunge in the market and got burned by a butcher, sassed by street urchins, finessed by a four-year-old, ogled by the "O-la-la" ladies, and served by a surly waiter. All in less than two hours.

If shopping in France was an art, I was still in the finger-painting stage.

Chapter 6

CALM BEFORE THE STORM. John and Mary strolling through Montpellier as if they hadn't a care in the world.

The Great Mayonnaise War

For me, the worst part about shopping was cooking all the stuff I had just lugged home. At the store, the artichokes had looked wonderful, fresh, and green, but how the heck do you cook an artichoke anyway? In fact, how do you peel the darned things before you boil, bake, roast, fry, or sauté them? And once you light the stove, how long did you have to fricassee them to achieve success? I was in the dark, which is why I stuck to simple dishes that required minimum competence in the kitchen.

Now, I don't like to say I'm a bad cook. . . . I don't like to say it, but it's true. The first meal I ever fixed for Frank, right after our gala three-day honeymoon in Midland, Texas, consisted of steak, baked potatoes, green beans, and apple pie. Frank took one look at his plate, then retired to the living room with a bottle of scotch. It had been downhill since then.

Let's face it: You have to enjoy cooking to be any good at it. You also need practice and patience. Frank's reaction to my first meal took the edge off my newlywed enthusiasm for the culinary arts.

Looking back, I realize that my entire experience prior to marriage had been, mercifully, cooking-free. My mother had prepared simple means on a regular schedule: pot roast on Thursdays and roast chicken after church on Sunday. But Mom had never offered to show me how to cook, and I had never asked. In college, I ate in the dining hall and, later on, at my sorority house. Working in Texas meant dates in restaurants, cafés, Tex-Mex dumps, places called Eats, and a fat burger at Fat Al's. I was woefully unprepared for haute cuisine, bourgeois cuisine, working-class cuisine, southern French cuisine, or to tell the truth, cuisine in general.

As I mentioned, a French housewife begins her shopping with 2,462 possible menus in her head. Then she surveys what's fresh, what's cheap, and what piques her interest at the moment. Using her vast experience (little French girls are always hanging around the stove picking up pointers from great-grandmother, grandmother, mama, and an aunt or two), she mentally prepares the day's meal from the ingredients that are readily available.

I, on the other hand, was used to nagging Frank at seven a.m. about what he wanted for dinner so I could call in my order before nine.

"Why don't you ever ask me what I want to eat at night instead of before I've had my coffee?" was his peeve.

"It's not all that difficult to decide," I would counter. And that was true, for I made only a few dishes that were edible. It didn't require much effort to say, "Number three."

"Why don't we go out to dinner?" Frank would often ask in self-defense. Music to my ears.

But with two kids, eating at home became a necessity. Fortunately, menu planning for an infant is a snap, thanks to those little glass jars of baby food. I had to hold my nose while shoving strained liver down the boys' throats, but the applesauce and apricots were quite tasty. Besides, if not for Mr. Gerber, the children would have probably been stricken with pellagra or rickets or some other dreaded disease. The boys thrived, but Frank, paraphrasing Winston Churchill, told one and all that I was a modest chef, with much to be modest about. I couldn't disagree.

In desperation I bought a copy of *The Joy of Cooking,* a book designed for novice but sincere chefs. I was doing pretty well with it until the author lost me on the chicken-boning business. Why not just cook up the whole bird and eat around the bones? A much more efficient solution, to my way of thinking.

I did manage to grasp some principles of cooking, probably by osmosis, and eventually expanded my repertoire to a half dozen semi-decent meals, and two or three potential disasters. Over-reaching had led to my downfall more than once.

I make all this clear because I don't want anyone to think I was an Escoffier in the rough. My culinary limitations were legendary, which was why I was stunned when Frank actually gave me a compliment.

He had returned from Grenoble, filled with enthusiasm for the town and the university. But four days of calculating the expense of moving and living there had soured him on the whole deal. No skiing lessons for me, I guess. But I was just as glad, for I was beginning to like Montpellier. Peter and Molly had capitulated, too. They decided to stick it out here, in spite of the monstrous M. Dufin.

"You know what would hit the spot?" Frank said a few days after he had returned. "A tuna fish salad sandwich."

My first thought was: *You brought me four thousand miles from home and now you want a tuna fish sandwich?*

"I like the way you make them," he continued. "They're the best I've ever tasted."

What was that? Were my ears working?

With my usual quick wit, I framed the mot juste: "Huh?"

"You remember, we used to have tuna sandwiches for lunch on Sundays at home," he said wistfully, as if he were being deprived of some great gourmet treat.

"Well, it's okay with me," I said warily. "They stock canned tuna at my favorite store, but I've never seen any mayonnaise."

"Oh, I'm sure they have it. Just look around," he said. "I miss the special way you make those sandwiches."

That morning, while Frank was busy enrolling at the university, I took the children with me for another adventure in shopping. The O-la-la ladies, whom I now knew as Mme. Perrin and Maman, welcomed us with their usual vivacity. A crowd of ladies was milling about the store, waiting for me to act like a lunatic. I didn't keep them waiting long.

Like a bird dog, I sniffed all over the cavernous store, in search of the elusive mayonnaise. Up and down the aisles I trod, my antennae alert, my eyes glued to the shelves. No luck.

Screwing up my courage, I told Maman about my problem.

"*Donde está,* this *el mayo?*" I said, unconsciously falling back on a mixture of high school Spanish and the pretend Spanish of Texas.

"*El mayo?*" Maman said, calling for her daughter to help her with this conundrum.

"John, what's mayonnaise in French?" I whispered.

"Mayonnaise," he said. "What's *el mayo?*"

"Nothing in particular, I guess," I said, looking at the perplexed ladies.

I talked on and on, using every language I could think of, except Morse code and semaphore. There were lots of understanding nods, but no mayonnaise ever appeared. It was a frustrating affair for all of us, and I finally bought the other items I needed and fled.

On the way home, we made the usual stop at our seedy café for *menthe, café crème,* and cider. This treat always cheered Stephen up considerably, so we never missed an opportunity to while away a few minutes there. Our friend, the surly waiter, had become remarkably more friendly the more we frequented the place and overtipped him. He would see us coming and have our drinks ready for us by the time we sat down.

We returned home in one piece, always an accomplishment, and Stephen fell into bed for his nap without a complaint. The house was as quiet as the Pension Louis, a scary thought.

That night I let Frank in on the bad news. There was no mayonnaise to be had in Montpellier.

"That's preposterous," he said. "The French use mayonnaise all the time. For God's sake, *mayonnaise* is a French word. They invented it."

"Then you go and ask them for me," I challenged. "Obviously I haven't gotten through to them."

"All right, all right," he said. "If only to show you the folly of your ways."

As if I needed to be shown!

The next morning at ten, we met with Peter and Molly, who were fully informed about my inability to buy a simple jar of mayonnaise, and the four of us, plus the boys, walked out of the house together. Frank, Peter, and Molly made a right turn. Stephen, John, and I made our usual left turn.

"Where are you going, Daddy?" John called out.

Frank stopped in his tracks. "To the store," he said.

"It's this way, Daddy," John said confidently. "*À gauche*. To the left."

Frank looked at me questioningly.

"Just where is this store?" he asked.

I pointed down the street. "Rue de Figuerolles," I said.

"Good God!" Peter gasped. Then he grabbed me by the shoulders.

"I can't believe you're still in one piece," he said, shaking me to make sure I was still in one piece.

"You've been shopping in the equivalent of the Bowery," Frank said. "I'm surprised you haven't been murdered."

"Oh, you're a bunch of sissies," I said. "The people there are fine."

"I told you to go to the new shopping district," Frank began, determined to get in his I-told-you-so's.

But I cut him off. "Come on, everybody, let me show you a *real* slice of France."

That got them. Grumbling, they followed me, while I kept up a running commentary on the way.

"And look at all the colorful posters," I said, pointing at a wall of them.

"Do you know what they say?" Peter asked me.

"Well, no. But I think they add character to the neighborhood," I said.

"That one says: 'Let's rip the guts out of the greedy capitalists,'" Molly said. "And that one says: 'Americans—go back to America!' Friendly little place you've found. Maybe they'll spare me because I'm Australian."

I ignored their comments. We were on my turf now.

"There's the café where we always stop," John said.

"Good Lord," Peter muttered. "Le Palais de Ptomaine."

But I wasn't going to let their attitude ruin the day. Those so-called experts on French culture could learn a thing or two from me.

We turned the corner and were confronted by a sight that still haunts me. There was a rally in progress, with scores of people cheering a young man who was gesticulating wildly from atop a horse-drawn cart. *Shades of the French Revolution*, I thought, wondering when the heads would begin to roll. But the speaker wasn't what caught my attention. Every lamppost up and down the street had been decorated with a life-size effigy of a German soldier—hanging by his neck from a noose.

"*Sales Boches*," Peter said, using the French equivalent of "dirty German."

"They're a bit late, aren't they?" Molly said. "Where were they in 1940?"

"Are they real?" John asked, pointing at the effigies.

"Not anymore," Frank said. "Thank God the war is over."

With the shrieking voice of the speaker in our ears, we skirted the crowd and headed directly for Mme. Perrin's store.

"Here we are," I said proudly.

"Couldn't you have found a more old-fashioned place?" Frank said in wonder.

"Oh, I love it," Molly said. "It's so . . . so medieval."

We entered the dim precincts of the store and stumbled around for a moment or two, waiting for our eyes to adjust to the gloom. Then Mme. Perrin spotted me and rushed over to say hello. I could barely see the other shoppers in the store, but I figured they were rubbing their hands together in anticipation of my performance du jour. Like a famous diva, I had my own fan club. They wouldn't be disappointed.

Frank introduced himself, Peter, and Molly. Then he held a rapid-fire conversation with the Madame. She threw me the occasional dark look; Molly and Peter were laughing, the dogs.

"Here's the upshot," Frank said at last. "Everyone in France makes her own mayonnaise, and Mme. Perrin was shocked—shocked—that you had been looking for it *en boîte*—in a container."

"Well," I said, relieved. "So much for tuna salad sandwiches."

"Not so fast," Frank said. "She's offered to show you how to make it."

"Couldn't we import a case of Hellmann's instead?" I asked.

"Mme. Perrin says any fool can make mayonnaise and it'll only take her two minutes to teach you," Frank said. "Of course, she doesn't realize she's not dealing with just any fool."

I was above responding to that remark.

Mme. Perrin herded us through the store, and along the way we picked up a squadron of women who wanted to be in on the excitement. We exited the rear of the store, where there were several picnic tables under a grape arbor. I hadn't even known the place existed.

Frank told me the makeshift picnic area was a way for Mme. Perrin to earn a little extra money from her customers. Some people would buy bread, cheese, chocolate, wine, or mineral water to take outside during the warm weather. It was a pretty little terrace, both shady and sunny, hidden away from the bustle and noise of the street.

Mme. Perrin produced a large green bowl, an egg, a bottle of peanut oil, and a silver spoon. I had the queasy feeling that I was about to send the honor of American womanhood crashing into the dust. But with Molly to translate for me, I gave it my all. Frank, Peter, John, and Stephen sat at a nearby picnic table because my fan club demanded front-row seats.

With a practiced hand Mme. Perrin broke the egg, drained off the white, then deposited the yolk in the bowl.

"Never, ever get any of the white in the bowl," Molly translated. "Or you can just throw the whole thing out and start over."

"Have *you* ever made mayonnaise?" I asked Molly.

"Certainly not," she said, wrinkling her nose. "I always buy it in the jar. But this is kind of interesting. It's positively—"

"Medieval," I said.

"Well, listen up because Frank says you make the best tuna salad sandwiches in the world and I want one," Molly said. "I'm starving."

"Don't get your hopes up," I said, eyeing Mme. Perrin's practiced technique.

"Shh. More information is on the way," Molly said.

Mme. Perrin took one of the eggshell halves, filled it with peanut oil, then began to beat the yolk with one hand while adding the oil with the other.

"You have to add the oil one drop at a time," Molly said. "Or you will be expelled from the League of French Housewives."

"Got it," I said, watching Mme. Perrin beat the daylights out of the egg yolk.

"My God," Molly said, looking around the table. "We're surrounded."

I looked up from the bowl to discover a dozen women dressed in black, like Mme. Perrin and her mother, hovering around us like curious crows. They were all widows, I learned later, from the 1914–1918 War. Joining the crowd was an old gentleman who was looking at Molly as if he had never seen a platinum blonde in a pair of bright yellow short-shorts. Come to think of it, he probably hadn't.

A woman leaned over my shoulder and said something. I looked at Molly.

"She asked why the Madame is using a spoon, when everyone knows you should use a fork," Molly said, waiting for Mme. Perrin's reply. It came fast and furiously.

"A spoon is better. *Fini.* That's all," Molly relayed to me. "Wait. Another voice heard from. That lady says a fork makes it lighter."

"Phhh!" Mme. Perrin snorted. I didn't need to speak French to understand that.

"Listen to me. Don't listen to her," Molly said, repeating Mme. Perrin's words of wisdom.

Resolutely, like a wayward pupil well reprimanded, I brought my attention back to Mme. Perrin and observed that something was beginning to form in the bottom of the green bowl. It might have been mayonnaise, even.

"Ask her how much you can make from one egg," I said. Getting eggs for breakfast was difficult enough around here. Eggs for mayonnaise might wipe out the store.

"About a cup," Molly said, after listening to Mme. Perrin's reply. "But you must be careful when starting out not to add too much oil at one time or it will *rater.* To go wrong, to curdle."

While the last of the oil was being added, Frank disappeared, leaving the boys with Peter. I kept glancing up to see where he had gone, distracting me from my studies.

"Attention!" Mme. Perrin said, bringing me back to the task at hand.

"Uh-oh," Molly said. "The fork lady says it's not that important to put the oil in slowly once the mayonnaise is started. After you've got it going, you can add the oil more quickly."

Mme. Perrin's face flushed with displeasure.

"The Madame says she's been making mayonnaise all her life, and she's never had a failure," Molly said.

The fork lady wasn't going to take that without a fight.

"And I've been making mayonnaise all *my* life. If you don't think it's good, I'll bring you some. Then you'll see what *real* mayonnaise tastes like," Molly translated, adding, "Ohhh, the gauntlet has been thrown down."

The fork lady crossed her arms over her ample bosom in righteous indignation, daring Mme. Perrin to contradict her. The Rubicon crossed, the observers now divided themselves into two factions, the fork people and the spoonsters.

"This could get ugly, darling," Molly said. "Old ladies dueling with forks and spoons. So medieval."

"This is more complicated than I ever imagined," I whispered to Molly. Before she could respond, Mme. Perrin took up the challenge.

"Thank you for the *extremely* kind offer to sample your mayonnaise," Molly translated Mme. Perrin's retort. "That is *exquisitely* polite of you, but I prefer not to take a chance. I'm trying to teach the American the right way to make mayonnaise. She must learn the *right* way, not the *wrong* way."

"Them's fightin' words where I come from," I said.

Several "hahs" arose from the crowd. These ladies recognized a good battle when they saw one.

Frank suddenly reappeared holding a bottle of wine in one hand and several glasses in the other. Since the pro-spoon ladies were blocking my view, and I didn't think it was polite to stand up during my initiation, I craned my neck to see what was going on. I hoped Frank wasn't giving the boys wine.

Frank had been known to give John a sip or two of wine, but as I mentioned, I strongly disapproved. France or no France, wine was not for children.

"What's going on?" I asked Molly as the two sides went after each other tooth and claw.

"Most of the spoon ladies champion slow oil; most of the fork ladies say it's unnecessary," Molly said. "Whose side are we on, darling?"

"We better stick with Mme. Perrin, or I'll have to find a new store to shop in," I said. "And I don't want to be responsible for the Great Mayonnaise War of 1950."

"Leave it to me," Molly said. Then she addressed the group. When she had finished, she told me what she had said.

"I praised the results of Madame's efforts," she said, pointing at the bowl. Miraculously, there was quite a pile of mayonnaise in it. "And I told them that in America, prepackaged mayonnaise is so good and so inexpensive that very few women make their own anymore, and that's why we're so interested in learning how."

"And what did they think?" I asked.

"That I was lying," Molly said, laughing. "But I praised Mme. Perrin's kind attempt to teach us. That pleased half the forkettes and all of the spoon people. So as far as I can tell, we've got about nine out of twelve on our side. A trip to the guillotine may be unnecessary."

"Thank you," I whispered, relieved that the ordeal was over. But I was wrong.

Mme. Perrin passed the bowl around for all the ladies to see what *real* mayonnaise looked like. Then she began speaking again.

"Now it is time for the vinegar," Molly said. "Just enough to thin down the mixture and make it set." Who knew mayonnaise had vinegar in it?

"Now a little salt," Molly continued as we watched Mme. Perrin work on her concoction.

"The fork lady says it is also time to add the dry mustard to give it flavor," Molly said, watching the crowd for signs of incipient revolution. "This ought to be good."

Mme. Perrin smiled sweetly.

"Yes, *some* people add mustard. But not the right sort of people, of course," Molly said, giggling.

The Madame's look confirmed to me her belief that adding mustard to mayonnaise was a most undesirable failing among the lower classes and that it would be up to me to eschew mustard in order to confirm my aspirations to a high-class pedigree. The fork lady, of course, was fuming and looking at me to come to her aid.

I took refuge in my patented vague smile that meant, "I would probably agree with you if I knew what the heck you were talking about. Or maybe not, if you don't want me to."

Finding no help from me and having lost the first two rounds, the fork lady made one more try. She took Molly by the arm, pulled her aside, and whispered in her ear. I waited patiently for the translation.

"She says that not everyone makes mayonnaise like the Madame. She offered to show you the one true method for the perfect flavor," Molly said at last. "I thanked her, but to prevent all-out war, I said it would have to be another time."

"Bless you," I said. "Now thank Mme. Perrin and let's get out of here before I collapse."

"Not until I get my sandwich," Molly said.

"Traitor," I said.

Later, in the privacy of my own kitchen, I experimented with what I had learned at the mayo clinic. I discovered that the fork lady was right. Mayonnaise was easier to make with a fork, and confidentially, I liked mustard in it, affirming, no doubt, my plebeian origins.

The world, however, is full of cowards and I'm one of them. I never breathed a word to anyone, because I didn't want to add fuel to a neighborhood feud or even start one.

The ladies drifted off once the excitement was over, and I joined Frank, Peter, and the boys. On the picnic table in front of them was a half-empty bottle of wine. John and Stephen were swirling the dregs of ruby liquid in their glasses.

"Frank!" I said. "You aren't giving those children wine, are you?"

"Well, let's see," he said. "John knocked off a magnum of champagne, but Stephen prefers the *vin rosé*. Peter and I are having Shirley Temples."

"I'm serious," I said, and I was.

"Oh, relax," he said. "I don't see anything wrong with giving John a spoonful of wine."

"*Vin rouge,*" John said, smiling.

"Frank!"

"I don't see anything wrong with it, but as it happens, the boys are drinking grenadine, pomegranate juice."

"You know my feelings about giving alcohol to children," I said, relieved.

"Sure, sure," he said. "Now, how about a tuna fish sandwich? The Madame has already made me pay for the egg, the oil, the vinegar, the salt, and the rental on the bowl and spoon."

"I'll need some bread. Loaf bread," I said, resigned to my fate.

"I'll get it," Peter said. "From what Frank says, the Tour d'Argent serves nothing like your famed tuna sandwiches."

That's for sure, I thought ruefully.

"Oh, and I'll need a knife, a fork, two cans of tuna, and a stalk of celery," I called out to Peter.

"I'm absolutely famished," Molly said.

"No matter how bad the sandwich is, just humor Frank," I whispered to Molly. "Please."

Peter returned with all the ingredients, and I set about to make our gourmet treat. Less than two minutes later, we were ready to eat. I couldn't help thinking that every one of the ladies in black could cook rings around me. Any one of them could probably whip up an award-winning meal—four courses, at least—at a moment's notice.

Frank, Peter, Molly, Stephen, and John dug in.

"Amazing!" Molly exclaimed. "This tastes *exactly* like a tuna fish salad sandwich!"

"That's a relief," I said. "Peter?"

"Uh, very nice," he said.

"Correct answer," I said. "Frank?"

"Absolutely the best tuna salad sandwich I've ever tasted. It must be the mayonnaise," he said as if he were feasting on ambrosial albacore. We looked at him as if he were nuts. Here was a man who criticized the menus in three-star restaurants absolutely transported by a very ordinary sandwich. There is no accounting for taste, but I was pleased.

We dodged a speeding truck on our way home, then ducked behind a horse cart, and evaded a police car lazily cruising the streets looking for trouble.

"Mama," John said, holding up a handful of dried horse dung. "What's this?"

"Throw that back in the street," I said, whipping out my trusty handkerchief to clean him up. "When we get home, wash that hand for five minutes by the clock."

"City boys," Peter said. "Don't know sh—"

"From Shinola," I interrupted.

"What's Shinola?" John asked.

"The opposite of sh—" Frank said.

"Don't start," I said to him.

We were spared an argument when Stephen spotted our café.

"Side!" he yelled and threw his legs out of the stroller, using his heels as a brake. I almost did a back flip.

"Side! Side! Side!" he chanted enthusiastically.

Molly looked at me, her face a question mark.

"He wants to stop for apple juice," I told her.

"There?" she asked, eyeing the dirty little café. "You're a brave woman, Mary."

I could see she was appalled. And our café did look a bit unkempt. However, I noted that M. Surly, our waiter, had brought out three drinks: coffee—cold, of course—*menthe,* and cider. Just the way we liked it.

"Frank, we *have* to stop," I said, explaining the situation. "Just for a moment."

Never a man to pass up a drink, he instantly agreed that a libation might be in order, and the six of us crowded around one of the rickety tables.

Frank, Peter, and Molly ordered *pastis,* a licorice-flavored drink that was an acquired taste—acquired, I was convinced, by people with no taste.

"Don't get your dirty fingers in that," I told John, who was busy mixing his menthe.

"His hand is probably cleaner than the glass," Frank observed.

"Mo' side!" Stephen yelled, flailing his glass around as if he were leading an orchestra.

"He really likes it," I said to Molly and Peter. "He'd drink ten glasses of it if I'd let him."

"It keeps him quiet," John said. "And he takes his nap without crying."

That remark attracted Frank's interest. He peered directly into Stephen's face. The child was a bit flushed, but he always got red in the face when he was excited. Frank took the empty glass from him and sniffed it.

"Have you tasted this?" he asked me.

"No," I said. "I hate apple juice."

"You may hate apple juice," he said. "But you might like this."

He handed the glass to Peter, who sniffed it, laughed, and passed it on to Molly. Then the three of them were laughing, setting Stephen off. John and I looked at each other. We weren't laughing.

"What's so funny?" I asked.

"Well, Carrie Nation, scourge of the drinking man, you've been giving Stephen cider from Normandy," he said.

"So?" Cider was cider as far as I was concerned.

"It's about twenty proof—stronger than wine," Frank said. "He's drunk."

As if to confirm this, Stephen burped, then broke into hysterical laughter.

"Side!" he yelled.

"You've turned him into a wino," Frank said. "And he's not even two."

"More like a side-o," Molly said.

"Molly!" Stephen screamed at the top of his lungs and threw his arms around her bare legs.

"I like a man who can hold his liquor," Molly said, patting him on the head. "How about a nice cognac to wash that down?"

"Side!" Stephen said, nodding vigorously. "Mo' side!"

"No wonder he's been sleeping soundly," Frank said. "You get him loaded every morning and he passes out every afternoon. Nice going."

I felt the tuna salad churn in my stomach and the mayonnaise *rater* with a vengeance. The coveted Mother of the Year Award slipped from my grasp.

"Can I have some cider?" John asked, not wanting to miss out on anything forbidden.

"No!" I said forcefully.

"Oh, come on, Mary," Frank said. "Admit it. You've been hoisted on your own petard, or perhaps on your own Pernod. If he wants a little side of side on the side, I'm on his side."

"No!" I repeated. "From now on, everybody drinks mineral water."

John then made things worse by doing an imitation of Stephen's drunken behavior that was savagely accurate. Everyone laughed but me. I was mortified.

Frank paid the bill and had a word with the waiter, telling him to stop serving hard cider to Stephen. Then we walked home to put poor, squiffed Stephen to bed to sleep it off.

I couldn't help thinking that for years I had somehow avoided poisoning my family with my erratic cooking, only to be done in by a fatal glass of cider.

I fully expected to find effigies of me hanging from the lampposts of Faubourg Figuerolles. The placard around my neck would read: "American. Can't cook. Poisons small children. Probably uses a fork to make mayonnaise—the peasant."

Chapter 7

WAITING FOR MAMA. The children of John's school, the Jardin d'Enfants, always sat on a long wooden bench waiting for their parents to pick them up. John (far right) was tremendously impressed by his friend Marc (left), the terror of the class.

Elves

Day One: "Did you find a little school for me, Daddy?" John asked.

Day Two: "It doesn't have to be a big school, Mama," John said.

Day Three: "Can't I go tomorrow?" John whined.

Day Four: "Oh, pleeeezzz!" John begged.

Day Five: "If you don't find me a little school, Mama," John threatened, "I'll tell everybody you're not a good cooker!"

Now, there was a revelation that would have made page one, but the poor child had a point. Since Bobo's removal, John had played halfheartedly with the occasional youngster we found in the park, but he didn't have any real friends.

Sending him to school, however, was such a giant step that Frank and I hesitated. First, there was the language problem. For all his bravado, John was still a beginner in French. How would he cope? Then there was his age. He was only four and too young by American standards to go to school. And finally, the thought of him attending school for the first time filled me with an irrational sadness. He was growing up too fast.

"If we were in Paris," Frank said, "we could probably find him an American or British nursery school. But down here in the sticks I think we're stuck."

"Well, please make some inquiries," I pleaded. "John's driving me crazy."

Frank mumbled something about a short putt, but he agreed to approach the alarming M. Dufin at the university and ask him about schools in the area.

A few days later Frank returned home from class, shaking with rage. He let out one of his patented bursts of creative profanity, one that shriveled the wallpaper and withered the plants. Stephen began to cry and I leaped up to cover John's ears for fear he would pick up a battery of new and unsavory words. By the time Typhoon Frank had blown himself out, I learned that M. Dufin had insulted my husband's intellect, linguistic ability, and manhood. It was all Frank could do to contain himself.

"That damned SOB!" Frank said, pounding a fist on the table.

"What's SOB?" John asked.

"Sob, dear," I said. "M. Dufin makes people sob."

"Oh," John said, losing interest. He only enjoyed learning words that made Mama's hair stand on end.

"Are you sure you want to go to school?" Frank asked John. "You'll hate it. I know I do."

"You go to big school. I want to go to little school," John said, a Mussolini jut to his chin. "Please, Daddy."

"Well, if Daddy has to talk to the egregious M. Dufin again, Daddy's stellar academic career may be tragically interrupted by assault charges," Frank said. "Then they'll send me off to the Chateau d'If—for life."

At the mention of the Chateau d'If, John shouted, "Monte Cristo!" and began swinging an imaginary sword at an imagined enemy. Frank had been reading *The Count of Monte Cristo* to him, and John wanted to go to Marseilles to see the famous chateau where the count had been imprisoned. I wanted to see it, too.

"I wish I had been armed with a sword this afternoon," Frank said. "M. Dufin would be shish kebab by now. I'm going to the Bar d'Oc for a drink. Here, read this."

He handed me two mimeographed pages and fled the house.

Shaken by Frank's outburst, I sat down and looked at the pages he had given me. They were in French, naturally, and my reading comprehension was about as good as my speaking ability. Still, I was curious and decided to give the translation a whirl.

The headline read: Lycée des Jeunes Filles.

I knew that *Lycée* was a school—a high school, I thought. *Jeunes* meant young. And perhaps *filles* was the French spelling for "fillies," meaning young female horses? A riding academy? I couldn't imagine why Frank was suddenly interested in equestrian pursuits, but I hoped we'd all be galloping through downtown Montpellier soon. How exciting!

After some incomprehensible paragraphs, there was another headline: Jardin d'Enfants. That was easy: It meant "Garden of Infants." I pictured a row of tiny tots in a cabbage patch, their little heads poking up above the ground. How cute! Although for the life of me I couldn't figure out what those botanical babies had to do with horses. However, I kept plugging along even without my trusty dictionary, which Frank had purloined and left at the university.

When my husband returned about an hour later, I was, needless to say, confused.

"Did you read the brochure?" Frank asked, pouring me a glass of red wine.

"Yes," I said. "But I've got a question."

"Shoot."

"Who are the elves and why are they expected to join the fillies at eight-thirty a.m.?"

Frank pursed his lips; looked at his glass of wine. Then he said, "You know, I think I've had too much to drink. I'm failing to grasp one word of what you're saying. I'm going to bed."

"No, wait," I said hurriedly. "Maybe you'd better read this to me in English."

"Maybe I'd better," he said with a sigh. "Show me the elves and fillies."

"Right here," I said, pointing at the words.

He shook his head and raised his eyes in supplication.

"First off, *jeunes filles* are girls, and your elves are *élèves*—pupils—pronounced *A-lav.*"

"Ahh," I said.

"You didn't understand a single word of this, did you?" he said.

"I got the gist," I said defensively.

Frank looked pained and said, "I had to suffer through twenty minutes with that supercilious bast—"

"Please, Frank, don't start," I interrupted.

"Look, here's the 'gist,'" Frank said after draining his glass. "There's a school near here called the Lycée des Jeunes Filles, a school for girls, which includes a kindergarten called the Jardin d'Enfants. Get it? Garden. Children. *Kinder* in German. No elves allowed and not a filly for a hundred miles. The kindergarten is open to both boys and girls."

"Sounds perfect," I said, vowing never to read anything again without consulting my dictionary.

"If M. Dufin recommends it, it's probably a dungeon," Frank said, grimacing.

The word *dungeon* sparked another solo sword fight from John, prompting me to exile him to bed.

"Why is he so anxious to go to school?" I asked Frank when I returned.

"Beats me," he said. "I guess he just wants to do what I do."

"Do you think we should make some inquiries?" I asked.

"Already done," Frank said. "I've made an appointment with the teacher, Mme. Lanval. We see her the day after tomorrow."

The next morning, with feelings as mixed up as a good bouillabaisse, I decided to head for the one place in Montpellier that I found restful, the Jardin des Plantes, the botanical gardens across the street from the university's medical school. The gardens seemed to stretch on forever: quiet, fragrant, and shady, even on the hottest days. All the plants and trees were marked with plaques describing them in French and Latin. The fact that I didn't understand either language only added to the mystery of the place.

Before we entered the garden, the boys and I stopped at a little store for a fresh loaf of bread and a thick slab of chocolate to make *pain au chocolat*, which is one of the great culinary inventions of all time. Imagine: hot, crusty French bread inserted with delicious dark melty chocolate and washed down with cold mineral water. Also imagine nothing to cook and nothing to clean up, other than two chocolately faces, and you'll know why *pain au chocolat* was my absolute favorite snack.

With our provisions stowed on board Stephen's stroller, we walked around the old part of town. No sidewalks in sight, just cobblestone streets so narrow you could almost touch the houses on either side. The medical school headquarters are in a former Benedictine monastery and near it is the wonderful Cathedral of St. Pierre, which looks more like a medieval fortress than a church. The two massive pillars in front are scarred with bullet holes and blasted with cannonball craters, but the church still stands, almost six hundred years old, more than three times as old as the United States.

Inside the hushed confines of the gardens we walked slowly, admiring the busts of famous botanists and doctors, having no idea who they were, but sensing their power and prestige. As usual, the gardens were almost deserted, so we had our pick of benches and sat in a secluded nook, breathing in the fragrant air. Or at least John and I did. Stephen decided that he would take his own tour and ran off around the corner. I could picture him ripping up priceless plants from Madagascar, so I sent John after him with instructions not to tackle his brother, but to keep him out of trouble. Then I took a bite of my *pain au chocolat*, closed my eyes, and envisioned myself enjoying this magnificent peace and quiet for a week or two.

"Pardon?"

The voice jolted me out of my reverie. Standing in front of me was a middle-aged man in a tight black suit. He was wearing a Homburg hat and was carrying a gold-handled cane. But what caught my attention was his forked Vandyke beard, which made him look like the movie version of the devil.

"*Oui?*" I ventured, determined to hold on to my soul.

He gave me a sharp look, then spoke in nearly flawless English: "You are the mother of two young boys?"

"*Oui,*" I said again, stupidly.

"They have climbed a tree and cannot escape," he said.

I jumped up and raced off to find them. And find them I did, stuck in a small tree. John had obviously climbed up first, then pulled Stephen after him, and now they were both trapped.

John passed Stephen down to me, then jumped to the ground.

"Stephen made me do it," John said immediately. When in doubt, blame your brother.

"You shouldn't have dragged him up there," I said.

"He would have cried," John reasoned, "and scared the birds."

"Nice try," I said to my budding ornithologist. "Let's go, and no more tree climbing."

When we got back to the bench, the man with the Vandyke was still there. I thanked him for alerting me to the boys' predicament. Then I asked him how he knew I wasn't French.

"French children wouldn't have dared climb a tree in the garden," he said. "So I decided you must be American."

I chose to take that as a compliment, and asked him about himself. He was, he told me, a university administrator, and he insisted I call him Jules. "That is the American custom, no? To address strangers by their Christian names?" We exchanged pleasantries for a few minutes; then I offered him some bread and chocolate. He accepted immediately.

"Are you aware of the history of these gardens?" he asked me.

"Not really."

"They are the oldest botanical gardens in France, perhaps in all of Europe," he said. "They were founded by Henri IV in 1593, but their significance goes back much further. In the 1200s Montpellier was on the trading route with North Africa, and as a result, merchants bought and sold exotic spices and plants. Following the lead of Arab physicians, doctors in those days used the spices and plants for medicinal purposes. For example, a tincture of violet and dried viper skin was the recipe for one miracle cure. And the penicillin of the sixteenth century was a pill made of two-thirds aloe and one-third myrrh. That was supposed to cure the plague, when taken with wine. Personally, however, I think the wine was the active ingredient."

I laughed.

"At any rate," he continued, "the Faculté de Médecine, as the medical school is called, has been a celebrated place of learning since the Middle Ages."

He shrugged, then said, "And why not? Anyone prescribing cinnamon and ginger for stomach cancer must be a genius."

"I take it you are not a big fan of doctors," I said.

"Ha!" he said. "Three hundred and fifty years ago there were two hundred students here studying medicine without knowing anything about germs. They were drunk most of the time and were rewarded for gluing plant leaves in a book and making wildly wrong guesses about diseases. Today there are seven hundred students, not quite as drunk, but still learning nonsense."

"Well, medicine certainly saves more lives today than it did back then," I said.

He sighed. "The one good thing about the sixteenth century was that students were forbidden to see patients until they earned their doctorate degrees. The penalty for practicing medicine without a license was to be paraded through the city, mounted backward on an ass. It is a punishment that should be pronounced on most doctors, with or without their licenses."

Since Jules was obviously getting upset, I steered the conversation away from medicine and told him something about why a nice Midwestern girl was eating *pain au chocolat* in the world's oldest botanical garden. After about twenty minutes, Jules dutifully tipped his hat and departed. I hoped I'd see him again.

When I told Frank about meeting Jules, my husband was unimpressed.

"Probably some underemployed old codger who's waiting for his pension," he said. "The university is lousy with them."

I didn't argue with him, but I had the feeling Jules was more than just some functionary. He had a scholarly air, and at least he had taken my mind off tomorrow's meeting at the school.

Stephen took the opportunity to scream all that night, resisting any and all attempts to quiet him. It was fortunate that the walls of our old house were two feet thick or Mme. Sauson would have evicted us long ago.

At eight o'clock the next morning, bleary-eyed and exhausted, the four of us lit out for the Jardin d'Enfants. Still in a fog, I couldn't help thinking about rows of small children growing out of the ground, but Frank's serious mood brought me back to reality.

"Don't judge the school by its physical plant," Frank warned in his best educationese. "Remember, the French are at the forefront of pedagogy."

I should hope so!

So, with my expectations lowered and fully expecting to find a run-down sharecropper's shack filled with pedagogically advanced children, I was pleasantly surprised by what we discovered. The girls' school was beautiful. The nineteenth-century building had been thoroughly modernized and was gleaming. Inside, the kindergarten classroom was decorated with nursery rhyme murals on the walls and filled with pint-size tables and chairs. There was a piano in one corner and shelves filled with toys for the children. The school was fully as modern as any we had ever seen in America and superior to many.

There was a large outdoor play area and a courtyard pretty with trees, shrubs, and flowers. On either side of the door were long wooden benches, which we learned later were there for the children to sit on while waiting for their parents to pick them up.

Most impressive, however, was the teacher, Mme. Lanval. She was young and attractive, and in five minutes she had charmed all of us with her quick smile and ready enthusiasm.

"Well, what do you think?" Frank asked me finally.

"I don't know," I said honestly.

"Let me put it this way," Frank said. "You'll be awarded the Légion d'Honneur for excellence in the French language before I beard M. Dufin in his den again. It's here or nowhere."

"Ask her if she thinks John speaks enough French to get by," I prompted Frank.

Mme. Lanval then posed a series of questions to John, all of which he answered quickly.

"She says he'll do fine," Frank translated.

I was still dubious when Stephen, bored by the interview, began to cry. Loudly. Mme. Lanval gave him a sharp look that shut him up instantly. Now, there was a woman who could handle children. That sold me. We all shook hands and the deed was done, but I felt as if I were throwing my baby to the wolves.

Frank and I were perplexed by John's school mania. Merely copying his father didn't seem to me to justify such enthusiasm.

"If he really wanted to copy you," I told my husband, "he would be smoking, drinking, and swearing like a ditchdigger."

Frank smiled. "At least his French is getting better and better every day. He's learning so much, I worry that he will forget his English."

"Not as long as I need a translator," I said. "With me, he gets plenty of practice in English."

"The point, I think, is that if a child has a burning desire to do something constructive, like go to school, I don't see how we can stand in his way," Frank said. "It's not as if he wants to go to the Bowery and live on the sidewalk—although bums generally make more money than students."

"But what if he has a terrible experience here?" I said. "He'll never want to go to school again," I said.

"He won't have to. I've got degrees enough for both of us," Frank said. "I'll give him one or two. Besides, he can always sell newspapers on the street, and Stephen can be his shill. His shrill shill. Think of all the dough we'll save with two self-employed children."

We let the discussion hang for several days, until it was too late to do anything except take John to school. Sometimes, the only way to make a decision is to make no decision at all.

The evening before the big day, Frank came home with an armload of school supplies for John.

"Now that you're going to be an *élève*," he said, "you're going to need the right tools."

Then he began laying out pens, pencils, a ruler, a protractor, crayons, ink, graph paper, lined paper, blank paper, chalk, a chalkboard, a notebook, and a pencil box.

John gave the pile of miscellaneous supplies a cursory look, selected a single pencil (there were No. 1, No. 2, No. 2 1/2, and No. 3 leads on display), and said, "Thank you, Daddy." Then he wandered away, totally uninterested in the rest.

"You're going to need all these things," Frank called after him.

"No, I won't, Daddy. I'm going to little school, not big school," John said with impeccable four-year-old logic.

"How do you like that?" Frank said, hurt. "I spend a fortune on all these supplies, and he turns up his nose at everything."

"Frank, he's going to kindergarten, not MIT," I said. "Besides, you forgot the slide rule."

"Next semester," he said, looking lovingly at the mountain of supplies. One thing you can say about my husband—he's organized. Here is a man who keeps color-coded checkbooks for various expenses and lays out the nibs for his fountain pens in descending order of thickness.

I find such behavior comforting. Frank always seems to be in control—even if he isn't. However, all his assurances couldn't make me feel easy about packing my son off to school. A foreign school, yet. With or without supplies, John's academic career, I feared, would be a disaster.

Finally the day arrived, and with John scrubbed, brushed, shining, and wearing his best blue corduroy overalls, we walked him slowly toward his new school. All along the way I fretted. Would he be accepted by the other kids? Or would he be miserable? Would he understand enough to follow along? Or would he just sit there, frustrated? I had a thousand questions to ask and no answers.

Frank, having gotten over John's dismissal of the supplies, was in a no-nonsense mood.

"For heaven's sake," he told me. "We're taking the child to school, not leading him to the gallows. Cheer up."

I smiled bravely, but my heart wasn't in it.

Mme. Lanval shook hands with us cordially, wished us a good day, and before we could barrage her with helpful suggestions or give her important last-minute instructions, she showed us to the door.

Suddenly, we were standing outside the classroom, stunned.

"That's what I'd call the bum's rush," Frank said, somewhat aggrieved.

"What have we done?" I said, my cold feet turning to ice.

Frank straightened his shoulders and said, "I'm not worried, and you shouldn't be either. Besides, I've got to get to class."

When I didn't move, he added, "What are you going to do, stay here all day?"

With a king-size lump in my throat, I looked at him scornfully. "Don't be silly," I said.

"And don't forget to pick him up at noon," he said, getting on his bicycle and pedaling away.

Forget! Oh, what a hard-hearted man I had married.

I couldn't think of an appropriate retort, so I returned home for a good cry.

By eleven-thirty, however, I had my sentiments well in hand, and with Stephen in tow, I set off to retrieve what was left of my elder son. The whole way there I criticized myself for being so emotional. Frank had been right: I was making this school business into a much bigger deal than it was. If my husband wasn't concerned, why should I be?

Class was still in session when I arrived at the Jardin d'Enfants, so I haunted the schoolyard and tried out all the benches. As I sat there reducing my nails to bite-size pieces, Frank whirled around the corner on his bike.

"I thought you might be late," he said lamely. "And since it's his first day, I thought I'd, uh, you know . . ."

The big softy, I thought, squeezing his hand. He was just as apprehensive as I. But I didn't have time to belabor the obvious because the classroom door burst open. Mme. Lanval stood in the doorway and out marched the elves. As each one passed her, they stopped, bowed, and shook hands as she rattled off their names and wished them *bon appétit.*

When John spotted us, he broke ranks and ran toward us, but Mme. Lanval called him back sharply. He had to return to the end of the line and go through the handshake before he came to us.

The handshake, we found out later, was mandatory. No one could leave without it. If Mme. Lanval was occupied, the *élèves* could shake her little finger or even her elbow, but "shake" they must before they left. We soon learned to get into the spirit of this little ritual, and so did John.

But now we flanked him protectively and started for home, bombarding him with questions like: "How did it go?" "Did you have a good time?" "What did you do?" "Did you like the other children?" John's eyes had a glazed, shell-shocked look, I thought, but he answered us in French that everything was wonderful.

Then seeing the surprised look on our faces, he quickly switched to English.

"It was okay, but we've got to hurry because I have to be back at two," he said. "You can't be late. Mme. Lanval said so."

And that summed up all we learned about his school from him that first day. It was fine, he liked it, and he wasn't supposed to be late. But I need not have worried about his being happy. He loved his school, the other children, and Mme. Lanval. School was five days a week with Thursdays off—corresponding to our Saturdays. I soon learned to dread "off" days, for John found them very dull and was always sorry to see them come. He even demanded to know why there was no school on Sundays or at night. Frank could only shake his head in amazement. "I hope he doesn't become a professional student like his father," he said.

After a few days I relaxed and decided that anything that aroused so much zeal couldn't be bad. My Sarah Bernhardt-like farewells took on less and less of a final parting atmosphere, until we were rushing off with no more than a quick 'bye to each other.

Our little *élève* had only two complaints that week. First, he demanded that we call him "Jeannot" from then on.

"John-o?" I said. What kind of name was that?

"It's a diminutive of Jean," Frank explained. "Johnny, if you like."

I didn't like. Normally, I disapprove of nicknames and diminutives. If you want to call your child Skip or Buzz or Biff, call him Skip or Buzz or Biff. Put it in writing, put it on his birth certificate, and knock it off with Chauncey, Hobart, and Sterling. I'm Mary (except in Texas, where I'm MAY-ree), Frank is Frank, and John is John. We are not Lulu, Chip, and Junior. But in this case I knew I had to relent. The poor child was trying so hard to fit in that it would have been cruel not to go along with him. So it was Jeannot—some of the time.

His other request was for short pants like the other boys wore. That was easy. I whacked off the legs of all his overalls. He thought this made him blend in better with the crowd, and although we never told him, Frank and I used to smile about this to ourselves, for John stood a good six inches taller than all his classmates. No matter what he wore, he would have stuck out like an oversize thumb.

We would take turns dropping John off at school and picking him up again. But I must admit that for the first few weeks I exhibited lurking and skulking skills I never knew I had before. I would descend upon the Jardin d'Enfants at odd hours, hoping to catch a glimpse of what was really going on there. What I saw made me smile.

At recess, the children would all troop out of the classroom and divide themselves into two groups: the boys and the girls. The boys would wrestle for a time; then they would take up a new game John must have taught them—Monte Cristo. This was a simple game: each boy grabbed a stick, shouted, "Monte Cristo!" and proceeded to sword fight everyone else. Boys, I guess, love any game that involves beating each other over the head with sticks. When Monte Cristo grew tiresome, they played *avion,* or airplane.

The boys would stretch out their arms, and making plane noises and machine-gun sounds, they would act out spirited dogfights. After they had warmed up, they would run over and dive-bomb the girls.

Veterans of this game, the girls sat quietly reading or playing jacks, but they kept a weather eye out for the boys. When the air raid finally came, they would all leap up, pretend to be scared, and run away screaming from the incoming bombers. I felt great sympathy for those sweet little girls until I realized that if the boys ignored them for too long, they would send out an emissary to find out why the attack hadn't begun. After some hesitation, the boys would realize they were late and swoop down on the impatiently waiting girls and the screaming would commence.

I thought this was strange behavior until I realized that I had attended many a cocktail party where all the men stood by the bar and all the women gathered in the living room to complain that all the men were at the bar. Besides, in Texas I knew plenty of real dive-bombers and fighter pilots who had the maturity of your average four-year-old. Some things are preordained, I suppose.

Still, like his current literary favorite, Monte Cristo, John seemed liberated at last. The months of imprisonment were over, he had a new name, and he was well on his way to making friends.

But the day we knew he really belonged was when he told us about the Blue Ladies.

Blue Ladies! We were intrigued.

"How blue?" I asked.

"Well, I mean, they wear blue uniforms," he said.

"And what do they do?"

"They help you on with your coat. They give out toys, and they keep the lines straight when you go to the bathroom," he said.

"You go to the bathroom in formation?" Frank asked, no doubt picturing a military kindergarten.

"Yes," John said. "The girls go first and then the boys."

We digested that in silence.

"They also help on the playground and make sure the boys don't push the girls in the mud puddles," he continued.

"That's nice," I said.

He went on about the school for a while and then announced, glorying in the memory, "You know, the Blue Ladies don't hit you half as hard as Mme. Lanval."

That was when we knew all was well. He was accepted and undiscriminated against. John would always be an outsider, but just the same, he had arrived.

He was one of the boys.

Chapter 8

LOVE AFFAIR. Elise, as usual, restraining a rambunctious Stephen. With absolute love, she absolutely tamed him, while becoming Mary's confidante and friend.

The Love Treatment

October 1950

Stephen had developed a drinking problem.

Not cider this time, but he downed a bottle of ink, the water in a vase, and heaven knows what else. I had to watch him like a hawk.

He had also been having fits lately. We would be walking down the street when suddenly he'd fly into a rage, turn purple, and begin ripping all his clothes off. I didn't know what caused this dreadful behavior; I assumed it was a phase—a phase John, fortunately, had never gone through.

And although Stephen had never been a great sleeper, his new routine was driving me to distraction. He would fall asleep at seven p.m. and wake up at midnight, screaming. He would keep on squalling until five a.m., then fall back to sleep for an hour. It didn't matter if I got up with him or ignored him: He cried all the same. Sometimes walking him up and down the living room pacified him, sometimes not. I tried eliminating his nap, but that didn't do any good either. His schedule: sleep for five hours; holler for five hours. It got to the point where I couldn't remember when he—or I—had slept through the night.

To add to our misery, we were undergoing the torture of toilet training. John was pretty well housebroken at sixteen months, but I didn't seem to be getting anywhere with Stephen. I tried to explain to him that going to the bathroom consisted of four easy steps: tell someone you have to go, go, flush, and wash your hands.

He had grasped these simple concepts, but their exact order continued to elude him. He would wash his hands, flush, then go in his
diaper and tell me about it later. Or he would go once in the toilet;
then just to keep me on my toes, he would go again in his diapers.
I was baffled, disgruntled, and frankly upset that I couldn't seem to
get through to him—about anything.

I don't claim to be an expert on child rearing, far from it, but I
do have one child who, other than suffering from the occasional
hallucination, seems to be fairly normal. How John wound up that
way was a miracle, I suppose.

Frank and I, being the youngest in our families, had never encountered any babies on a regular basis, and we didn't have a clue
about caring for an infant. To his credit, Frank threw himself into
researching pregnancy and childbirth. He read every work on the
subject and made a catalogue of file cards, organized and indexed
by symptom and disease. If I had a twinge, he'd run for his file and
pull out the appropriate card.

"Are you in a coma and/or vomiting blood?" he would ask.

When I told him it was just a small pain, he would reassure me
that I was not in the grip of eclampsia, dyspepsia, or some other
deadly condition. All I was looking for was a little sympathy; what
I got were medical horror stories. I soon learned to keep my mouth
shut, or Frank would have had me confined to the hospital for the
remainder of my pregnancy.

John was born a month early and weighed in at just five pounds.
The doctors kept him in an incubator for three weeks, then turned
him over to us. When we got him home, we were helpless as babes.
Fortunately, the babe knew exactly what to do. We just watched
him in awe, hoping he wouldn't expire or spontaneously combust.
So great was our fear of damaging him that it practically took both
of us to transport him from room to room. We would hold nightly
debates about milk temperature, diaper tightness, and breathing
and heartbeat rates.

After a harrowing week of excruciating attention to detail and
an overwhelming sense of impending disaster, a Mrs. Odell rang

our bell. She was a nurse sent by the hospital to make sure incompetent new mothers like me weren't killing their babies.

Frank and I watched with our hearts in our mouths as Mrs. Odell manhandled our son, tossed him in the air, and splashed him in the kitchen sink for a bath. She scrubbed him within an inch of his life.

"Now see here," my husband thundered. "You can't do that! It says so in Sanderson and Von Engle, *Child Care: The First Year,* Chapter 7—uh, I have the reference in the next room." He rushed off to consult his card file.

When he had gone, Mrs. Odell said, "They won't break, you know. They're tough little buggers. This one here is a fine, strong boy."

By the time Frank returned with the correct citation in hand, Mrs. Odell had John bathed, powdered, and diapered. I was amazed that his head hadn't fallen off, but her confidence about the toughness of babies did a lot to calm me down.

I mention all this because I want to make it clear that I was not some hysterical young mother, but a four-year veteran of the motherhood wars. I thought I could handle any situation with grace and aplomb and a bit of help from Frank (although grace and aplomb were usually more helpful).

Raising a child, after all, does not require a degree in physics or the ability to split the atom. It seemed to me that parents needed only two ingredients to do it properly: a little common sense and a lot of luck. All those useless books I read when John was born were long on theory and short on practicality. My approach was to take each day as it came and try to do what was sensible. Lo and behold, it seemed to work for John. But with Stephen I had met my Waterloo. Common sense had failed and my luck had run out.

All I knew was that this incessant crying was turning the rest of the family into nervous wrecks.

"Can't you control your son?" Frank asked me one night at three a.m. as we lay in bed listening to Stephen's howls.

"No, and you can't control him either," I said.

"Well, this time just let him cry," Frank said, rolling over.

About an hour later we heard a thunderous crash from the boys' room. I woke with a start. Frank was already out of bed and loping down the hall. When he returned, he was shaking his head in disbelief.

"Stephen cried so hard, he knocked the crib over. When I got there, he was lying with his head on the floor and his feet in the crib," Frank said.

"Is he all right?" I asked, getting out of bed to check on him for myself.

"Yes, I put him on the mattress and told him to go to sleep, not that it will do much good," Frank said, crawling back into bed. "I'll put the crib back together tomorrow."

"We can't just leave him there like that," I said, aghast.

"Sleeping dogs can't even sleep around here," Frank muttered enigmatically. "Let him alone."

I checked on Stephen anyway and he didn't seem injured, but I couldn't sleep the rest of the night for worrying.

The next morning, Stephen was as perky as I was peaked. He seemed to have suffered no ill effects from his fall.

"We have to face reality," Frank said, sipping his coffee. "He'll probably cry until he's twenty-four, so I've got an idea."

I was sitting at the kitchen table, my head in my hands, woozy from lack of sleep.

"I think it's time to get you a *bonne*," he continued.

"A bun?" I said, picturing a gooey breakfast roll. "No, thanks, I couldn't eat a bite."

"No, no," Frank said. "A *bonne à tout faire* is a maid—an all-purpose cleaning woman, baby-sitter, chief cook, and bottle washer."

A maid? Now that got my attention.

"I talked with Mme. Sauson and she told me about a woman who is looking for a family to care for," Frank said. "We pay a few francs a day, and she can look after the kids while we take naps."

Bliss!

"It's not a real solution, but if we have to stay up all night, we might as well sleep in the afternoons," he said. "What do you think?"

"What's her name and when can she start?" I said.

"Her name is Marie, I think. She's a countrywoman who lives on a farm outside of town. Her own kids are grown up, and Mme. Sauson tells me Marie is pining for the company of children," Frank said.

"Foolish woman," I said. "Is she available this afternoon? I'm *so* tired."

"Don't you even want to meet her?" Frank asked. "I mean, given your rather checkered career as the hirer of household help?"

"Delilah!" we both said at once.

Two years ago, I had interviewed a woman named Delilah, who had come highly recommended by Richard Widmark, a young actor who lived in our village. According to Mr. Widmark, Delilah was a gem, a woman of almost Renaissance capabilities, who could have, had she wished, taken over the management of Buckingham Palace. I was willing to believe that and hired her on the spot.

The first week was uneventful. Then Frank began to look at me in a peculiar manner. I asked him what was wrong, but he made some silly excuses and told me everything was fine. The second week Frank was still acting peculiar, which was not all that peculiar for him, but I was tired of being studied in silence.

"What is it?" I finally asked. "You look at me as if I've grown a third eye. It's disconcerting."

"I don't like to mention this," he said finally, "but do you have a drinking problem?"

"What!" I said, both insulted and mystified. One highball was my usual limit, and even that was mostly water. "What on earth are you talking about?"

"Now, don't get mad, but last week when I made myself a cocktail it didn't taste right," Frank said. "So I checked the bottle and found it had been watered. I figured you had drained most of it and filled the bottle with tap water."

"For heaven's sake," I sputtered.

Seeing my ire, Frank quickly retreated.

"Then it must be Delilah," he said, almost wistfully.

I think he hoped it was me. Delilah, after all, was a pretty good cleaning woman. But we couldn't have her emptying the liquor closet three times a week. Frank, tired of supporting her habit, began leaving the adulterated whiskey out in the open and hiding the good stuff.

"Talk to her," Frank said, transferring the responsibility.

I spent the next few days dithering and working up my courage, which, as I have said, was in short supply. Should I really talk to her or take the coward's way out and just fire her?

That decision, fortunately, was taken out of my hands. One day I sent her out to the playground with John while I puttered around the house. She was to return at three, but by four I got worried. I went to the playground. No one had seen her. Getting panicky, I walked up and down the streets nearby until I came to a vacant lot strewn with the remains of a recently demolished house. Amid the wreckage I spotted John's stroller perched precariously on a mound of rubble.

I rushed across a minefield of broken boards, crushed cement blocks, and sharp shards of glass to find, to my relief, John dozing peacefully. Then I heard singing. Delilah was sitting on a cracked and chipped toilet, her hat at an odd angle, her coat thrown on the ground. In her hand was a bottle of rye from which she took the occasional swig between verses of "Bringing in the Sheaves."

"What's the meaning of this?" I demanded, sounding eerily like my mother.

"Can't drink no more of your damned watered-down whiskey," she slurred. "Had to buy my own, you cheapskates!"

I stormed off with my baby, furious that I hadn't had the grit to fire her a week before.

I learned a lot about my deficiencies as an employer from that incident, and I only hoped that Mr. Widmark had better luck in choosing his roles than he did in choosing domestic help.

Having played Samson to Delilah, I was realistic about hiring help, especially in a foreign country. My major worry was about the traditional method of discipline practiced by parents in the south of France. The favorite method of correction, it seemed to me, was to slap children on and about the head. A cuff or two from Mme. Lanval or the Blue Ladies wouldn't do John much harm, but my choice has always been the seat of the pants. I didn't want our children to grow up hearing the bells of Notre Dame ringing in their ears.

Would Marie be a head knocker? Would she be able to handle the children since she spoke no English? More important, would she even like them? These were the thoughts that swirled through my head as I waited to meet her. Frank, whose brilliant idea this was, unfortunately had to be in class, so I was on my own.

At first glance Marie looked like any other of the women in France who scrubbed, cleaned, and did heavy menial work for a living. Her forty-five years had not treated her kindly, and her dismal black cotton dress and felt shoes, the uniform of her trade, did their best to wrap her in a cloak of anonymity. But when she laughed and her dark eyes shone with warmth and friendliness, I could feel the force of her personality. She had a dignity about her that belied her work-roughened hands and lined face.

With John as my translator and inventive sign language learned from years of playing charades, I tried to get across two points. First, Stephen was difficult to manage, and I expected her to do nothing more than supervise him and take part-time care of John, who was now in school.

This came out, through John, as something like: "Stephen's bad, bad, bad, bad!"

And second, that as far as I was concerned, the house could sink under a mountain of dust, the unwashed dishes could be stacked to the ceiling, and the dirty laundry could be allowed to stay where it lay. My only hope was that she would be able to cope with the children.

John's translation: "The house is dirty. Don't worry. It's always dirty."

Marie smiled a smile of polite disbelief at the dark picture John and I painted. The children, she said, were beautiful, well-mannered little gentlemen, and they would have a fine time together. She held out her arms and the boys drew close to her, as to a magnet, and two pairs of round blue eyes looked and passed judgment. Both of them, as instructed, raced to hand her an apron, and they positively glowed when she thanked them. As she began methodically to wash the pile of dishes in the sink, she kept up a conversation with them, and they did their best to be as polite as she. I stared in disbelief at their display of company manners.

The interview was obviously over and she thought of herself as fully employed. I guess she was because as she worked she spoke to me through the children. She told them that she had one son, now a grown man and hard at work all day. Sometimes she was so lonesome for a little boy of her own that she was downhearted. Then she had heard about us. The new American family in town with two boys to love, and she knew we must be looking for her. The children positively wriggled with pleasure at being chosen by Marie.

Reassured by her talk, I went to get dressed. Frank, in a valiant effort to improve my French, had suggested that we attend the opera, where by osmosis the words would flow into my head—and stick there. It was a nutty scheme, but I loved the idea of going to the opera, even if it was only a special matinee given for the students at the university.

Still nervous about leaving the children, I met Frank at l'Oeuf, the heart and soul of Montpellier. It's called that (the Egg) because of the oval shape of the plaza, which is studded with restaurants, bars, cafés, bistros, and shops. No matter what your mood, l'Oeuf cheers you up simply because of the number of people there having a good time. Knots of students drinking beer or coffee and engaging in philosophical arguments were common; lovers locked in torrid embraces didn't raise a concerned eyebrow; and old married couples promenading about must have been a part of the scene for hundreds of years.

You can get anything from a quick snack to an eight-course dinner on l'Oeuf; buy trinkets or treasures; drink expensive wine or sit over a cup of espresso all day without the waiter telling you to move on. Believe me, in New York if you're not spending serious money, they want their table back.

"How did it go?" Frank asked when I met him in front of the ornate Fountain of the Three Graces, which serves as a meeting place in Montpellier, rather like the clock in Grand Central Station.

"All right, I guess," I said truthfully. I really didn't know how Marie was going to work out.

"You're not worried about the boys, are you?" he asked.

"Of course I am," I said.

"Well, maybe she'll set fire to the house first—as a warning—before she kills the children," he said.

"Frank!"

"Come on. We'll be late," he said. But his mordant sense of humor set me to worrying again.

We purchased tickets for a stall on the second balcony, and an old lady in a black dress checked our stubs, then produced an enormous key and unlocked our private box for us. I felt just like Irene Dunne in a period picture, expecting at any moment to feel the heat of the spotlight on me and to hear the crowd below request that I sing a song. Fortunately, no one did or I would have driven the audience out of the house.

The box was covered with red plush to match the chairs and the curtain. The fact that it was so far over on one side that we had to hang over the edge to see the stage never dulled a moment of the first act. For a time I forgot all my troubles and was swept away by the music and the powerful voices of the singers.

At the conclusion of the first act, we went to the bar for a cigarette and a glass of wine, but I quickly discovered that I was the only woman puffing away. It seemed that the southern ladies just didn't smoke in public. I felt like a scarlet woman, and that made me think that any self-respecting person wouldn't be smoking and drinking in the middle of the day. I was not only scarlet, I was irresponsible. All I could see were our two infants cowed in a corner, or crying, or being hit on the head—maybe even bleeding! Finally, I could stand it no longer.

"Frank, I've got to go home. Right now!"

"What for?"

"I've got to see if the children are all right," I said. "Why did we ever leave them? We don't even know that woman or what she's doing to them. I've got a bad feeling."

"Why do I get the impression that things are more dramatic here than they are onstage?" Frank murmured.

But I married a real man. He knew when it was useless to argue with a woman. After a vexed silence he took me by the arm and led me out to the entrance. There he commandeered a taxi, a rash extravagance in Montpellier, and we hurtled back to the rue de Claret.

"And don't spare the horses," Frank said sarcastically.

We screeched to a halt in front of the house, and while Frank paid the driver, I ran up the stairs, knowing in my heart that I would find the boys in distress—if they were even alive.

Outside the door ominous silence prevailed. *Where were they? What had happened?*

Silently, I opened the door and peered in.

And what to my wondering eyes did appear? A scene right out of a Norman Rockwell painting. Marie was sitting at the kitchen table darning socks; John was beside her cutting out pictures from a magazine; and Stephen, our wildest little Indian of all, was sitting on the other side of the table, placidly making chalk marks on a slate.

The apartment breathed of serenity and it was spotless. The day's washing was flapping off the balcony, and a gorgeous smell came from a pot on the stove. The Rockwell painting could have been called *Domesticity—French Style.*

I came all the way in. I had to. Our offspring were eyeing me critically.

"What are you doing home, Mama?" John asked while Stephen stared at me as though we had never met.

"I—I . . . forgot something," I said, fleeing to the bedroom. I grabbed a handkerchief, waved it ostentatiously, and said au revoir to Marie.

"Who's Marie?" John asked, swiveling his head around as if he were trying to find an unknown person hiding in the room.

"There," I said, nodding toward Marie.

"You're so funny, Mama," John said. "Her name is Elise. Don't you know that?"

I smiled wanly and slipped out of the apartment. At that moment I didn't know what I knew anymore.

"This is all your fault," I told my husband as we sat in our favorite watering hole, the Bar d'Oc. "You said her name was Marie."

"Marie, Elise. What's in a name?" Frank said. "The point is, we've stumbled onto a nice woman who loves the children. Let's be thankful for that and have another bottle of this extraordinarily ordinary *vin ordinaire*. After that taxi ride, we can't afford anything better."

"You've got to apologize to her for me," I said. "I feel like such a fool. And I'm sorry about getting so worked up."

"I've never been a big believer in women's intuition before," Frank said. "But I really believe that you are blessed with reverse women's intuition. Whenever you predict disaster, nothing happens. I'm just worried that someday you'll think things are going great—then the world will suddenly come to an end."

But he was wrong. Things did get better and the world kept spinning along as usual. The nameless dread that had spooked me that day had made me forget Elise's bright eyes, her upturned mouth, and the laugh crinkles at her eyes. But I never doubted her again. She became not only my maid but my friend, my conversationalist, and my tutor who tried, without much success, to correct my French. The children, of course, fell headlong in love with her.

In a week she was not only in command of the boys, but, at her insistence, the house and the cooking. At the end of the day the house sparkled with cleanliness, and the children were scrubbed and sweet. Elise, with no signs of wear or tear, would present our two for damp good night kisses and whisk them off to bed.

The first week I prayed she wouldn't quit. The second week I raised her wages. The third week I would have done anything for her. But the little demon of curiosity kept gnawing at me. How did she manage everything so easily? What was her secret?

Then, using my newfound skulking and lurking skills, I began coming home unexpectedly, sneaking in the door, and giving John the third degree. And suddenly a whole world of child psychology opened up before me.

How did she keep Stephen from his favorite tricks of turning on the gas stove, eating or destroying anything within reach, teetering from high places, and breaking bottles? Elise told him not to, as I did, but when he continued, she didn't spank or scold him. She picked him up, hugged him, and smothered him with kisses. She told him he was a perfect treasure, a little chicken, a little cabbage, and that she loved him. Then she set him down again, and as John declared, "It really works!"

And work it did. Before my disbelieving eyes, Elise was actually loving him out of being disobedient. She sang songs to him about himself and told him stories in which he always turned out to be the central character.

From the time she arrived until she sang him to sleep at night, a stream of flattery, praise, and affection poured over him. No matter how naughty the act (and there were many), no matter how obstinate he grew, or how violent his temper tantrums, Elise would brush back her salt-and-pepper hair, twinkle at him with her dark eyes, and maintain an iron calm.

As I got to know her better, I learned of her past life and wondered at her happy nature. She had lived through two world wars in embattled France, and her life had been hard and joyless. But her cheerful nature dismissed these hardships. She summed up the bad years with "It's finished now."

And that was her attitude toward the children's misdeeds. Once it was over, "it was finished," and she would smile at the funny things they did next. She constantly showed them things to be happy about and divided her attentions equally when she was with both boys and taught them to respect and love each other.

She talked always of the boys' best characteristics and ignored their bad ones. When I explained to her that I had not been able to train Stephen to stay dry during the day, she looked surprised. Not at him, but at me.

Toilet training is not something southern French parents think much about. Their superior, if unhygienic, method is not to put pants on kids until they have reached an age when they can "indicate what is desired." Children are encouraged to relieve themselves wherever they are: the streets, the park, the garden. After his adventure atop of the Eiffel Tower, John was charmed with this idea, but his straitlaced Midwestern mother was not. French men, however, had no such inhibitions, and when nature called, they answered. Needless to say, between the men, the children, and the dogs, you had to be careful where you walked in France.

Amazingly, within two weeks, using the French system, Elise had convinced Stephen that only dry pants were fitting for such a perfect baby. One by one his black moods became fewer, and that was not surprising. When someone is holding you, loving you, and laughing with you, it's hard to remain a desperate character for long, even if you're only eighteen months old.

When Stephen was in my care, I adopted Elise's tactics and found that they worked, even for me. The Mr. Hyde in him receded to a manageable degree, and wonder of wonders, he began to sleep through the night occasionally.

"I think I'll divorce you and marry her," Frank said, only half kidding. As a housekeeper and surrogate mother, Elise could not be equaled, especially by me. For what I had left out of my calculations on child rearing was a prime ingredient—not just love but absolute and unqualified love. Sure, it takes common sense and luck to raise a child, but Elise taught me the greatest lesson of all. No child can long withstand the furious and unstoppable onslaught of The Love Treatment.

Chapter 9

CAFÉ SOCIETY. Stephen (with his ubiquitous bib), Mary, and John in front of the Café-Bar, one of their many haunts in Montpellier, generously explored and inspected by Frank.

My Affair

Soon after our arrival in Montpellier, Frank, in an act of supreme self-sacrifice, volunteered to make a survey of the local bars and cafés. His plan was to choose one that would become a headquarters for us, a place where we could catch up on the gossip, grab a quick snack, and generally get to know the people of our district.

"Besides," he said, "once you mingle with the local people, you'll pick up the language."

I was skeptical. No, I was an out-and-out unbeliever. I knew I couldn't pick up French if it were featherlight, lying all around, and I had a bushel basket. My doubts, however, were cast aside by my enthusiastic husband, who made a scientific search of fifty-two bars and restaurants, leaving me home with the kids. That man would do anything for me.

The results of his exhaustive research trickled in slowly. He nixed the Bar Général: "Wild-eyed Communists, bomb-toting anarchists, and very little drinking going on there. No girls allowed."

After considering the Café Sud, Frank rejected it out of hand. His description: "All laborers, cheap drinks, and centuries of dirt on the floors, the walls, and the waiters."

He likewise condemned L'Argent: "Snooty poseurs, expensive drinks, stupidly expensive food, and a general air of Balzacian bourgeois ignorance."

Gee, I wouldn't want to go there.

No, the place he chose was the Bar d'Oc, just down the street from us. It got Frank's highest rating: "Good service, good food, the occasional free drink, and on weekends free movies."

But what really sold Frank, I think, was that the bar was a hotbed of sedition. It was filled with mysterious men speaking a mysterious language called Occitan. Frank was fascinated.

"Think of it," he said. "Here are these men who refuse to speak French to show their disdain for the central government."

"Are they dangerous?" I asked apprehensively.

"Not very," he said. "The idea of a secession of Occitan speakers from Paris is ludicrous. But I admire their tenacity in keeping a virtually dead language alive for almost six hundred years."

As Frank explained it, all Gaul was divided into two linguistic groups: The *Langue d'Oil* (French) and the *Langue d'Oc* (Occitan, Provencal, Limousin, and others). When he wasn't consigning souls to the Inferno, Dante had apparently come up with that classification.

Montpellier, I learned, was the traditional capital of the region known as Languedoc—*Langue d'Oc,* the language of Oc. This was the place where Occitan separatists were active, especially at the end of the nineteenth century. But nationalist movements were all but wiped out by the world wars, and the old gentlemen fomenting revolution at the Bar d'Oc were considered by nearly everyone as slightly ridiculous—rather like the ancient relics in the American South who hoard their Confederate money, fully expecting Robert E. Lee to ride again. Still, I was charmed that the language of the troubadours was alive and well and having a drink at the Bar d'Oc—even if the speakers themselves were far from romantic.

Frank would quiz these old men about their language, making notes and marveling to me that each tiny village in the region had different words for common items, different pronunciations, and even different verb forms.

"I could get a Ph.D. in Occitan," Frank said, "and never leave the bar."

So, from almost our first moments in town, "our spot" was the Bar d'Oc, creaking revolutionaries and all.

I loved to sit outside, under a green-striped umbrella, sipping espresso and watching the world go by. Inside, there was a long mahogany bar on the left and little tables sporting spotless linen and fresh flowers on the right. The owner, Pascal, always made a big show of welcoming me, but I was under no illusion that my sparkling personality was the reason. Frank was. He was the most popular guy there. His lavish tipping (fifty cents, on occasion), his willingness to stand a round, his interest in all the patrons, and his penchant for bringing in crowds of paying customers from the university to listen to the Occitan speakers made him the man of the hour. The children and I were fortunate that Frank's celebrity rubbed off on us.

One day, with John in tow, I stopped into the Bar d'Oc for lunch and ordered a tomato, onion, and lettuce salad. Pascal insisted that I have it with *poulpe,* whatever that was. So I smiled and said, "*Mais, oui!*" That was a phrase that everyone liked to hear. But when the big wooden salad bowl was placed before me, I almost had a heart attack. Sitting serenely atop the greens were three baby octopuses, their tentacles entwined in a macabre fandango.

Now, I'm not a picky eater. I've eaten moose, elk, and bear steaks; I've enjoyed shark fin soup and thousand-year-old eggs; I love snails and cockles and mussels alive, alive, oh! I've even learned to sample tripe, and the way the French prepare sweetbreads is simply wonderful. Out on the range, I've eaten rattlesnake stew and even chowed down on Rocky Mountain oysters, a dish you really don't want to know about.

But everyone has to draw the line somewhere. I won't eat horse. In my opinion, horses are God's most perfect creation. They are so beautiful, they take my breath away. Unfortunately, the French have no such qualms and even find it delicious.

As I was considering what to do about the octopuses without offending Pascal, John looked up from his *croque monsieur,* a kind of toasted ham and cheese sandwich, and said, "Wow! Can I have those?"

I glanced around the crowded room, hoping that no one would notice, and nodded. John had no intention of eating them but he spent the next few minutes boxing with the little creatures, even naming one of them Sugar Ray Robinson, after the prizefighter.

"Think how good he'd be with eight arms," John said in wonder as Sugar Ray defeated his brethren in a two-round fight.

I spent the rest of the meal rooting around suspiciously in my salad to make sure there weren't any more little critters lurking in the lettuce.

But before Pascal could ask me how I had enjoyed my lunch, I made John wrap the octopuses in a napkin and deposit them in my purse—a trick I would never have gotten away with on board the *Veendam*. Later, I washed the napkin and secretly returned it to the Bar d'Oc. And nobody was the wiser—except me.

That humiliating episode perfectly illustrated how my lack of French prevented me from fully enjoying our stay. I was like Stephen, just learning to talk, and overwhelmed by the number of words I needed to know in order to be understood and to understand.

Mme. Perrin and her mother, who knew a cash customer when they saw one, complimented me on my improving French. And the lady at Le Bon Lait, where I bought my milk, was likewise impressed with my progress. But in my heart I knew they were wrong.

The reason I knew they were wrong was because Frank and John teased me mercilessly. The mere sound of me speaking French sent them off into gales of laughter.

"Mama's talking French" would always gather my family around, as if I were a street performer or a circus freak. They couldn't get enough of me. Once I think I even caught Stephen sniggering at my accent. It was all mildly irritating, but I soldiered on, even putting my own personal stamp on the language. I'll only mention one locution that brought down the house.

The phrase, to my mind at least, was perfectly understandable. When Frank wanted order at the table, he would point and say to the boys, "*À ta place!*" That meant, literally, "To your seat," but the implied meaning was, "Sit down and shut up," a useful phrase when dealing with small children who are prone to leap up from the table at odd moments.

One evening Stephen was acting up as usual, spilling his milk, throwing his food, and sliding off his chair so he could crawl around under the table. Sick and tired of his nonsense, I scolded him: "Stephen, sit in your *à ta place!*"

Frank almost blew a sip of wine through his nose at that one. But Stephen understood me perfectly well and returned to his seat, chastened, for at least a minute or two.

Despite my continuing problems with the language, I couldn't live in a shell, and once I was comfortable in a place, such as the Bar d'Oc, I would throw restraint to the wind and really try to talk to people in French. I found to my surprise that my listeners hung on every word, whether because they didn't understand me or because they were interested, I couldn't tell. But they would pump me for information about America, to them a land of myth. They considered the most mundane facts about the U.S. to be as fantastical as the novels of Jules Verne. First, there was the sheer size of our country. In Europe you can ride two hours on the train and cross four national boundaries. When I explained how long it took to get from New York to California, they were amazed. The customers were also fascinated by my stories about Texas—everyone had heard about cowboys and Indians and wanted to know more. They especially wanted to hear about rodeos, because one venerable gentleman, M. Paradis, had actually seen Buffalo Bill perform in Paris many, many moons ago.

M. Paradis, by the way, had convinced himself that I was part Apache Indian and would greet me with a raised palm and a hardy "How!" each time we met. I could understand his confusion because I still spoke like the Lone Ranger's Tonto. "Me Mary. Nice meet you. Weather heap good. Thank you. Good-bye," was probably the way I sounded to him.

It was Tonto, however, who showed me the way to speak French. Instead of trying to learn the myriad tenses and cases in the language, I would speak in the present and use simple words. I would quit attempting to sound like a Frenchman, and I would simply be an American trying to communicate. After all, when Tonto says, "Him bad. Me shoot," we all understand what he means. And if a trusted and resourceful Indian scout doesn't bother with the pluperfect or the subversive perpendicular (or whatever it's called) why should I?

One of the benefits of being a regular customer at the Bar d'Oc was that we got good seats for the Saturday evening movie. For weeks we had been watching flickering black-and-white French films of dubious vintage, but the big news was that Pascal had managed to get hold of a real Hollywood movie—in color! How he managed such a coup was shrouded in secrecy, but Frank told me that the local fixer, a man named Lucian, had had a hand in it somehow. I had never met this Lucian, but every time something shady happened, his name was invariably mentioned.

The great Hollywood film was called *Destination Lune* or *Destination Moon*, a George Pal science fiction epic. Frankly, I was disappointed. I would much rather have seen a romance or a Fred Astaire–Ginger Rogers musical, but at the Bar d'Oc you got what you paid for—and this was free.

John and Frank, however, couldn't wait to see the film. Frank had been reading Jules Verne's *From the Earth to the Moon* to our son, and John was bug-eyed about the prospects of space travel.

"Did you ever fly a rocket, Daddy?" John asked his father.

"Only once," Frank said. "When I blew up Tokyo."

"Really?" John asked.

"I can't talk about it. Top secret," Frank whispered.

"Frank!" I interrupted. "Don't fill his head with such nonsense. Nobody's ever ridden in a rocket to the moon and no one ever will. It's all made up. Like a fairy tale."

Going to the moon, indeed!

Frank winked at John as if to say, "Don't listen to her. It's all top secret."

That Saturday I made both the boys take naps so they could stay up to see *Destination Lune*, and at seven-thirty we walked over to the Bar d'Oc. There was a general buzz of excitement in the place, for it was not often that an honest to goodness American film—in color!—made it to the Bar d'Oc. Instead of paying forty cents at the local movie house, you could spend five dollars on drinks and dinner and think of all the money you could save. What a bargain!

Pascal stretched out a white sheet on the back wall, dimmed the lights, and started the projector. I gritted my teeth, cleared my head, and got ready to read the subtitles. It was slow going at first, and I found that I was missing most of the action, for by the time I read the subtitle and translated it in my mind, the story had moved on—leaving me in the dust.

A few minutes into the film, I heard a hysterical laugh that sounded mighty familiar—Woody Woodpecker. Suddenly it dawned on me: The picture was in English. I had been reading and translating the French subtitles like an idiot. I felt like such a fool, but I began to enjoy the show. The premise was ridiculous, but the costumes were wonderful—blue, yellow, red, and purple space suits and black velvet skies filled with twinkling stars. I even found myself explaining, in my lame French, to our neighbors what was happening on the screen when the subtitles got vague. Boy, did I feel in charge that evening. And did I ever like that feeling. I wanted more.

But it is difficult to be a social success in a foreign country when you don't really speak the language. After months in France, I could count on one hand the number of friends I had made among the local populace.

I was, however, the only resident on our block who was chums with the garbage man. I didn't know that anyone else wanted to be chummy with him, but I know that he singled me out for special attention. No one else in the neighborhood got the red carpet treatment that I did. He never saw me without tipping his cap and smiling. We even talked, in my halting fashion, about the weather and especially about his horse, Bruno.

For me it was an affair of the heart—with Bruno, not his master. Bruno was absolutely magnificent. He was a dapple-gray Percheron standing seventeen hands high. He had a sensitive face, a flowing white mane, meltingly tender brown eyes, and giant hooves the size of garbage cans. I never knew a more gentle or intelligent horse, and not many people measured up to Bruno's high standards.

The garbage man, whom I came to know as Giles, was nice, too. But that was probably because we were his best customers. I didn't have the French knack of producing a delightful stew or soup from bits and bones. And I bought those rusty old canned goods from Mme. Perrin because for me it was quicker and easier and less likely to send my family to the hospital. As a result of my profligate ways, I probably had more garbage and debris than anyone else in the neighborhood.

The garbage on our block was collected each Tuesday and Thursday, and on those days we were supposed to put our pails out in front of the house early in the morning. I was always embarrassed that my overflowing pails and supplemental boxes and bags towered over Mme. Sauson's neat little bundle. The French, in my opinion, make the Scots look like a nation of Diamond Jim Bradys when it came to thriftiness.

"The difference between our cultures," Frank said, "is that Americans take a three-thousand-pound cow, cut one steak out of it, and throw the rest away. The French use it all—the eyes, ears, horns, and tails. Nothing goes to waste."

And since Giles was in the waste business, he couldn't help but appreciate my efforts to make sure he had a full wagon. I might have been a big customer, but I wasn't exactly a *good* customer. My problem was the Thursday collection. Thursdays, as I've mentioned, were the equivalent of our Saturdays, so both John and Frank were off from school. Even Stephen had learned to keep relatively quiet until seven o'clock on Thursdays, so we slept in and ate a late breakfast. As a consequence, I forgot more days than I remembered to put out the garbage.

At six a.m. I would hear the rumbling of the wooden wheels of the wagon and the clomp-clomp of the horse's hooves on the cobblestones.

"The garbage wagon," I would gasp in dismay, and throwing on my clothes, I would grab the pails and race out into the street just as the wagon passed the house. "Monsieur!" I would cry. "Wait, *s'il vous plaît.*"

He would give me a fierce, speculative look, then whistle to Bruno, who would stop in his tracks. The horse would slowly back the wagon up to my front door. Giles would toss the garbage into the wagon and hand me back the pails. Then he would give another whistle, and Bruno would move on down the street. Giles never touched the horse or steered Bruno in any way, except through a series of whistles.

Our house was the next to last on the block, and when the last container on our street was emptied, Giles, standing on the sidewalk, would whistle again and the big horse, without any guidance, would turn the wagon around. Bruno couldn't make it in one circle, so he would go halfway around, back the wagon up, then come forward again, this time making the turn complete. Then he would slowly start down the opposite side of the street, while Giles emptied the pails.

Sometimes I would watch them with admiration, thinking that this team—man and beast—had figured out their life's work to such a degree that they got the utmost out of their job with the least expenditure of energy and motion. It was a pleasure to see them work together, Bruno often anticipating the commands of his master.

One Thursday morning, after one of my frantic rushes with the garbage, I stood watching the horse back the heavy wagon up to my door, then strain to pull away. I felt called upon to make an apology for all the extra work and blurted out, "The *cheval*, he is *merveilleux.*"

The garbage man looked startled, but my French always had that effect on people. Then he began to smile and introduced himself and his horse. He looked at Bruno as if he were seeing him for the first time.

After that, I always had an apple or a carrot for Bruno on Tuesdays, but found myself constantly late on Thursdays. That was embarrassing to me, not because I was late, but because it meant poor Bruno had to stop and back up for me once a week. He was no colt, I knew, but an aged country gentleman, and no matter how politely and skillfully he accomplished his task, I still felt bad about making extra work for him.

Recently, however, I had caused a major neighborhood scandal. I had completely forgotten to take the garbage out, as usual, but unusual for me, I was sound asleep. I never even heard the creaking wagon or the slow hoofbeats on the cobblestones. Instead, there was a knock at our door. Frank, the victim of a late-night party at the university, was snoozing peacefully, so I got out of bed in a daze.

When I opened the door, there was our landlady, Mme. Sauson, gasping for breath. That well-upholstered soul never climbed the many steps to our apartment unless there was an emergency. It was just too much exercise for her and left her utterly winded.

She leaned against the doorjamb, her hand on her heart, and explained in a shocked sort of way that the garbage man had rung her bell. The garbage man, of all people!

"He says his horse won't go on until you bring out your pails!"

Chagrined, I grabbed the pails and raced down the stairs. There at the open door was the garbage man. At the curb, looking over his shoulder at me with reproachful brown eyes, stood Bruno. I didn't know who to apologize to first, the man or the horse.

Bruno was *fatigué*, Giles explained slowly. His horse was tired of going past our house and then having to back up again just to get my garbage. This morning he had stopped at our door, and all his master's whistles brought no response. Bruno refused to go on until he heard the slam-bang of the proper number of pails from our address.

It was difficult for the horse to back the wagon up, Giles informed me, so Bruno would rather wait for me. It was less of a chore for him.

I felt like blushing with embarrassment, and I also had an uncomfortable feeling from the way Giles averted his eyes that he was not accustomed to chatting with ladies standing around on the sidewalk wearing nothing but their negligees. For that was what I was wearing—no robe, no slippers.

To add to the confusion, all the neighbors on the block were leaning out their front windows, standing in their doorways, or frankly staring at me from the sidewalk. They were all dressed in their plain black morning dresses and wearing their felt slippers, the standard uniform of the French housewife. I felt like a bird of paradise and a bit of a scarlet woman in my satiny bedroom ensemble.

I patted Bruno on the nose and promised him I would do better in the future. That brought a round of giggles from my neighbors, one of whom called out something about an intelligent animal, while a second, referring to my remarkable outfit, gave me the inevitable "O-la-la."

After many thanks all around, and smiling nods from neighbors and garbageman alike, Bruno went back to work as usual. I dove into the house to escape further notoriety and slunk upstairs, my cheeks ablaze with color.

I never again forgot to put out the garbage, and I never again wore a negligee in public. My reformation, however, was rather disappointing to the neighbors, I think. My mad dashes gave them a little early morning gossip—would she make it to the wagon in time?—until they got to the market to find out what was really going on.

I thought that the neighbors, Giles, and maybe even Bruno missed the spice in their lives of those early mornings. My antics did break up the dreary routine. But I knew at least one person who was glad to see me fade into obscurity—Mme. Sauson, our landlady. I believe she thought I was giving her house too much publicity, for she was a very proper French lady. She told me that, in all the years she had lived in Montpellier, she had never, ever spoken to a garbageman until Giles had rung her bell that morning. The way she said it made me think that she liked things that way. I had forced a social situation on her that had shocked her to her bourgeois soul. Now, she said, whenever she saw Giles, he tipped his cap to her, too, and she didn't share my enthusiasm for the man and his wonderful horse. She was pathetically grateful when I never again called attention to her home by getting a personal request for my garbage.

Chapter 10

ON THE EGG. John (above) and Stephen hanging out at the "Fountain of Three Graces" on the Oeuf ("the Egg"), the oval-shaped piazza in the heart of Montpellier.

A (Foggy) Day in Montpellier

"A foggy day in London town," Frank sang in a clear tenor voice. "The coffee's done, and Mary's not around."

It was six a.m. and I was getting my morning weather report and being chided for staying in bed. (If the day was really nasty I'd get a refrain from "Stormy Weather," while bright skies and sunshine brought on "Sunny Side of the Street." Frank never sang more than a line or two of any song and preferred to make up his own lyrics. The Frank Hit Parade included everything from the slightly salacious "I'll be *seizing* you in all the old familiar places" to the downright dumb "I didn't know what time it was . . . so I bought a watch.")

My husband was a tolerant man in many ways, but he needed only four or five hours of sleep a night and he couldn't understand those of us who couldn't function on less than seven. He always made me feel morally and ethically bankrupt if I didn't greet the sun. The only good part of Frank's urge to rise with the chickens was that he kept Stephen occupied until I dragged myself out of bed. He sang to Stephen and they held long conversations in French baby talk. They even played a game called, "Shhhhh." When the coffee was ready, Frank poured himself a cup, put his finger to his lips, and said, "Shhhhh." Stephen copied him, and for a few minutes, just enough time for Frank to fortify himself with the first cup of the day, silence would reign. Then all you-know-what would break loose, and that was my signal to get up.

I gulped down my coffee, which by now was pretty good. When we had first arrived in Palavas, I was shocked to find that the people in the south had no idea how to make a decent cup of coffee. They drank something called *café filtre*, a weak brew that made dishwater seem flavorful. They also served espresso, which was much better and stronger, but espresso was considered déclassé and much frowned upon in better establishments.

In desperation, I had my mother send me a ten-cup aluminum percolator like the one I used at home. A few days of tempering, by letting it stand full of coffee, made it into an adequate coffee-maker—but still not like the battered pot I was used to.

The coffee itself was another problem. In New York, Gristede's ground and packaged it for me. Here, I had to deal with the beans themselves. Mme. Perrin, at the general store, had bags and bags of the stuff, but I couldn't tell one bean from another. Only by a long process of experimentation (and some monumentally lousy coffee) did I find the right blend of beans.

Frank brought home a peculiar-looking coffee grinder that had probably been designed by a tea drinker. I didn't have the strength to work it. Frank had to start it for me, or I had to have John stand on it while I turned the crank with both hands and all my might. Eventually, Frank took over the grinding detail out of sheer caffeine desperation. I was grateful. A cup of strong coffee was something—perhaps the only thing—to look forward to at dawn.

Once I got John up, dressed, and fed, either Frank or I would drop him off at school. If Frank pulled drop-off duty, I would putter around the house with Stephen until nine forty-five; then it was time to go shopping.

Mme. Perrin at the general store always greeted me with a big smile and Stephen with a big cookie or a piece of cake. Then, using my newfound confidence in simple words and phrases, I would get what I needed for that day. I also became unintentionally involved in a family battle, a move that I would live to regret.

Mme. Perrin had a niece named Sophie, a fifteen-year-old, who worked part-time in the store. Sophie had dropped out of high school and was intent on marrying a seventeen-year-old named

René. Mme. Perrin and Maman disapproved—vehemently. René was *"un criminel,"* according to Maman, an unemployed delinquent with a motorcycle who had a bad reputation in town—just the kind of guy any teenage girl would find fascinating. Sophie had dark hair and flashing eyes, and she was mature beyond her years physically. Mentally however, she was still a romantic child, incapable of knowing what was best for her. Still, as a once goofy teenager myself, I could sympathize. Being bossed around all day by Mme. Perrin and Maman would get anyone down. I tried to be nice to Sophie and answer all her questions about America, which she found exotic and glamorous in the extreme.

Almost every day I would hear about René's latest outrage or Sophie's latest complaint about her overbearing aunt. I smiled and shook my head in commiseration, regardless of whose side of the story I was listening to.

Then it was off to the Boucherie d'Or, the Golden Butcher, where my status as a celebrity had definitely dimmed. Only new customers were agog at my presence while the old-timers treated me like one of the gang. I had even made a few friends standing in line there. Fortunately, the butcher, much calmer now, no longer got apoplectic at my accent and simply filled my order.

Stephen and I would then saunter over to Le Bon Lait, where I bought milk fresh from the farm. It wasn't pasteurized, homogenized, or reverberized, just plain old milk straight from the cow. At first I was skeptical about this policy of ignoring Dr. Pasteur's scientific breakthrough, but the boys seemed to be thriving on it and I hadn't heard of anyone who had been hospitalized from drinking the stuff. Le Bon Lait was one of Stephen's favorite stops. He was always sure of getting not one, but two *grisettes de Montpellier,* a honey-and-licorice hard candy covered with sugar.

With Stephen happily sucking away on his *grisettes,* we would next visit the wine seller. I would carry our empty wine bottles to the store and fill them from big wooden casks. Wine was the single most important product of our region, but unlike Bordeaux or Champagne or Burgundy, the grapes grown in the south went into the vast quantities of *vin ordinaire* drunk by ordinary people. At

twenty to forty cents a fill-up, wine was a bargain, and though
Frank complained that he would have much preferred a good
twenty-year-old Bordeaux, I couldn't tell the difference. The lady at
the wine store was also good for a chunk of chocolate, which
Stephen stuffed into his mouth along with the *grisettes*. Come to
think of it, for Stephen shopping was a lot like trick-or-treating on
Halloween. Every place we went, he got a treat.

We would also go to the fish store and the vegetable market in
this run-down part of town. Stephen liked to manhandle the vegetables and poke the recently deceased fish as he used to do in
Palavas. Then we would head for our seedy café and our personal
surly waiter, whom we now knew as Jean-Paul.

"No *café*," I said to Jean-Paul one day. I had finally worked up
the courage to change my order.

"*Non?*" He looked hurt, but I was not going to drink any more
café filtre, that disgusting devil's brew masquerading as coffee.

"*Non!*" I said firmly. "*Je* Daisy-Ray *chocolat. Chocolat chaud.*"

That meant hot chocolate.

I hoped.

Shaking his head sadly, as if he had just lost his best friend,
Jean-Paul retreated into the bowels of the café. I wondered what he
would bring forth from its depths.

He returned with a little espresso pot and placed it before me.
Suspiciously, I poured a small amount into my none too clean cup.
I sniffed it; then I took a tiny sip. It was delicious. Better even than
the hot chocolate at the Bar d'Oc, and that was darned good.

"*Bon!*" I said, smiling.

"*Oui?*" he asked, worried.

"Okay," I said, placing my thumb and forefinger together in the
international symbol of okayness.

I would have gladly whiled away a half hour enjoying my
chocolate, but at eleven-fifteen on the dot, Stephen would become
anxious to leave.

He would polish off his (nonalcoholic) cider and begin chanting, "*Allez, Maman! Allez vite!*" Translation: Let's vamoose!

And off we would fly, heading toward home and the absolute highlight of Stephen's day: His extravagant reunion with Elise.

When we neared the house, he would leap out of his stroller because I wasn't going fast enough, trot along beside me, then pull ahead. When he got near the front door, he would begin calling her name. At the bottom of the stairs, he would be shouting. And when he burst into the apartment, he would fall into Elise's arms as if he hadn't seen her for a decade. If for some reason she wasn't there, he would throw himself to the floor and weep real tears. Believe me, Mama never got a reception like that.

I would stay and chat, as best I could, with Elise and catch up on all the neighborhood gossip. Amazingly, although she lived way out of town, Elise knew every detail about everybody in Montpellier. Did I know that the vegetable seller's young wife had run off with a student at the university? *No!* Did I hear that the shoemaker had cancer? *Oh, no!* Did I know that there was an irregularity at the local bank? *A good thing we have no money!* And of course you knew about Sophie. *Sophie? Mme. Perrin's niece?* The very one. With that awful boy René.

Although I admit I was fascinated by the intimate details of other people's private lives, I tried to stay aloof. I knew all about rumors. Small-town gossip was the lifeblood of my newspaper job back in Texas. I reported the "society" goings-on—weddings, engagements, parties, anniversaries—and I could print only a tenth of what I knew. We were in the business of giving nice coverage to as many people as possible so they would subscribe to the paper or buy an advertisement. All the dirt got spiked. Which was probably just as well because I once found myself on the wrong end of the gossip.

A week before Frank and I left Texas for Florida, he withdrew all our money from the bank. The nosy teller made some comment like, "Gee, that's a lot of money."

Irritated at the woman's presumption, Frank said, "Yes. I have to cover my wife's gambling debts and gin bills."

That story spread faster than measles in a kindergarten. My

friends began looking at me with horror in their eyes; people would point me out in the street and whisper behind their hands. Suddenly, I was shunned by my colleagues at work and didn't know why. Finally, I stormed into the publisher's office and demanded an explanation.

"Well," he said, "it's a shame. I mean, everyone knows about your gambling and drinking."

"What!"

"Your husband had to close his account at the bank to pay your debts, and I suppose that's the real reason you're leaving town."

How anyone who knew me could possibly have believed such claptrap defied explanation, but that was the power of malicious gossip. We left Texas under a cloud entirely of Frank's making, and I haven't dared go back since. And Frank had better not joke around like that again. I still don't find it funny, although he practically falls on the floor laughing every time he thinks about it.

But I didn't have time to gossip much with Elise because I had to race off to pick up John. He and the other children would be sitting on the long wooden benches, waiting. The last parent to arrive was a rotten egg, and it was bad form to be late.

It was also bad form to interrogate the teacher during lunch break, and John would be mortified if I approached Mme. Lanval.

"No, Mama," he would say. "We have to go. Now!"

On the way home from school, John would stop every few minutes and try to coax a cat to come out of a yard. In France, cats aren't really pets. They are guard cats or mousers, big, mean creatures who look as if they could take your leg off at the knee. John, however, was optimistic that he could make friends with the scarred old veterans, and he approached them with the French equivalent of "meow," *minou, minou.* The cats would spit and growl, and we never had any luck.

We would either return home for lunch or, as a special treat, dine out at the Bar d'Oc. John, of course, preferred the Bar d'Oc, but not because of the food. He had become addicted to a game played at the bar. I would give him a few *sous* and Pascal would produce a wooden board with rows of holes in it. Each hole was stuffed with a tiny piece of paper with inscriptions like "Try again" "Not this time" "Almost" and even a few winners like "A bottle of grenadine" "Free drink" and "Two francs." John would take a matchstick and, after long moments of consideration, make his choice, and plunge the match into the board and extract the paper. He won a few drinks, a few francs, and the occasional bottle of grenadine. I suppose it was gambling which, despite my husband's wild stories, I'm against. But the look of rapture on John's face when he won silenced my fears.

The afternoons I devoted to working on my writing. I had conceived a grand notion that I would produce a series of stories for the *International Herald-Tribune*, a series about life in the south. I never had the temerity to send my work to Paris, but it was fun to be writing again. With two children, my time was limited and my journalistic skills were rusty. What used to take me ten minutes to write now took me an hour. So I struggled. But since my livelihood didn't depend on my typewriter, I was free to go window-shopping or used-book buying, and I had plenty of free time to get involved with the social life of Montpellier, and especially with John's school.

One of the highlights of John's school year was the "Gala," an outdoor fun fair designed to raise money for the French equivalent of the PTA. Frank was reluctant to go at first, but when I assured him I could handle it alone and impress Mme. Lanval with my new French technique, he hurriedly agreed to attend for fear that John would be expelled.

We arrived on the campus of the Lycée des Jeunes Filles at the appointed hour, Frank still grumbling, and the first person we met was John's friend Marc.

"Hi, *Américain*," Marc said to John. Then he grabbed my son's hat and dashed away, with John in hot pursuit.

"What was that all about?" Frank asked.

"It's a game they play every morning," I said. "Don't you watch him when you drop him off?"

Frank shook his head. "I just leave him at the gate and assume he can walk five steps to the school."

"Well, you've missed all the fun," I said, filling him in on my skulking, lurking, and third-degree procedures. The hat-snatching game was a morning ritual, and John felt that this was a mark of distinction and thoroughly enjoyed both the snatch and the chase.

I was interested in John's schoolmates, but I got scanty reports about them from my son. The one boy I did remember vividly, however, was Marc. He was, as my mother might say, "a caution," the Peck's Bad Boy of the class.

John, of course, admired him tremendously, for it seemed that Mme. Lanval spent most of her time telling Marc to sit in his *à ta place,* be quiet, and stop wrestling with the little girls. The Blue Ladies, it seemed, could not make him behave either. And, I believe, they didn't try very hard, for one look at Marc, with his round, rosy-cheeked, bright-eyed little imp's face, always split with a big grin, made it easy to see why even the strict Mme. Lanval couldn't stay angry with him for very long.

I followed with breathless interest Marc's crimes and punishments. One day he would have to sit on a stool in the corner; another day he would get a few well-placed whacks on the side of the head. And finally, the crème de la crème of all punishments, he was placed in the closet, where he was once confined for most of a morning. Yet we could see that his spirits were never dampened but momentarily. I suspect that Mme. Lanval knew this, but felt she had to go through the motions.

Marc chose this "gala" occasion to interview my husband about something slanderous John had said.

"Is it true?" Marc asked, staring wide-eyed at Frank.

"Is what true?" Frank said.

"That you go to school?" Marc said.

Frank admitted the awful truth.

"But you're a man. They can't make you go to school. Why don't you have a job?"

The idea of a grown man going to school of his own free will was just too ridiculous for Marc to believe. He was shaken that the monstrous rumor about Frank had been confirmed. It left him convinced that all Americans were mad.

Frank was still laughing when two pixyish little girls, the twins Annette and Anni, came over to speak to him.

"Are you poor?" Anni asked.

"Very," Frank said, smiling.

"We thought so," Annette said. "That's why we have to share our *goûter* with Jeannot."

"What was that all about?" I asked Frank, who was laughing again.

"Don't you pack John an afternoon snack?" he asked. "It's called a *goûter*."

That was a new one on me. I asked for details.

"Well, apparently, John has been bumming the little girls' snacks for some time, and I get the impression they aren't too happy about it."

I called John over and confronted him with this new information.

"I eat half of Anni's *goûter* and half of Annette's," he said, as if this were the most natural thing in the world.

"But you come home for lunch," I said.

"Everyone else goes home for lunch, too," said John. "But they still bring something to eat in the morning or afternoon. I never do." He gave me the abandoned-orphan look.

Frank had a word with Mme. Lanval, and we soon learned all about the *goûter*, which is a snack consisting of bread and chocolate squares, my beloved *pain au chocolat*, or an apple and chocolate squares that helped reinforce the children's breakfast or tide them over until dinner. I pointed out to John that French children ate only cereal and drank coffee well laced with milk for breakfast. They seldom had dinner until eight. Living *à l'Américain,* John started off his day with juice, eggs, toast, and hot chocolate and was in bed by seven p.m. All in all, I thought that a *goûter* was rather superfluous, but I couldn't have him gulping down Annette's and Anni's snacks. Besides, children are the biggest conformists of all and positively cringe at the thought of being "different." Saddled with a decidedly "different" family, we decided we should go along with the crowd in this minor manner.

I was mulling all this over when Frank presented me with a glass of champagne.

Champagne at a PTA fun fair?

"The greatest innovation I ever heard of," Frank said. "A champagne booth. This would really bring out the parents and teachers back home—in droves."

We were sipping bubbly and feeling very sophisticated when John brought his friend Michel to meet us. Michel was a pale blond boy whose parents had sent him to the south from Paris, believing the mild winters would help his precarious health. Since Michel was no physical match for the other children and was an outsider like John, it was inevitable that they would find each other.

Frank quizzed Michel about where the boy lived in Paris and how he liked Montpellier. It became painfully obvious, even to me, that the poor child missed his mama and papa back in the capital, but he was being brave about the situation.

Even though it was a warm fall day, Michel was clad in his trademark gray fur coat. His aunt, with whom he was living, made him wear it from September to June, no matter how hot the weather, believing that it would keep him from catching cold. Michel had beads of sweat on his forehead, but he was an obedient little boy who had been told that he would die if he removed the coat.

While we were talking, John pulled a few hairs out of the fur coat and showed them to me.

"If Michel likes you, he lets you pull hairs out of his coat," John boasted. "Since I'm his friend, I get to pull as many out as I want, anytime I like."

Visualizing a piebald coat by spring, we convinced John to pull sparingly and not to abuse this beautiful friendship.

In the evenings we would have friends over for cocktails or meet them for dinner in town if we could get Elise to stay late to baby-sit. We became friendly with a group of students at the university, including our old buddies, Peter and Molly; a couple from New York, Ron and Lisa; a single man from Hartford, Connecticut, Dick

Robinson, and his girlfriend, Dominique. We would have bridge parties or go to the movies together, or just sit and talk. Oh, how I loved to hear English spoken.

Frank, John, and I were also suddenly thrust into the social and political life of Montpellier. It all happened one misty fall evening as the whole family was on its way to the Bar d'Oc to see a movie— a French one this time, with no subtitles. But before we arrived at our destination, it began to rain lightly, prompting Frank to burst into a few bars of "Stormy Weather."

"Don't know why," Frank sang, "there's no sun up in the sky—"

"Because it's night, Daddy," John interrupted. "There's no sun at night."

"Can't fool you, can I?" Frank said and switched to "White Christmas" for some reason.

But Frank didn't get past the first few bars before we were suddenly confronted by three men who kidnapped him. They grabbed him by the arms and hustled him down the street.

"You go ahead," Frank shouted over his shoulder. "I'll meet you later."

I suppose I should have been worried, but I recognized Frank's cronies from the Commune Libre, which was a sort of community center and the political headquarters for the movers and shakers in our district. Through the Commune Libre we became enthusiastic supporters of our local bicycle racers and attended all the events to cheer on our champions. I didn't understand the details of the bike races—sprints and things like that—but I could sense when my fellow residents were happy or disappointed and joined in.

The Commune Libre also sponsored the famous waiter races. We applauded and shouted to our favorite waiters as they raced down the cobblestone streets, in full uniform, carrying a tray, a bottle, and two full glasses of wine. When a waiter from the Bar d'Oc came in third, the entire place went crazy. Apparently it had been twenty years since any Bar d'Oc employee had done so well. Frank, naturally, stood a round for a grateful house.

The men of the Commune Libre had taken a shine to Frank. Perhaps it was his general spirit of bonhomie or because we were the best customers for their newly installed, industrial-size ice machine. The locals had been slow to embrace this new contraption, which made rumbling sounds and looked as if it could supply ice cubes for the Sahara Desert. But as Frank said, "A Manhattan is supposed to be dry, not hot."

Whatever it was, Frank was one of the boys there, and according to him, he was considered an impartial outsider with no vested interests. "They let me be the umpire," Frank said, "because I don't have any family feuds going back four hundred years." And besides, the Commune Libre, like the merchants in town, knew a real customer when they saw one.

With Frank absconded, I said, "How" to M. Paradis and settled the boys into our usual table at the Bar d'Oc. John got his *menthe à l'eau* and instructions to translate the movie for Mama. Stephen got his second cider of the day and a piece of bread to chew on, just to keep him quiet. Although quiet didn't really matter on movie night. There were babies, toddlers, teenagers, and grandmas all carrying on their own conversations. And I knew from experience that both boys would soon grow weary of the movie, desert their seats, and crawl around on the floor with the other kids. Nobody seemed to mind. I didn't know if this laissez-faire attitude was for me, but it seemed to work for the French.

Before the movie began, I took the opportunity to covertly study the leaders of the Occitan separatist movement, Fricor and Gobert. Fricor was at least seventy with a drooping white mustache. He had been a farmer in his youth, but he had sold the farm for a tidy profit. With his carefully stashed cash (he didn't believe in banks), Fricor purchased three cognacs and three Pernods during his twelve-hour stint at the bar. No more, no less, according to the owner, Pascal. I never saw him eat anything, though I suppose he must have since he weighed more than two-hundred-fifty pounds. With his lined face and gnarled hands he looked like a retired army sergeant.

Gobert was his lieutenant and acolyte. He was a mere spring chicken, maybe sixty. A lean and nervous man, Gobert treated Fricor as if he were a combination of God and Charles de Gaulle.

He was always hopping about doing Fricor's bidding, and "Yes, sir-ing" the man to death. I think that Gobert's obsequious manner covered up the fact that he wasn't very competent. The plotting for independence had gone nowhere for decades because, as Frank observed, Gobert spent most of his day ordering bottles of wine for himself and putting them on Fricor's tab.

Everybody at the Bar d'Oc liked Fricor and Gobert the way you like your dotty old uncle. They showed the two men a kind of humorous respect, never intruding on their constant whispering. Secretly, I fancied the two men liked me. After all, if I didn't really understand French very well, they must have known that I would have been hopeless in Occitan. They could have plotted to blow up the Eiffel Tower with me listening, and I could never have testified against them in court.

Hugo was just serving our drinks when Frank came rushing in. "Quick," he said, "I need to borrow John."

"Make sure you return him," I said, wondering what *this* was all about.

Frank grabbed John by his shirt and lifted the child out of his seat like a sack of potatoes. Then they were gone into the night. Stephen looked up at me, his face a question mark, but I could only shrug.

Twenty minutes into the movie, a costume drama set in the court of Louis XIV, Frank returned with John and a huge smile on his face. He looked as if he had just won the million-franc lottery.

"What happened?" I asked.

He shushed me, but after the movie he said, "You won't believe this, but I'm the new Boss Tweed of Montpellier."

My husband a politician?

"When I got to the Commune, the place was in an uproar," Frank said. "Today was the annual appointment of the new president, and since it is an honorary title, they don't bother with an election. Usually, everyone knows who's going to get the job at least a year in advance. But not this year. Three guys swore up and down that it was their turn, and bad feelings almost caused a riot."

"And they dragged you into it?" I said.

"It was Lucian's doing," Frank said.

"The fixer?" *I had to meet this character.*

"That's Lucian. I never met a man who had more connections in more places in my life. He was the one who finagled the ice machine, organized the bicycle races, and even got me those books I couldn't find in the store," Frank said. "Lucian decided I was the one to play Solomon."

"So with your Monte Cristo sword you cut the candidates in thrice," I said, laughing.

"Better than that," Frank said. "I solved their problem using abstruse mathematical equations, quantum physics, and celestial mechanics."

"And just how did you do that?" I asked.

"I told them a four-year-old could resolve the matter," Frank said. "That's why I needed to borrow John."

"For the celestial mechanics part?" I said. My husband lives in space most of the time.

"Exactly," Frank said. "I put the names of the three candidates in a hat and had John pick the winner. And *voilà*. No more problem."

"That's it?" I said. "After all that buildup? You drew a name out of a hat?"

"I told you I was a political genius," Frank said, leaning back in his chair, his hands clasped across his stomach, a thoroughly satisfied man. "I believe I shall run for mayor next spring."

That was an idle threat, I hoped, but with Frank you never knew.

I dozed off to the haunting strains of: "Don't know why you must cry, Stormy Stephen" and "A foggy day in Montpellier . . . quit your cryin' and hit the hay."

Unlike Stephen, I recognized sound advice when I heard it—even if it came from a politician.

Chapter 11

FRENCH SMALL FRY. Stephen strikes a particularly Gallic pose on the rue de Claret, bringing home the bread for a disastrous Thanksgiving dinner.

Fowl Play

November 1950

The French rarely invite friends to their homes for dinner, as we do in America. Instead, they entertain their guests in restaurants or bistros or brasseries. At first I found this custom to be cold and impersonal, but the more I thought about it, the more it made perfect sense—especially for someone with my skills in the kitchen.

That's why I was surprised when Frank suggested that we give a traditional Thanksgiving dinner for our friends at the university. Surprised and apprehensive. Thanksgiving was on a Thursday—Elise's day off.

"Are you sure you trust me not to kill everyone with my cooking?" I asked him.

"You've cooked a turkey before," Frank said. "What's the big deal?"

He had a point. Of all the meals I made, all five of them, the turkey dinner was far and away the best in my repertoire—that is, if you exclude the first one I ever made, the one where I left all the guts and brains and necks and things inside. That was pretty gruesome, but I had learned my lesson.

"Well, it might happen," I said vaguely, hoping he would forget all about it. Besides, Thanksgiving was weeks away, and I was consumed with two other problems that were making my life less than sensational.

First, we had all been gripped by *la grippe*. Both the boys had come down with the flu and had been confined to barracks while

Elise and I tended to them like latter-day Florence Nightingales. Stephen was his usual weepy, cranky self, but John was inconsolable. For him, missing school was the biggest tragedy of his young life; being ill was of no consequence. The poor child got up every morning, hacking, coughing, and sometimes vomiting, and demanded to go to school. But since he had a temperature of 102 degrees, I wouldn't let him out of the house. Oh, how he missed his friends, and oh, how he let me know about it.

The flu had come with the colder weather. I had noticed that in places where the residents prided themselves on the mildness of the climate, they never admitted to themselves or to others that it sometimes got darned cold. In Florida, where Frank was stationed toward the end of the war, people would simply deny it was winter, even when they could see their breath in the air. Here in Montpellier, all I heard was *"pas chaud,"* which loosely translated means, "not hot."

The second thing that was not so hot was our apartment. When we had moved in, M. Sauson had explained that we were his first tenants. The house had stood empty for many years before he had bought it, and he couldn't understand why. Now we knew, for this was not an ordinary, complacent house, but rather a stubborn, veritable delinquent among houses, and deep within its heart and vital works, lay a menacing spirit. That spirit, like the flu, manifested itself when the weather turned.

I had been looking forward to the cold ever since I took my first bath here. The water had been freezing cold and I had to boil about a thousand gallons of water on the stove to fill the Brobdingnagian tub. Frank complained to M. Sauson and reported back to me that there would be no hot water until the furnace was turned on. That would be when winter arrived. But in spite of all Frank's questions, he hadn't been able to find out just when that would be. I was feeling positively wintry at the beginning of November, but so far it was only *"pas chaud."*

Our baths were sketchy events throughout September and October, but I was hoping now that I had turned blue, winter had officially begun. Then, last week, wonder of wonders, Mme. Sauson huffed and puffed her way up the stairs to inform us that the workmen would soon be there to start the furnace so that we could all revel in the joys of central heating. With frost on my nose, I anxiously awaited their coming.

The next afternoon two workmen dressed in blue jeans arrived, accompanied by M. Sauson, who had shed his usual blue suit for his working costume: a dark red bathrobe worn over an old pair of trousers and a blue beret perched on his balding head. The men began about two o'clock and worked off and on until seven, banging and hammering. They made many trips up and down the stairs, draining water out of the radiators and assuring me frequently that everything was going to be shipshape.

When they finally left, the radiators actually began to get warm. I took Stephen on a tour of the house and explained to him about the hazards of hot radiators, but later on I saw him sitting on one in complete comfort. In fact, that radiator remained his favorite perch all winter, and he never even got singed. Still, the fire in the furnace did take the chill off the house, and I managed to have a few lukewarm baths. But believe me, it required a pioneering spirit.

Then one night the water refused to go down the drain of the giant gilded tub. We reported this distressing fact, and M. Sauson contacted a plumbing concern, Le Grand Frères. The brothers Le Grand, all six of them, made a Le Grand entrance one morning at dawn. Frank and Stephen met them at the door, and they all trooped into the house, followed by M. Sauson in his working garb. When everyone had assembled, and the handshakes and bows were completed, the Monsieur, in his courtly manner, explained the problem and directed the men to the bathroom.

Work began.

Work stopped. Stephen decided this would be a good time to show off his mastery of bathroom procedure.

Work began anew.

Work stopped. In case I hadn't been appreciative enough, Stephen decided an encore was in order.

Work began again.

John and Stephen were as fascinated as I, and we gathered

around the doorway to watch. To the best of my knowledge, although I was out much of the day, the five men who perched themselves on the side of the tub never lifted a tool. The Monsieur stood in a corner glowering darkly at them all, and one little man, perhaps the youngest of the Le Grand brothers, did all the work. He worked all morning, creating a fearful racket, and then they all stopped for lunch.

Lunch in southern France was no sandwich affair but lasted from twelve to two, so that gave me a chance to sneak a peak at their progress. The mammoth tub, twice the size of the little plumber, had been moved to a corner of the bathroom, and where the pipes ran down through the floor, a square-foot of tile was missing, giving me a good view of the Sausons' kitchen below.

All this exertion for a clogged pipe.

The next morning at six, the crew of plumbers arrived to renew their assault on the problem. This time they came armed with an array of equipment that would have done a medieval torture chamber proud. They ripped and scraped, banged and slammed, and generally made enough noise to clear the clog by sheer vibration alone. Elise and I decided that we had better leave the house and take the children with us. When we returned, the Le Grand brothers told us they would have everything fixed "in a day or two."

On the fifth day, Frank said, "It only took God six days to make the universe. If these guys were in charge, we'd still be waiting for the light."

On the afternoon of the sixth day, M. Sauson announced proudly that the job was done. The floor was patched up after a fashion, and I could no longer peer down into the kitchen below and see what was cooking for dinner. That was a relief, except for one thing: The bathwater still wouldn't run out of the tub. Frank and I talked it over and decided to keep this information to ourselves. We felt sorry for the Sausons and could imagine how much the brothers Le Grand were costing them. In America, six plumbers working full-time for six days would put a dent in the Rockefeller fortune.

Frank, as usual, found a solution to our problem: a giant tin of

Drāno. That helped a little, but it still took more than an hour for the water to seep out of the tub, even if it was filled only a quarter of the way up.

Much more fun than the flu and the pipes were my visits to the Jardin des Plantes. Almost every Thursday I would take John and Stephen there in the afternoons while Elise enjoyed her day off. My friend Jules and I would sit on a bench and talk while the boys played happily amid the cool splendor of the gardens. But even after all this time Jules remained a mystery to me. My vaunted third-degree skills, which worked so well on a four-year-old, failed to get much information out of him. I did, however, learn something of Jules's life and why he hated doctors.

Jules had been born in Montpellier and had gone to the university as an undergraduate. He had done his advance work in Paris and lectured there for many years. Then the war came and Jules disappeared into the underground resistance movement, rightly fearing he would be imprisoned by the Nazis. He only hinted at his activities during the war, but they must have been dirty and dangerous. In 1946 he had returned home to Montpellier to teach and take up his present administrative duties, but his real passion was French history.

Soon after his return, Jules's wife had become ill and died, despite the attentions of the famous doctors at the university. He blamed all doctors for the loss of his wife and was still bitter four years later.

For my part, I kept Jules informed about my progress in French (a very short subject), about the boys, and about Frank's wartime experiences, which seemed to interest him greatly. He was also fascinated by my secondhand tales of Peter Lord's heroics, as well as the details of our other friends' war stories. Jules was amazed that everyone in our circle was a veteran. Somehow he had the idea that Americans hadn't contributed much to the final victory over the Nazis, but I soon put him straight on that accord.

We would share a *pain au chocolat* or sometimes cheese and bread (my own personal *goûter*), while the boys wolfed down the ice cream that Jules insisted on buying them. For John and Stephen,

Jules was the Good Humor man. Jules always put me in a good humor, too, with his lectures on the history of our city.

"Montpellier is an upstart," Jules said. "A baby, a parvenue. Many of the towns and cities in Languedoc are much older and have a much more interesting history—going back to pre-Roman times.

"Beziers, Narbonne, and Nimes, for example, are probably a thousand, twelve hundred years older than Montpellier, which really did not exist until the late tenth century.

"What finally made Montpellier into anything more than just a dusty village was the spice trade with the Levant," Jules said, sweeping his arms around the garden.

"The local merchants got filthy rich dealing with the Arabs and the Jews who taught them to use their imported spices as medicine. Thus, the founding of the medical school around the year 1000. Two hundred years later Montpellier was prosperous enough to boast of twenty-five towers shaped like an escutcheon—our famous *l'écusson.*"

"That's what they still call the old part of town," I said.

"Exactly. Eight hundred years later and the name is the same," Jules said. "A strange concept to Americans, I think."

What amazed me was not the antiquity of Montpellier, but the fact that it wasn't even particularly French. The city had once belonged to a princess named Marie, who married Pedro of Aragon, bringing Montpellier with her as a dowry. Then, somehow, Montpellier wound up as a part of the Kingdom of Majorca. Majorca, of all places! That sounded like the equivalent of Boston once belonging to the Kingdom of Miami. But what was more intriguing was that the city, the whole kit and caboodle, was sold in the fourteenth century to France for 120,000 gold coins. It seemed to me that the Dutch got a better deal buying Manhattan for $24 worth of trinkets, but the whole idea of buying and selling cities willy-nilly was boggling.

"Montpellier was a center of the Protestant Reformation," Jules said. "A rebel city that for almost a hundred years defied Paris and the Catholic Church. Louis XIII, in the seventeenth century, put an end to all that by force of arms. The idea of Montpellier as a merchant republic was hateful to the central state. After all, France had paid good money for Montpellier and wanted the benefits—the taxes.

"We have been pretty quiet for the last three hundred years," Jules said. "Except for your friends, the Occitan separatists. They yearn for a time that never really existed, other than in folklore. But they also represent the unconventional, the refusal to yield to 'foreign' powers, such as Paris."

That sounded to me a lot like the American South, where all Yankees are foreigners and the people pride themselves on their orneriness and individuality. The South, it seemed, was the South, no matter where you went.

Although my conversations with Jules made me more comfortable with my surroundings, it was the North, not the South, that was on my mind. Specifically, the Massachusetts Pilgrims and their famous Thanksgiving dinner.

"Are you ready for the party?" Frank asked me a week before the big date.

He had remembered, darn it, and the feast was on.

"Okay," I said. "Who's coming?"

"Peter and Molly, Bob and Sylvia, Ron and Lily and Dick Robinson," Frank said. "They're all looking forward to having a good, old-fashioned Thanksgiving dinner."

"Me, too. I just don't know where to get one," I said. "What are they bringing?"

"Peter's got four bottles of scotch he picked up in London, Bob has a half case of prewar Bordeaux, and Ron is the proud owner of six bottles of champagne, the good stuff."

That sounded like a well-balanced meal.

"What about Dick?" I asked.

"He's bringing Dominique, the campus dish," Frank said with a leer.

"Speaking of dishes," I said, "isn't anyone bringing food?"

"That's your department," Frank said.

"All right," I said. "Now tell me where I can buy a turkey."

"Hey, I discovered the secret of mayonnaise. It's your turn to find out where the turkeys are hiding," he said.

So the great Montpellier Turkey Hunt began. I was encouraged by the fact that there is actually a word for turkey in French. It's *dinde*. Unfortunately, that's also the slang word for a stupid woman, so I had to be careful how I phrased my question.

The first person I approached was Elise. She had an encyclopedic knowledge of the local meat and game, as did all French women, but on the question of turkeys, she drew a blank. Elise had never eaten or even seen a turkey. She suggested I ask my butcher.

But before I attempted that, I quizzed Mme. Sauson. She said she had once had turkey for dinner in Toulouse, but she had never seen it served or for sale in Montpellier. That was not good news. But I girded my linguistic loins and went to the Boucherie d'Or with my request. All the ladies in the shop and I discussed the best way to approach our choleric butcher without having him fly off the handle. One lady, who I knew as Mme. Borel, volunteered to do the dirty work.

With more courage that I could ever muster, she asked the red-faced butcher why, if he were really a butcher, he didn't have turkey for sale. All the ladies, she lied, had decided to cook turkeys. All the ladies nodded in agreement.

The butcher turned as purple as an underdone piece of beef. He sputtered and screamed, saying he had been in business for forty years and not once—not once!—had anyone ever asked for turkey.

"Well, times change, and *professional* butchers know what their customers really want," Mme. Borel said smoothly.

"*C'est impossible!*" yelled the butcher. "*Dinde! Mon Dieu! C'est impossible!*"

Mme. Borel put her nose in the air and sniffed; all the other ladies followed suit. I cowered in the corner, wishing I hadn't started this whole business.

"Come, ladies," Mme. Borel said. "We will take our business where it is appreciated."

All the ladies murmured their consent and marched out of the shop en masse.

Good grief, I thought. *I've put the poor man out of business.* And I raced outside to join the crowd. If they had had signs, they would have made a perfect picket line.

I thanked Mme. Borel for her efforts, but told her I didn't want to cause any trouble with the butcher.

"Serves him right," Mme. Borel said. "Him and his high-and-mighty ways. What he needs is a little knocking down; then maybe prices will be lower and service better. But don't worry. We'll all be back tomorrow."

I fled to the sanctuary of Mme. Perrin's general store, remembering that I had just barely avoided the Great Mayonnaise War of 1950 and I didn't want any part of the Infamous Turkey Uprising of the same year. After I had hidden in the shadows for a few moments to make sure the butcher wasn't tracking me down, cleaver in hand, I put the question to Mme. Perrin and Maman.

"Dinde? O-la-la!"

That was about all I got out of them, a flurry of O-la-las and vigorous head shakes. But I didn't despair. I had two more possible sources.

After I picked John up from school, we wandered about the new shopping district on the assumption that the bright, shiny stores would be home to such an oddity as a turkey. Three butcher shops later, I had to admit I felt like a real *dinde,* in the colloquial sense.

My last chance was Pascal, the owner of the Bar d'Oc. If he couldn't find me a turkey, they didn't exist in France.

"Now see here, Pascal," I said after ordering John a *menthe à l'eau* and myself an espresso, "I've got a problem."

"Oui, Madame?"

"A turkey, a *dinde? Compris?* Understand?" I said.

He nodded. *"Pour se soir?"* he asked. "For tonight?"

"Non, pour la semaine dernière," I said. "For next week."

Pascal rubbed his chin, mulling that over. Then he spoke to John.

"Mama, did you want the turkey last week or next week?" John said.

"Next week, of course," I said.

"Then you say, *la semaine prochaine,*" John said, laughing.

"Ah," said Pascal.

"He says he'll see what he can do," John advised me.

"*Merci,*" I said and drank my coffee, feeling, as usual, like the village idiot.

True to his word, Pascal made inquiries as far away as Paris. And he was successful. We could have a turkey, packed in ice, delivered by Grande Vitesse, the French Parcel Post, for only forty thousand francs—two months' rent. Frank thanked Pascal effusively and reimbursed him for the long-distance phone calls, but declined to spend that much for a darned (not his word) bird.

"We've established that turkeys do exist in France," Frank said later that day, "although they cost more than caviar. There must be some way of getting one cheaper."

"They used to be cheaper," I said knowingly.

"Really?"

"Jules told me that Montpellier had quite a flock of turkeys in the 1550s, brought over from the New World," I said. (Yes, I had even interrogated poor Jules about the elusive fowl.)

"They were said to live outside town, and on market day they waltzed into Montpellier on their own accord and offered themselves for slaughter," I said.

"Maybe I should just stand outside the door with a two-by-four and wait for them to saunter by," Frank said.

"How about a nice chicken instead?" I suggested.

"No, there's got to be a way," he said.

"Use your political connections," I joked.

"That's it!" Frank said. "Lucian. He can get a B-29 with a complete set of spare parts, if you want one."

"A turkey will do," I said.

"That should be no problem at all," Frank said.

I wondered. It had been my experience that, when people tell you "no problem," there is nothing but trouble ahead. Still, Frank's enthusiasm was as infectious as the flu, and I soon found myself getting into the spirit of Thanksgiving.

The day before the projected feast, I attempted to buy a pumpkin pie, a *tarte au potiron.*

Why a pumpkin was called a pot-iron I had no idea, but I harangued the poor woman at our local pâtisserie until she produced a yellow-orange thing that might have even tasted like pumpkin. Just to play it safe, however, I also bought a selection of beautiful little chocolate cakes and even some delicious *marrons glacés,* candied chestnuts from Provence. Chestnuts. Thanksgiving. That seemed almost traditional.

With the desserts settled, it was on to the side dishes. I decided on *haricots verts,* green beans to which I would add almonds, a snap to prepare; creamed baby onions, which no one would eat, but they do provide a nice contrast to the green beans; mashed potatoes; candied yams, which fortunately came in a can at Mme Perrin's; wonderful flaky rolls from the pâtisserie; and my world-famous stuffing. Okay, only Frank and I like it, but it's easy to make.

Stuffing. People go crazy preparing stuffing. They add giblets (something I wanted no part of, considering where they had been), oysters, mussels, raisins, dates, pomegranates, chestnuts, acorns, pork, ground meat, cauliflower, headcheese, whale blubber, and sheep's eyes to produce some kind of grandiose effect. My stuffing, like my tuna sandwiches, was simplicity itself: day-old bread, onions, salt, and pepper. Period. No cardamom, soy sauce, brandy, or nasturtiums. The bread picks up the flavor of the turkey, and it doesn't have to fight with the other ingredients. By the way, my stuffing is delicious with a good turkey gravy. Unfortunately, I had yet to make a good turkey gravy, but this year Molly had volunteered to do the honors. She claimed to be an expert, and I was more than willing to turn the whole sordid business over to her.

I stocked up on tomatoes and lettuce at the vegetable market to go with the hunk of Roquefort cheese I had at home. The town of Roquefort is north of Montpellier, and Frank had taken me there to see the caves where the cheese is ripened. Probably the best blue cheese in the world, Roquefort is made from ewes' milk and gets its blue veins from the bacteria it picks up in the caves. The result is a tangy, creamy, and utterly delicious cheese that I like to crumble over a plain oil-and-vinegar salad. What a great way to start or, as Frank and the French prefer, to finish a meal.

I bought some cider for Stephen and John, and as far as I was concerned, we were all set. Except, of course, for the turkey. That was Frank's bailiwick. He assured me that Lucian was on the case and a turkey would be delivered to our door. It had only cost us ten thousand francs—two weeks' rent. I was wary but hopeful.

Yet sure enough, at eight o'clock on Thanksgiving morning, I looked out the window and there was a large package wrapped in butcher's paper at the front door. Lucian had delivered as promised.

"John, go downstairs and bring the turkey up here, will you?" I said, rubbing my hands together and getting the kitchen ready for the great Thanksgiving feast. I busied myself, checking to see that I had all the necessary ingredients, and opened *The Joy of Cooking,* zeroing in on the cooking tables: A ten-pound bird requires so many hours at such-and-such temperature. Based on past disasters, I always made a point of rechecking the turkey-cooking figures with Frank, my expert accountant.

I laid out the potatoes, the onions, the stale bread, the beans, the almonds, and the condiments, surprised that I hadn't forgotten anything. Then I wondered what was keeping John so long.

"Need some help?" I called down the long flight of stairs.

"No," John said manfully. But it was obvious that the turkey was too big for him to carry. He looked like Sisyphus pushing his rock up the hill. My poor son was grunting and groaning, trying to roll the package upstairs, one step at a time. At that rate Thanksgiving would be a memory before he reached the landing. So I went down to help him, and together we managed to get the bird into the kitchen. It must have weighed twenty-five pounds.

I unwrapped the greasy and, by now, lint-covered brown paper to discover . . . something. It was a bird of some sort, I suppose, but it was too big to be a chicken and too small to be an ostrich. Its ghastly purple skin was studded with random white feathers, and blood was trickling out of its raggedly cut neck. I looked dubiously at its black webbed feet and I knew in my heart that this—whatever it was—had never been a turkey.

Stephen came trundling out of his room, took one look at the creature on the kitchen counter, and burst into tears. I felt the same way.

This is all Frank's fault, I thought.

"Stephen, go wake your father up," I said to divert his attention from the scary thing on the counter. "Tell him I need to see him right now."

Dutifully, he trotted off to wake Frank, who had been out with Peter Lord until the wee hours. John and I gingerly examined the bird, trying not to get too close to it.

Two minutes later Stephen came out of the bedroom and said Frank wouldn't wake up.

"Try again," I said, then went into the living room to ponder what to do.

Suddenly, there was an agonizing cry from the bedroom and Stephen scooted past me, a mineral water bottle clutched in his hand. He was followed by a bleary-eyed Frank, holding his head with both hands.

"He conked me on the head with a bottle," Frank said, rubbing his scalp.

"He's up now," Stephen said.

"Happy Thanksgiving," I said. We were certainly off to a rousing start.

There are times when disaster seems imminent but you are powerless to do anything about it. I felt like the captain of the *Titanic* watching the iceberg coming closer and closer. The good ship Thanksgiving, I feared, was now about two feet from its own berg.

"Come into the kitchen," I said to Frank. "And see what Lucian hath wrought."

"My God!" Frank exclaimed. "What the hell is that?"

"Our turkey," I said. "Our ten-thousand-franc turkey."

Frank stood back, eyeing the creature.

"Turkeys aren't supposed to have black legs and webbed feet, are they?" he asked.

"Not that I ever heard of," I replied.

"Is it a goose?" Frank asked.

"Pray it's not," I said. I had once cooked a goose and had turned it into a gelatinous mess which went directly from the oven to the garbage can.

"The feet would indicate a waterbird," Frank said scientifically, pacing about the kitchen, his hands clasped behind his back as he inspected the corpus from every possible angle. "A monstrous duck perhaps?"

"Got me."

"A heron or a flamingo?" Frank said.

"A flamingo?" I said, laughing. The idea of one of those awkward pink birds gracing my Thanksgiving table struck me as funny. "I can't wait for the leftover flamingo hash."

Frank, however, was serious. "Could it be a stork?" he wondered aloud.

"The legs are too short," I said, suppressing a giggle. "And I don't think they have webbed feet."

"Well, I'm going down to the zoo," Frank said, leaving the kitchen.

"Why?"

"To see if their emu is missing," Frank called back.

"Frank, what am I going to do with this thing?" I cried piteously.

"Cook it up and let's see what it tastes like," he said, disappearing into the bedroom. "And please disarm Stephen. My head hurts enough already."

While Frank took a nap, I screwed up my nerve and plucked the giant bird of its remaining feathers. Then I took a break to read more of *The Joy of Cooking*. The index yielded no information about flamingos or emus, so I pretended the thing on the counter was a turkey. The way I figured it from the chart, I needed to cook the bird for one hour at 800 degrees or eight hours at 100 degrees. That didn't seem quite right, but then neither did this turkey.

I scrubbed the carcass down, buttered it, salted and peppered it, and then began to prepare my special stuffing. Ten seconds later, I was done. The only problem was, I couldn't lift the bird to put it in the oven. So I took another break. We were *this* close to the iceberg.

I was roused out of my dreams of nautical disaster by a knock on the door. It was Molly.

"Thought I'd pop by to give you a hand," she said. "Peter's still sleeping it off."

"Thank goodness you're here," I said. "I'm in big trouble."

After surveying the situation, Molly advised two courses of action.

"We could all go to the Hotel Montpellier for a fabulous meal, or we could attempt to cook this dinosaur," she said. "I opt for the former."

"Let's cook it. Maybe it will be all right," I said feebly, though the entire idea of a traditional Thanksgiving seemed to have come unglued.

With Molly's help I heaved the giant bird onto a pan and squeezed it into the oven. It fit. Barely. But those big black legs hung outside the oven door.

"Should I cut them off?" I wondered.

Molly looked green. "I need a drink," she said.

"I'd like to join you," I said, "but I think I'll need to keep my wits about me this morning."

The rattle of ice cubes woke Frank instantly. Perhaps he could hear our own personal *Titanic* about to plow right into that berg.

"I've got an idea," I said to my husband. "Why don't you go down to the Commune Libre and throttle Lucian?"

"And get your money back," Molly added.

Frank looked abashed but said nothing.

"Why don't we wait for Dick Robinson?" Frank said finally. "He's a med student. Maybe he knows something about the local fauna."

That sounded good to me, so I poured myself another cup of coffee and sat down to talk with Molly.

We had invited everyone to come over at noon under the assumption that the turkey would be ready about two. Now, if I started cooking at twelve the bird wouldn't be ready until five or so. A long, long cocktail hour. However, an overabundance of cocktails was not something that would dismay our guests. I got dressed in my best suit, and the guests began to appear, loaded down with liquor of all descriptions. Frank was his usual efficient self at the bar, making and dispensing drinks with a machinelike regularity.

When Dick Robinson and his girlfriend Dominique arrived, they were sent to the kitchen immediately. Dick was a short, stocky man who had been a Marine pilot during the war. He had been shot down twice and had parachuted into the Pacific. The man was afraid of nothing except Dominique, the campus dish. He treated her as if she were made of glass, though in reality she was made of flesh and blood. Especially flesh, distributed in all the right places. Molly, no mean looker herself, said she felt like a dowdy old maid by comparison. "Dominique seems very nice," Molly had once said. "But I hate her on principle."

In the kitchen, I pulled the oven door open to let Dick inspect the bird, but his medical opinion was not needed.

"The feet, the feet!" Dominique cried. *"C'est un cygne."*

"A swan?" Dick said.

"Mystery solved," Molly said, pouring herself another drink. "Is it edible?"

Dominique had no idea. She had grown up on a farm and the swans there were used as watch animals to prevent poachers from stealing the ducks and geese.

"Of course they're edible," I said knowingly. "At least they were in the Middle Ages. My friend Jules told me that gangs of roving students, penniless and starving, used to steal swans and eat them. How apropos for a room full of penniless, itinerant students."

"Look, Mary, I'm not penniless. Let's go buy chicken or a duck," Molly said.

"Nonsense," I said, determined now to cook the swan to tender perfection—if such a thing was possible.

"Dick, please chop off its legs for me so I can get it into the oven," I said.

"Why me?" he asked.

"You're going to be a surgeon, right?" I said. "Here's a good chance for you to practice your technique."

He looked pained, but set about his work with grim determination.

With Frank in charge of the drinks, the party really got rolling. After the ritual denunciation of the evil M. Dufin and his latest crimes against humanity, the talk was mostly about Korea. Last month the war was won. This month a million Chinese soldiers were threatening to kick us off the Korean peninsula. Frank had been wondering what to do, whether to go or stay, as had all the American students.

"If it gets really bad," Dick said, "they'll start trading atomic bombs."

"Let's hope it doesn't come to that," Frank said. "But have you heard about Nick Cass? He was recalled to active duty. The poor SOB was a B-29 pilot."

"And will be again," Peter Lord said. He had arrived late but made up for it by quickly downing Manhattans at a Frank-like rate.

"Are they going to get you?" Frank asked Peter.

"I've already been notified to be ready," Peter said. "Give me six more Manhattans."

"Maybe we should all go home," Ron Freeman said. "If this is going to be World War III, I'd feel better dying on my own soil than here in Montpellier."

"Don't talk like that," his wife, Lily, said.

Somber talk for somber times. On November 11 we had gone to the Armistice Day ceremonies held at the Oeuf. I had expected a big parade, bands, tanks, and airplanes flying overhead, just as we have at home. Boy, was I wrong. What a solemn occasion. Hundreds of people stood around the Oeuf, and not a sound was heard. There was only one band and it played *La Marseillaise,* which sent shivers down my spine. Then came a muffled drumroll, and the parade began—a parade of death. The veterans of both wars shuffled past the crowd. It was pitiful, pitiful, pitiful. The amputees in their wheelchairs, in little carts, and on crutches shambled by, supported by friends and wives and children. Blind men proudly wore uniforms and medals they could no longer see, gassed soldiers were gasping for breath through damaged lungs, and tiny old men were shaking and weeping with emotion. I didn't mean to, but I cried. I wanted somehow to salute them, but what could I say to a man with one arm or to a widow draped in mourning clothes? How lucky we all were to have survived the war. Would we be as lucky in Korea?

Molly, working on her umpteenth drink, took me aside for a private conversation.

"I don't want to upset you," she said, "but have you noticed the smell from the kitchen?"

I sniffed the air. I didn't smell anything and said so.

"Shouldn't a cooking swan smell like *something*?" she asked.

I dashed out to the kitchen to investigate. When I opened the oven door, not a trace of heat emerged. The swan was cool to the touch.

"I lit the stove," I said to Molly. "I'm sure of it." The bird should have been cooking for more than two hours, and now I had to start from scratch.

"Give it another whirl," Molly suggested. "Then we can eat around midnight."

I struck a match, but before I could light the oven, Stephen came rushing into the kitchen shouting, *"Au feu, Maman! Au feu!"*

"My sentiments exactly," I said, smiling and patting him on the head. "Oh, foo is right."

"Non, Maman. Au feu! Au feu!" he shouted, pulling on my skirt, trying to drag me into the other room.

"Mary, I think he's saying there's a fire," Molly said.

Just then I heard a whooshing sound and smoke began billowing into the apartment. I ran out into the hall and saw flames under the stairs. I could hear Mme. Sauson shrieking at the Monsieur to do something, *do* something!

The men in the living room swung into action. "Frank, save the children. Ron, come with me. Bob, protect the women," Peter ordered. Then he rushed downstairs to help fight the blaze.

Frank told me to go to the balcony and be prepared to jump.

"Not on your life," I said, brushing him aside and walking out to the landing. Ron and the Monsieur had brooms and were beating the flames, while poor Mme. Sauson sagged against a wall, holding her hand to her heart, her chins wobbling with fright. Peter, who was a foot taller than M. Sauson, grabbed the broom from our landlord and in short order had extinguished the blaze.

"That was exciting," Peter said when it was all over. "I believe I'll have another drink."

For the next two hours we sat in our smoke filled apartment, speculating on the cause of the fire, while Frank poured drinks all around. Our guests ripped through the rye, slurped up the scotch, bolted down the Bordeaux, and chased everything with the champagne.

By five o'clock, when I went to check the bird, I found it, like my bathwater, lukewarm. I didn't know if the fire had somehow affected the gas line, but the stove just didn't seem hot enough to me. At this rate, as Molly had predicted, dinner would be served sometime after midnight.

However, I had underestimated Frank's heavy hand on the drinks. Our guests were in no condition to eat anything; they were barely able to walk.

"Lovely dinner, Mary," Dick Robinson said as he and Dominique were leaving. "Best I ever had."

Dominique looked at him with a peculiar glint in her eye. I suppose the French are not big on imaginary dinners and, for some imponderable reason, prefer actual food.

"I think we'd have been better off with your internationally famous tuna sandwiches," Molly said, gripping a swaying Peter by the arm. Our hero firefighter was hosed.

One by one they drifted off into the night, leaving Frank and me stunned. I fed the children an omelet and put them to bed early. Frank drifted off in his chair. The good ship Thanksgiving had gone down by the bow.

I inspected the bird in the oven. It was still *pas chaud,* so I just turned off the stove and let it sit in its own grease. Perhaps Elise could do something with it in the morning.

I didn't know it then, but that was just the first in a series of being smoked out of our rooms and watching M. Sauson attack the flames in different ways. Sometimes he would throw a pan of water up at the ceiling, and other times he used his well-singed broom while we waited hopefully in our apartment, wondering if we would be required to jump from the balcony to the street below.

A plasterer was called in and took the better part of a day to plaster around the offending pipe where it entered our apartment. But that provided only temporary relief, for in a few days the smoke came puffing out from around the new plaster and into our apartment. We got so hardened to the fire-fighting scene downstairs that after a while we lost interest.

At last M. Sauson decided he was using too much coal in the furnace, and as a result our apartment got colder and colder until I feared for our health. But amazingly while we were often uncomfortable, and went about in layers of sweaters, *la grippe* released its grip on us and we survived the winter without a sniffle or a cough or a fever. I guess we were lucky, or it was much too cold for germs to germinate in our apartment.

The shadowy Lucian never revealed where he had acquired a swan and declined to return our ten thousand francs, saying he had had "expenses" and was making no profit on the deal. I suppose a hearty band of swan-nappers don't come cheap. But the whole affair had left a bad taste in my mouth, or rather, no taste at all in my mouth. Just what the heck did swan taste like anyway? Frank said it probably tasted like chicken, but that's what they told me about rattlesnake stew in Texas. I would never know. Gristede's would have canceled my account if I tried to order a swan back home, and that Thanksgiving was, if you'll pardon the expression, my swan song in the field of waterfowl cookery.

As I mentioned, the French rarely invite friends to their homes for dinner, and now we all knew why. Practical people, the French, and they probably get to keep most of their friends, too. But as I cleaned up the wreckage of the party that night, I couldn't help thinking about the awful Armistice Day display of human wreckage. For all our carping and complaining, we had it easy in comparison, and although we had been flamed, smoked, and had gone turkey-less on Thanksgiving, we had much to be thankful for.

Chapter 12

HOME FOR THE HOLIDAYS. Mary and Frank in front of their house on rue de Claret, presumably to keep the wolf from the door. Christmas was coming, but the VA check hadn't.

Away in a Manger

December 1950

"Marley was dead. As dead as a doorknob," John intoned. "I am the Ghost of Christmas past. God bless me, every one!"

That was his summary of Dickens's *A Christmas Carol,* the seasonally appropriate story Frank had been reading to him.

"I predict a great future for him as a *Reader's Digest* editor," Frank said. "John could turn *War and Peace* into a two-page book selection. Something like: 'Bang. Boom. So long, Nappy.'"

Despite Frank's fears that John was headed for a career in condensation, my son had become an apparition aficionado. He was fascinated by ghosts and claimed to see them everywhere. They visited him at night, disrupting his sleep, and even followed him as far as the gates of his school. They were not allowed inside, however, because Mme. Lanval did not approve of ghosts. Thank goodness for Mme. Lanval.

More embarrassing, John had decided that Stephen was born to play Tiny Tim and taught his brother how to limp. Stephen threw himself into the role with such gusto that people on the street would shake their heads sadly as the poor little lame boy hobbled by.

"*Mal à la jambe, Maman!*" Stephen would crow and give me a demonstration of his bad leg. "*Je m'appelle Petit Tim!*" he would cry and limp for all he was worth. John, as Scrooge, would treat him badly, but when I complained, my older son told me he was only following the book. Silly me. I never thought I would yearn for the sword-fighting days of Monte Cristo. Or for the days when we had a few francs to fling around.

It has been my experience that for money to be the root of all evil, you have to have some in the first place. On that score, Frank and I must have been the purest people in all of Montpellier. We were stone-cold broke. The Veterans Administration had not sent us a check since July, and we were burning up our limited resources at an alarming rate. A dozen letters and telegrams had finally disclosed the root of our evil problem: The VA had lost John's birth certificate and now presumed he didn't exist. As much as John wanted to be a ghost, I had undeniable proof he was alive, and I had even offered to take him to Paris for the bureaucrats and administrators to inspect.

Always more practical than I, Frank suggested that we send Stephen out into the streets with his limp and a tin cup to gather the rent money. And in truth, we were reduced to begging, not only the VA but Frank's brother, John, who saved us from being evicted with a timely check for a hundred dollars. I would have put the touch on my mother, but she had just gone loco.

My mother is a nice conservative lady who taught school to make ends meet after my father died prematurely. She had lived in St. Louis all her life, and her idea of a big adventure was going to the movies on Saturday night—but not too often because that might indicate an unhealthy interest in popular entertainment. She had retired last year, and I expected she would continue living as she always had—quietly and conservatively. Then I got a letter saying that she was moving permanently to St. Thomas in the Virgin Islands. The thought of my prim and proper mother moving to the equivalent of the South Seas threw me for a loop. I couldn't even find St. Thomas on a map, let alone imagine my mother in a sarong or grass skirt, doing the hula on the beach. That was just too ridiculous, and I told her so in a letter.

Her tart reply suggested that someone living in an obscure city in Southern France was in no position to criticize her choice of abodes. She had me there, but this was a woman who made Queen

Victoria seem slightly racy, suddenly becoming a character out of Somerset Maugham's "Rain." Frank thought Mom's move was great and suggested that St. Thomas probably made St. Louis seem like Hobbs, New Mexico. Still, having a beach bum for a mother was upsetting. The next thing you knew, she'd be taking up surfing.

My mother's peculiar behavior, combined with our financial woes and Frank's continuing agony over whether or not to stay in France, made life in Montpellier about as secure as my reputation as a linguist. I didn't know if I should pack, unpack, or pack it in. Two of our friends at the university had decided to leave. One poor man was recalled to active duty, and the other, our medical student friend Dick Robinson, was convinced that with the U.S. tied up in Korea, the Soviets would invade Europe. He said he didn't want to wind up in a Communist concentration camp. Frank dismissed the idea, but talk like Dick's was not uncommon at the time.

With Christmas only a week away, Frank and I made a pact. We would save money by getting each other only one small present and then we'd spend what we had left on the children. That might have been a mistake because John, at least, was ambivalent about the big holiday.

"Aren't you excited about Christmas?" I asked him one day.

"'A poor excuse to pick a man's pocket once a year,'" John said, quoting Scrooge.

"What do you want Santa to bring you?" I insisted.

"There is no Santa," he said.

My heart sank. I had hoped he would believe in Santa for at least another year or two.

"Really?" I asked warily. "What makes you say that?"

"Because Michel told me so," John answered.

"Who are you going to believe?" I asked. "Me or some little boy in a balding fur coat?"

"Michel," John said firmly. "He lived in Paris."

That explained it.

"You don't understand, Mama. In France, Père Noël gives you presents—if you're good."

I breathed a sigh of relief. At least he believed in something.

"Poor Stephen, all he'll get is a whipping from Père Fouettard and a lump of coal," John said mournfully. "He cries too much."

"Well, maybe you can share some of your Christmas loot with your brother," I said.

"Humbug!" John said, overflowing with Christmas spirit.

I had been planning a traditional American Christmas for the boys, and I hoped to pull it off with more style than my traditional Thanksgiving dinner. But John's sudden belief in Père Noël made me change course. I badgered Frank to tell me about the local customs so I could make sure I followed them correctly.

"Christmas here is pretty much the same as it is at home," Frank told me. "Except that it is Père Noël who checks the record and hands out gifts and Père Fouettard who administers the whippings of bad boys and girls."

"Poor Marc," I said, thinking of John's school friend who was always in trouble.

"Christmas in France is very family-oriented," Frank said. "There's not much in the way of public celebration. Also, Christmas trees aren't particularly traditional. That's a German custom that made its way south from Alsace."

"Would the neighbors think we are German sympathizers if we got a tree?" I asked.

"Alsace sympathizers perhaps," he said. "But why not?"

He went on to tell me about the French custom of putting out shoes for Père Noël to fill with gifts and about the traditions from every part of the country. In the north, he said, they were big on Yule logs and they liked to give out gifts on St. Nicholas Day, December 6. Brittany celebrated with buckwheat cakes and sour cream. Alsace wouldn't be Alsace without a roast Christmas goose (thank goodness we lived far from Alsace); and in Paris, to see the holiday in without oysters was a sin. As far as he knew, Frank said, celebrations in Montpellier were a mixture of traditions from all over France, so we could pick and choose the ones we wanted. That suited me fine.

My first step was to buy a tree—a feat, I hoped, that would be easier to accomplish than finding a turkey. The word for tree in French is *arbre*, which makes sense if you think about Arbor Day. An evergreen tree is *un arbre à feuilles persistantes*—a tree with persistent leaves. I liked that. But trying to say *un arbre à feuilles persistantes* with my accent, I knew, would leave many a mouth agape and many a head scratched in wonderment and confusion. Still, I was not about to turn this matter over to the shadowy Lucian, fearing he might show up with a poison ivy plant or a two-hundred-foot-high redwood.

Fortunately, I was saved by Mme. Perrin and Maman, the O-la-la ladies at the general store. They stocked holly, evergreen boughs, and fir trees planted in terra cotta pots. I bought a tiny tree and hauled it home in Stephen's stroller, while I hauled Stephen home by the hand.

Setting it up in the living room, I stepped back and appraised the tree. Well, appraised the bush. It was a rather tired-looking specimen, but I figured I could, ahem, spruce it up with a bit of creative decoration. The first thing I did, however, was take the tree out of the pot and put it in a cardboard box. That way Stephen could pull it down on top of himself without risk of death or dismemberment.

I wrapped a white tablecloth around the box and warned Stephen not to touch it—a warning that was sure to make him wild to bring it down on his head at the first opportunity. Still, I had to try.

That afternoon, after I had picked up John from school, the three of us went to the Oeuf to visit my least favorite store, Galeries Lafayette. The largest store in town, Galeries Lafayette is part of a giant department store chain with branches all over France.

I disliked the store for two reasons. First, when I made a fool of myself in public, I preferred to do it before a limited audience. At Galeries Lafayette there were always hundreds of customers milling around, waiting for me to make a spectacle of myself. And second, the service there was slow, slow, slow. That's because they have an odd way of selling things. The customer chose what she wanted, got a ticket, and then stood in line for an hour to pay the cashier. Then she had to go back to the original clerk, stand in line again to show the bill of sale, and finally get the item. Ridiculous. The owners should take a trip to New York and see how Macy's handles thousands of customers an hour. Shopping at Galeries Lafayette was time-consuming, annoying, and intimidating. But I hoped I would find something suitable for Frank.

Pulling Stephen's stroller through the revolving door and preventing John from making more than three complete circuits got us off to a distressing start. I grabbed John and plucked him from the doors just in time to prevent him from knocking down a package-laden old lady. Then it was on to the main floor, a marble-and-gilt museum of a department store studded with little outposts or kiosks selling various merchandise.

Galeries Lafayette was decorated for Christmas in a big way. Pillars were draped with greenery, gold foil, and red berries, and at one end of the store, mounted on a platform, was a life-size manger scene, illuminated from below. Mary, Joseph, shepherds, and farm animals were clustered around the baby Jesus lying in his cradle. It was an inspiring display that dominated the floor, although it seemed to me that the Three Magi and their camels cast baleful eyes on the shoppers.

Going from kiosk to kiosk, just poking around, I didn't find anything immediately, so on a whim I stopped by the lingerie counter to buy myself a new slip. That was an impulse, I admit, and I hadn't researched the word for *slip* before leaving home. Still, sometimes I was lucky applying a French accent to an English word.

"*Un sleep?*" I inquired, figuring that *sleep* might be the way Maurice Chevalier would say the word in the movies.

The girl behind the counter nodded vigorously and pointed to the next station over. Dutifully, I followed her finger, elated that she had understood me.

A salesman behind that counter also understood me perfectly, but produced several pairs of men's bikini bathing suits.

"No, no," I said. "*Un sleep.*"

"*Oui, Madame,*" he said, pointing at the truncated trunks.

I mimicked putting on a slip, but all I did was confuse the poor man, who was trying his best to get me what I wanted. I found out later that a *slip* is not a slip, but one of those overrevealing bikini bathing suits French men wear.

Disappointed, I thanked the clerk and wheeled away with Stephen's stroller. I had only gone a few paces when I realized something was wrong. I turned around and was horrified to find that Stephen was gone.

"John!" I said. "Where's Stephen?"

He didn't answer me, because he, too, was gone. The store was swarming with shoppers, and I couldn't see the boys anywhere. Trying not to panic, I made a methodical search of the immediate vicinity, but failed to locate them.

Imagining all sorts of dire possibilities, I stashed the stroller and strode through the store with mounting anxiety. Had they been kidnapped? Had they run out into the street? Where were they?

I tracked down a floorwalker and tried to explain to him what had happened.

"*Mes enfants!*" I sputtered. "*Mes garçons,* two of them . . . gone. Vanished. Poof!"

He seemed to comprehend and snapped his fingers. Immediately, two employees ran to their boss; then with a burst of French that eluded me, the floorwalker apparently instructed his men to fan out and look for the children. Then he took me firmly by the arm and led me on a tour of the store.

Up and down the aisles we trod, ducking into corners and detouring down passageways that the average customer never saw. Fifteen minutes later we wound up back where we had started, and we were joined by the two employees. They looked concerned but shrugged the Gallic shrug. John and Stephen were lost forever.

"*Gendarmes!*" I said. I wanted the police.

But before anyone could react, I heard a small, familiar voice: "Hi, Mama."

I whirled around, looking in all directions, but I didn't see anyone.

"Where are you!" I shrieked.

"Up here," John said.

I looked up at the manger scene and was horrified to see that Stephen had dispossessed the baby Jesus of his cradle. He was lying in the manger, snoring away, pretending to be asleep. If only he would do that at home.

Worse, John was sitting on a plaster donkey, urging it on with a hearty "Hi-ho, Silver!"

"Don't move!" I yelled to them.

Then the floorwalker, his two men, and I all rushed off to rescue the children before they destroyed the nativity scene or fell and broke their necks. A crowd of disapproving shoppers had gathered around to gawk and shake their heads at us.

A cleaner, it turned out, had left a ladder standing at the rear of the crèche—a magnet for small boys. John and Stephen had taken full advantage of that oversight and had thoroughly enjoyed playing with the holy family and their attendants.

"Je suis le bébé Jesus," Stephen said. "I am the baby Jesus."

Be that as it may, I spent the next few minutes apologizing to the floorwalker and screaming at the children. Then with as much dignity as I could muster, I left Galeries Lafayette—too embarrassed to ever go back.

The boys both got a good spanking, and they deserved it, but although I may have dented the seats of their pants, I'm sure I didn't dampen their enthusiasm for escaping Mama and running off at odd moments.

When we got home, I sent the boys off to their room in disgrace, telling them to stay there until Christmas or New Year's. I was thoroughly shaken and darned mad. I had no hesitation about taking it out on Frank.

"I was humiliated," I said. "Why won't they ever stay put?"

Frank was unsympathetic. "They're children, not miniature adults. They do dumb things because they don't know any better."

"Well, they had better shape up or it's lumps of coal for them," I said.

"You've got to admit it must have been pretty funny," Frank said, laughing.

"That's because you weren't there," I said. "And you'll be lucky if you don't get a bikini bathing suit for Christmas."

The following day I had almost recovered, which was good because, with only four days until Christmas, all sorts of things began to happen. Grande Vitesse, the French parcel service, delivered not one but two enormous boxes. The first one was from Frank's mother, who had sent toys for the children and a new blue snowsuit for John. I was delighted to get the snowsuit because the weather in Montpellier was certainly no longer *pas chaud,* it was downright chilly. The little boys and girls at John's school had begun wearing cotton smocks over their shorts or dresses, but except for Michel in his gray fur coat, they all looked cold to me.

The second package came from Paris. That was mysterious enough, but there was no note inside. What the box contained, however, was glorious: two bottles of vintage champagne, a tin of Beluga caviar, a loaf of pâté de foie gras, and two wrapped packages marked JEANNOT, and ETIENNE. (Etienne, pronounced A-tee-yen, is French for Stephen. The diminutive is 'Tienne, presumably "Steve.")

"André must have sent it," Frank said, surveying the contents of the box. "Who else do we know in Paris?"

"Mr. Scrooge," John said, peeking out of his room.

Frank laughed. "How do you know?"

"The Ghost of Christmas told me," John said.

"Back to your *à ta place,*" I said. "You're still in Coventry."

"Humbug," John groused.

"Well, who cares who sent it? Let's open the wine," Frank said. "It's not often we get to drink the good stuff."

"Oh, let's save it for Christmas," I said. "We'll have a feast to make up for Thanksgiving."

"Humbug," Frank said, but he agreed to wait.

The next afternoon I went shopping for Frank's Christmas present—alone. As I walked through my favorite run-down neighborhood, I noticed that even in this rough part of town, the merchants had gone to some trouble to decorate their stores: a bit of greenery, a few ribbons, and nativity scenes everywhere. I stopped into a gift shop—okay, a junk shop—and discovered a treasure trove of Christmas ornaments. I bought a silver wine cask, a ceramic Père Noël, a glass angel, a clay shepherd, and half a dozen other balls, bells, and bijoux to decorate our spindly little tree.

In the same dingy, dark store I found what I wanted to give Frank: a briefcase. That sounds pretty dull, I know, but watching Frank riding his bicycle with one hand on the handlebars and the other arm full of books made me nervous. He had to fight crowds of motorcycles, bicycles, cars, and pedestrians on his way to the university, and I knew I would feel better if he had two hands on the wheel, so to speak. I figured he could strap the briefcase to the fender of his bike and he would be a hundred times safer than he was now.

The briefcase was made of dark brown leather, with straps and worn bronze buckles. It had obviously been well used, but the price was right, and for the purpose I imagined, it was perfect. I don't think it would have been appropriate at a corporate board meeting, but for a student, why not?

When I got back home, the boys were busily engaged in projects Elise had created for them. John was painting a picture of Père Noël and Stephen was sitting on her lap, "helping" her sew on buttons.

"We're having a party tomorrow at school," John informed me. "Can I go?"

"May I go?" I said automatically. "Of course you may."

"Then you aren't mad at me anymore?" he asked.

"Look, I don't want to be Mr. Scrooge," I said. "But you might have hurt yourself or Stephen. You have to mind me and not run off willy-nilly."

"God bless me, every one," John said in wonderment. "Thank you, Mama."

Frank came home that afternoon with a minature crèche, probably just to remind me of my misadventures in Galeries Lafayette, and he spent a long time with the boys setting it up beneath the Christmas tree.

"Stephen slept in Jesus' cradle," John said.

"So I heard," Frank said. "At great length."

"Does that mean he'll get Christmas presents?" John asked.

"Probably," Frank said.

John looked disappointed, but he continued to arrange and re-arrange the small figures called *santons,* little saints. These beautiful figurines are made in Aix-en-Provence, and some can be quite expensive. They include not only the traditional nativity characters but townspeople like the miller, the baker, the fishwife, and even the village idiot (a character I could commiserate with). This set contained figures that were just the right size for Stephen to swallow. But stern warnings from Frank, Elise, John, and me had so far kept him from choking to death. However, it was early yet.

At seven o'clock that evening, the usual fire broke out downstairs and we listened to the familiar sounds of Mme. Sauson's screams and the Monsieur's frenzied broom work on the stairs. Ahh, domestic tranquillity.

But our peaceful evening came to an abrupt end when Peter and Molly arrived (literally) in a puff of smoke. They were beside themselves with rage. In unison, they rattled on in French at a pace that left me breathless.

"Well, I won't go," Molly said in English, her face red. In her hand was a telegram.

"Go where?" I asked.

That set them off again and I was sorry I had asked. Finally, Frank made them sit and cool off.

"This is truly bizarre," Molly said. "Could it be a practical joke?"

"Frank?" Peter said accusingly.

"Not me," Frank said, oozing innocence.

"What is going on?" I asked, irritated because I couldn't understand their outraged French.

"Here, read this," Molly said, thrusting the telegram at me.

Then she realized how futile an act that was and read it aloud. "You are cordially invited to *le réveillon.* L'Hotel Du Midi. *Joyeux Noël.*"

She paused dramatically.

"It's signed . . . Dufin!" she whispered as if she couldn't bear to mention his name.

"M. Dufin? That's a hot one," I laughed. "And what's a *réveillon?*"

"I had thought it was a celebration held after Mass on Christmas Eve," Peter said. "But if Dufin's the host, it probably has something to do with devil worship."

"Then it must be a joke," I said. From what I knew of the satanic M. Dufin, he would be the last man on earth to throw a party—especially for the students he hated.

"What are you going to do?" Frank asked.

"Leave for Spain tonight," Peter said. "I want to be out of town—hell, out of the country—in case the old SOB has lost his marbles."

"Say," Molly said to Frank, "how come you didn't get an invitation?"

Frank shrugged. "He must hate me more than you."

"He hates everyone," Molly said. "Are you sure you didn't send these telegrams?"

Frank was busy protesting his innocence when a singed M. Sauson, fresh from his fire-fighting duties, pounded on the door.

He had a telegram for Frank and said he hoped it wasn't bad news.

"If it's what I think it is," Frank said, "it's very bad news indeed." Sure enough, it was addressed to M. and Mme. Littell and contained the same invitation Molly and Peter had received.

"Frank probably sent it to himself," Molly said, "to make ours seem real."

"Frank is many things, but he's not a practical joker," I informed Peter and Molly. "Besides, we hardly have enough money left to send one telegram, let alone three."

They thought about that for a moment; then they left as bewildered as they had come. When they had gone, I told Frank he could level with me: Had he sent those telegrams?

"I wish I had," he said, "because if it's true . . ."

I thought I detected a shudder.

*   *   *

The next morning dawned clear and frosty. I knew that even before I got out of bed because Frank was on his second made-up verse of Gene Autry's new song, "Frosty the Snow Man," much to Stephen's delight.

I dragged myself out of bed and gratefully accepted a cup of coffee. As soon as my head cleared, I said, "You sent those telegrams, didn't you?"

Frank looked pained. But then he's an expert poker player, with the face for it. I could never tell when he was being serious or stringing me along.

"I'll get to the bottom of this," he vowed, putting on his hat and coat.

"I hope so," I said, "because I certainly don't want to meet this awful Dufin character, not on Christmas Eve."

"Is it Christmas?" John asked, wandering into the kitchen dressed in his pale blue Dr. Denton's. His face was as droopy as his pajamas.

"Two more days," I said. "Then a visit from Père Noël."

"Not for me," John said. "I was bad in the store. Père Fouettard will spank me."

"You can never tell," Frank said. "Sometimes Père Noël is a soft touch."

"Or maybe Santa Claus can find me in Montpellier?" John said, brightening.

"That's the great thing about Christmas," I said. "All kinds of unexpected things happen."

"Like Mr. Scrooge being nice and sending us presents from Paris?" he asked.

"Exactly," I said. "Now go get dressed. You've got a party to go to."

Because the weather was cold, I decided that John should wear his new snowsuit rather than receive it as a present on Christmas Day. Even opening presents is no fun if you have galloping pneumonia. So with Stephen bundled to the eyeballs in his stroller and

John proudly outfitted in his snowsuit, we made the familiar journey to the Jardin d'Enfants.

When we got there, however, I was in for a shock. The classroom was filled with children, and every single one of them was wearing a costume. The twins, Anni and Annette, were dressed as little Dutch girls; Marc, appropriately, was a lion; Michel was wearing a World War I soldier's hat and a makeshift uniform; other children were dressed as fairy princesses, magicians, pirates, and animals. They made a colorful sight, but it was a sight I was appalled to see.

"Why didn't you tell me this was a costume party?" I stage-whispered to John.

"You didn't ask," he said.

Silly me.

I have a friend back in America who told me about taking her five-year-old daughter to the child's first ballet class. When they arrived, all the other little girls were wearing their ballet slippers and leotards while my friend's child was in her street clothes.

"Mary," she had said, laughing, "it was awful. All the other mothers were looking at me as if I were some kind of moron without enough sense to outfit my child correctly. That was when I knew I was a bad mother and would always be."

I had been amused by her story, but now I didn't find it so humorous. Most mothers, it seemed, were privy to some mysterious maternal grapevine. They always knew where they had to be, when they had to be there, and what their children had to wear or bring. I was hopelessly disconnected from that grapevine, which I imagined growing on a soaring trellis. I felt like an uninformed squash lying on the ground, looking up with envy.

Oh, what a terrible mother I was. If only the floor would open up and John and I could escape. I spun on my heel, intent on fleeing, when I heard Mme. Lanval's voice.

"*Oh, c'est joli,*" she said, putting her hands on John's snowsuit. "*Le costume.*"

Saved! The teacher thought John's snowsuit was a costume.

"But, Mama—" John began.

"Shhh," I said. "Pretend your snowsuit's a costume and not another word."

He shrugged and joined the other children, hood up, sweating profusely, but gamely trying to fit in. At the end of the party, all the children rushed out of the classroom, the boys to play *avion*. I sat on the long wooden bench with Stephen and watched as the pirates shot down the bears and the lion leaped on the little Dutch girls.

I knew in my heart I was a bad mother, but at least I was a lucky one. My children had practically desecrated a holy shrine, yet so far the Archbishop of Montpellier hadn't ordered their arrests. The costume party could have been another fiasco, but again I had gotten off scot-free.

Perhaps, I thought, my glib comments to John were true: All kinds of unexpected things do happen at Christmastime. Why, if Stephen could lie quietly in a manger, M. Dufin could throw a party, and my mother could find work as a model for Gauguin, anything could happen. And probably would.

Chapter 13

A CHRISTMAS WISH. John and Stephen had high hopes they would be visited by Père Noël or Santa Claus or, preferably, both.

A Christmas Peril

After the potentially disastrous costume party, I got John to help me wrap a few presents while Stephen took his nap.

"Now remember," I said, producing the briefcase from the top of the closet, "this is supposed to be a surprise for Daddy, and you have to keep the secret or you'll spoil all the fun. Got it?"

John assured me he would be as silent as the Ghost of Christmas Yet to Come.

"That ghost didn't say a word," John informed me. "Not one word."

"Good," I said. "Just remember that."

When Frank came home from the university at about five, he was in no mood to be trifled with.

"I am in no mood to be trifled with," he said, glowering. "I think I'm having a nervous breakdown."

"What's wrong?" I asked.

"What's right?" he said. "My whole world has been turned upside down. The invitations from M. Dufin are no joke. They are terribly, terribly real."

"Oh, no," I said. "Are we going to go?"

"I talked it over with the other students—all of them got invitations, by the way—and we decided that if we don't go, Dufin will get even worse. So we'll get very drunk, go, and see what that old SOB is up to," Frank said, his head in his hands.

"At least I'll get to see this monster in the flesh," I said. "Besides, the Hotel du Midi is a pretty fancy place. I'll bet the food's good."

Frank got up wearily from his chair and limped to the kitchen to make himself a drink.

Limped?

"What's wrong with your leg?" I asked, worried he had had an accident on his bicycle.

"Nothing," he said. "I'm auditioning for the role of Petit Tim. Maybe M. Dufin will have pity on me."

At the mention of Petit Tim, Stephen, who had been playing quietly, leaped up and went into his act. Soon Frank, John, and Stephen were all hobbling about the living room to beat the band. The Three Stooges had nothing on these boys.

"Sorry, Frank," I said after they had all collapsed on the couch. "Stephen was the most convincing. You don't get the job."

"Humbug," Frank said. "Tomorrow night's going to be the humbuggiest night of my life. Oh, to be in Hobbs, New Mexico, right now, listening to the soft sighs of the vampire bats, the sweet howls of the rabid coyotes, and the delightful maraca-like resonances of the rattlesnakes. Paradise!"

"Don't be sad, Daddy," John said. "We got you a present."

"That's nice," Frank said. "A train ticket to Rome?"

"No, it's a surprise," John said.

Pause.

"And it's a secret," John said.

A longer pause.

"And it's a briefcase."

Oh, well. So much for surprises. Keeping secrets, I should have realized, was an acquired skill, like archery or sheep shearing, and not something we are born with. Four-year-olds need a lot of practice.

"John!" I said. "You've ruined the surprise."

"Show him, Mama," John said. "He needs a present now."

Looking at Frank's grim countenance made me realize the child had a point. I took the briefcase from the closet and handed it to Frank.

"Ah, what could this be?" he said, shaking the wrapped package.

"It's a briefcase," John said, looking at his father as if Frank had lost his mind.

"No, I think it might be dueling pistols," Frank said, putting his ear to the package. "Or a box of fine Cuban cigars. Or perhaps a swan."

"*Un cadeau!*" Stephen shouted. "A present!" Then he leaped for the package, intent on wresting it from his father.

"No, it's for Daddy," John said, trying to grab it back.

But Stephen would not be denied. When you're eighteen months old, all presents are for you, no matter what anybody says. Stephen ripped off the paper; then he ran to his room with the briefcase dragging on the floor behind him.

Frank laughed. "Do you know the word for briefcase in French?" he asked me.

I didn't.

"It's *serviette*. As in, '*Madame, la serviette, s'il vous plâit!*'" Frank said in perfect imitation of our napkin-crazed waiter aboard the *Veendam*.

"'I'm dreaming of a white Christmas,'" Frank sang. "'Just like the ones in Hobbs, New Mexico. Where the treetops are a-hissin', and the snakes are a-pis—'"

"Frank!" I shouted from the bedroom.

"'And the snakes are a-glistenin','" he revised with a discreet flourish. Stephen clapped his hands in appreciation; I clapped the pillow over my head. It was only six a.m., and from the song selection in the kitchen, I decided it must be snowing. On Christmas Eve.

Wait a minute . . . snowing in Montpellier?

I jumped out of bed to confirm my singing weatherman's forecast. Sure enough, it was snowing lightly. How wonderful! I stumbled out to the kitchen and was greeted by Frank and Stephen whispering conspiratorially.

"Okay, 'Tienne," Frank said. "Belt it out."

Stephen giggled, then in a tinny little voice sang, "'Hap birf, hap birf, *cher Maman*. Hap birf you.'"

"Well, thank you," I said, kissing him on top of his head. "And thank you, maestro."

Yes, Christmas Eve is my "birfday," which proved beyond a doubt that my mother, in addition to being loco, had an unusually bad sense of timing. How could a mere birthday of mine compete with the extravaganza that was Christmas? I won't go into the gory details, but birthdays are to me what the conquest of Europe was to Napoleon: a passion and a curse.

"I have a present for you," Frank said.

Pause.

"And it's a secret."

A longer pause.

"And it's a pink negligee from Paris," Frank said. "Are you surprised?"

"Bowled over," I said. And I was.

"*Un cadeau!*" Stephen shouted, going into his present-grabbing routine. Frank went to rescue the box, but he was too slow. If you've ever seen those awful nature films in which a school of piranha devours an entire cow in ten seconds, you'll have an appreciation of Stephen ripping at that box. He had the heavy gold-foil paper on the floor in seconds and was clawing viciously at the top of the box when Frank snatched it away.

"It's for *Maman*," Frank said, taking the present out of Stephen's reach.

"*Non! Pour moi*," Stephen cried. "For me!"

So we compromised. Stephen got the box, the paper, and the ribbons, and I got a wonderful pink chiffon negligee, the likes of which I had never seen outside of the movies. Marlene Dietrich, eat your heart out.

"Oh, Frank. It's absolutely lovely, but it must have cost a fortune," I said, holding it up to my frayed flannel nightgown.

"It did," he said. "I spotted it last August and had Peter pick it up in Paris last month, back in the days when we were still semi-solvent. Hope you like it."

"It's gorgeous," I said. What a happy beginning to a day Frank feared would be a disaster. "Hap birf me," indeed.

Frank, John, and Stephen went outside to build a snowman in the backyard, while I sat at the kitchen table to do some last-minute wrapping. Elise had knitted both boys scarves, one blue, one green. I was touched by her generosity and concern for the children. In turn, we had given her just about the last of our money as a Christmas tip, although we practically had to hold her down to get her to accept it.

"Hey, Mary!" I heard Frank shout.

I went to the window.

"What do you think?" Frank called up.

"About what?" I answered.

"Our snowman," he said.

I looked all around the yard, but for the life of me, I couldn't see a snowman.

"There!" Frank said, pointing.

I had to laugh. By his right foot was a teeny snowman that couldn't have been more than a foot high. It had two raisins for eyes, the tip of a carrot for a nose (Stephen was noisily chewing on the rest of the carrot), and a quarter-inch piece of ribbon for a scarf.

"It's not a snowman," I said. "It's a snow baby!" There wasn't enough snow in the yard to build a proper snowman. "It's *un bébé de neige*," I said, making up the term on the spot.

"*Bonjour, bébé de neige,*" Stephen said, bending down to get a closer look at the miniature snowman. Then he slipped and fell on top of the little lump of snow, crushing it.

"You've killed the snow baby!" John shouted. "You'll get coal in your stocking and Père Fouettard will spank you."

Stephen burst into tears and fled back into the house, calling pitifully for Elise. Unfortunately, she was on holiday, so he had to make do with me—a poor substitute, I admit, but I did my best to calm him down. Bribes, I've found, often work in these circumstances, and a candy cane sent to us by Frank's mother soon soothed troubled waters.

"Frosty the Snowman was as dead as he could be. Killed by a falling Stephen, now he's his-to-ree," Frank sang.

"Oh, Frank," I said. "The poor child feels bad enough."

"He looks okay to me," Frank said. "Although he's so sticky from that candy cane, we could probably attach him to the wall as decoration."

"Decoration!" I said. "That's what we've got to do. Decorate the tree."

Frank looked at his watch. "I don't know if I've got thirty seconds to spare," he said. "Besides, there's no tinsel."

The tinsel was Frank's favorite part of tree decorating. He put the long silver strands on the tree one at a time. An eight-foot-tree took him hours to finish, but he enjoyed it. The year before, he had tried to show John how to do it, but John just took handfuls of tinsel and flung it at the tree. Frank was so furious that he went back, untangled the tinsel, and restrung it in flawless fashion.

"No tinsel this year," I said. "The tree's too small."

So we spent a few minutes attaching red ribbons to the old collection of ornaments I had purchased at the odd little junk store. The results were, well, odd.

"It looks like a cat covered with Christmas ornaments," Frank said, standing back and eyeing our creation.

But the children thought it was beautiful, and that was all that counted.

"Are you sure you want to go to this *réveillon* thing?" I asked Frank as we were sitting around drinking eggnog that afternoon.

"I'm sure I don't," Frank said. "But I must. And by I, I mean we."

Frank and I debated whether or not to attend midnight services at St. Pierre, but we decided that the children would be hardpressed to sit still for an hour, then endure two more hours of being civilized at the Hotel du Midi. Thoughtful person that I am, I volunteered to stay home with the boys that evening, but Frank was determined to share his misery with me, thoughtful person that he is.

Resigned, I put the children to bed at the usual hour for a long winter's nap. I just hoped that they would get enough sleep to take the edge off any bad behavior. Then I followed suit. I had been to many parties that lasted until dawn, but I had never gone to one that started at one a.m.

At twelve-thirty in the morning, we all trooped out of the house like the four dwarfs: Sleepy, Cranky, Nervous, and Despondent. There was a biting wind, but the weather had cleared and the moon cast a silver sheen over the wet cobblestone streets.

"Let's sing a Christmas carol," I suggested, trying to cheer everyone up.

"No," John said. "I'm worried."

"About what?" I asked.

"We're Americans, right?"

"Right."

"Suppose Père Noël only visits French children?" he said.

"In that case, Santa Claus will find you," I said. "They work together, like Abbott and Costello."

"But if Santa comes, he won't fill up my shoes. He'll be looking for socks," John said.

"Then we'll hang up your stocking when we get home," I said. "That way we'll cover all bases."

"Yes," Frank said. "But who's on first?"

"Exactly," I said.

The Hotel du Midi was located in the old section of town, just off the Oeuf. It was an area of graceful eighteenth-century buildings, including the opera house. Every time I visited there, I felt as if I were taking a journey back in time—a journey to an era of gas lamps and horse-drawn carriages.

The hotel lobby was plush with red and gold velvet, and everything had a brittle shine to it, a shine that you find only in old and haughty hotels.

We were ushered into a Rube Goldberg–type of elevator and taken to a private dining room on the second floor.

"More victims," Molly called from across the room, beckoning us to join her and Peter. We said hello to everyone, but they seemed glum and listless. Thirty people—students, wives, husbands, girlfriends, boyfriends, and children—all sat around, looking as if their best friend had died suddenly.

"Gee whiz," I said, sitting down. "You folks are taking all this much too seriously. Let's have a party and to heck with the odious M. Dufin, who isn't even here yet."

Frank, Peter, and Molly looked at me as if I had just burst into song at a funeral.

"Come on," I insisted. "What's that cake on the table? It looks delicious."

"It's a king's *galette*," Peter said. "Baked inside is a favor—a ring, a miniature doll, or something. Whoever gets the favor in their piece is king for the evening and gets to wear a paper crown."

"How wonderful," I said. "Let's cut it up and see who the winner is."

This time the three of them looked at me as if I had spat on the flag at a veterans rally.

"Let's have some wine," Frank growled and reached for the bottle.

"Oh, come on," I said. "Stephen, do you want some cake?"

"*Gâteau!*" Stephen shouted, waving his arms.

Now, that was the kind of enthusiasm I was looking for. I reached over to the king's *galette,* but Molly stopped me.

"To do it right," she said, "the youngest member of the party—mercifully Stephen and not me—has to get under the table and tell you which of us gets the first piece of cake."

"Fine," I said. "He'll be under the table soon anyway."

"That's where I want to be," Frank said, draining his first glass of wine.

I ignored him and lifted Stephen down from his hotel-supplied high chair. He was thrilled that I actually wanted him to crawl around under the table instead of trying to get him to sit in his *à ta place.*

"All right," I said, cutting the cake into six pieces. "Who gets the first piece?"

"*Moi!*" Stephen said.

"If I were a betting man, I would have won a bundle on that answer," Frank said sourly.

"Okay," I said. "Back in your *à ta place.*"

"*Non,*" Stephen said.

"Come on," I urged. But Stephen wouldn't budge.

"Let him stay there," Peter said. "Perhaps he'll be spared Dufin's wrath when the old . . . gentleman arrives."

So I put a piece of cake on a plate and shoved it under the table, feeling as if I were feeding a dog.

The cake was delicious, but I didn't find any mysterious objects in it. Neither did John, Frank, Peter, or Molly. Then I heard a gagging sound from under the table, and I knew at once that Stephen was the king and that something was lodged in his throat.

"Frank!" I yelled, but my husband was already under the table. He brought up a kicking, gasping, blue-faced Stephen by the ankles and began pounding the child on the back.

Too stunned to move, I watched incredulously as a gold-colored ring shot out of Stephen's mouth and onto the red carpeting. Frank stopped the shaking and pulled Stephen upright, checking his mouth to make sure there was nothing else in there.

"*Gâteau,*" Stephen rasped. "*Gâteau!*"

He was crying loudly, but that was good. It is difficult to cry if you are choking to death.

By now we had attracted a crowd, all offering suggestions and advice. Knowing how Frank felt about creating scenes in public, I took Stephen from him and hurriedly exited the dining room to give my baby a checkup in private. I sat with him in the hotel lobby, suddenly realizing that my heart was pounding. Only quick thinking on Frank's part had saved the day—and our son. I hugged Stephen and kissed him until he got tired of all the fuss and demanded more cake. Babies get over things quickly; mothers never do. But I took him back upstairs, intent on corralling the rest of my family and dragging them home, where we should have stayed in the first place, M. Dufin or no M. Dufin.

When I walked back into the dining room, I could almost smell the resentment. A man dressed in a dark suit had his back to me and seemed to be addressing the students.

The abominable M. Dufin, I thought, wondering if I should simply take Stephen home or try to edge my way past the monster and get back to the table where I had my coat, my purse, my other son, and my husband.

"*Gâteau!*" Stephen screamed, pointing at a piece of king's *galette* on a nearby table.

The man in the suit turned around slowly. I was thunderstruck. It wasn't M. Dufin at all. It was Jules, my friend from the botanical gardens. He gave me a devilish grin.

"Jules! *Joyeux Noël!*" I said, rushing up to him and giving him the traditional busses on both cheeks.

You could hear the oxygen being sucked out of the room.

"What are you doing here?" I asked.

"*Joyeux Noël*, Mary, Étienne," Jules said.

I looked over to our table. Frank had developed a ghastly pallor, and Peter Lord looked as if he were about to faint, but when Stephen calmly abandoned Mama and settled himself in Jules's arms, the entire company was on the verge of hysteria.

Jules walked us back to our table and deposited Stephen in his chair. Then he faced the panicked crowd and said: "As you see, I do not eat small children, despite the rumors. And if you'll excuse me, I believe I shall address you in English—for Mary's benefit."

"Daddy, where's M. Dufin?" John asked.

"Right there," Frank said, nodding toward Jules.

"No, that's Jules. He buys us ice cream," John said. "Right, 'Tienne?"

"*Oui*," Stephen confirmed enthusiastically. "*Glace!*"

"For those of you who have not met me," Jules said, "my name is Jules Dufin, and I am the dean, as you would say, of the Institut des Étudiants Étrangers. Many of you have crossed my path and have probably wished you had not. Seeing all of you together, I want to ask your apology for my past behavior and to trust me when I say that all that—malarkey?—is in the past. I shall endeavor to be a mentor and a friend, not an enemy.

"I thought it was appropriate at this time of year, the time of *le réveillon*, the wake-up or first call of the new year, to declare my intentions. The birth of Christ gave us all a second chance, and I hope that you will give me a chance, too."

Twenty-eight people sat in silence, awed by a changed M. Dufin. Two people, however, were not impressed.

"Jules!" Stephen called out, breaking the awful silence. "*Je suis le roi!* I am the king!" He had pulled the golden paper crown down around his eyes.

Jules gave him a smile.

"Jules, can we get ice cream?" John asked. "We always get ice cream."

"Why not?" Jules said. "Ice cream all around!"

The ice cream seemed to break the ice, and although some of the guests remained wary, most of them accepted Jules at his word—and the party really took off.

We were served the traditional thirteen desserts, samples of what is sweet and good in the world. We drank champagne with our oysters, and for good measure, we went through a *bûche de Noël*, a chocolate cake rolled with mocha whipped cream and shaped like a Yule log. It was enough to decay the sweetest tooth. Stephen and John were blissfully covered from head to foot with the sticky remains.

"Is Jules really Mr. Scrooge?" John asked, moving the whipped cream on his nose to the back of his sleeve.

"That's just a book," I said. "Jules is a very nice man who has had a difficult life."

"I like him," John said, plunging into his sixty-eighth piece of cake.

I had always known that dessert was delicious, but I never knew it was redemptive.

Jules sat with us for a few minutes and asked Frank and me how we had enjoyed the wine and pâté he had sent us from Paris.

"That was you?" I said. "There was no note inside the box."

Jules apologized, saying he had been so rushed, he had forgotten to include greetings.

"Thank you, Mr. Scrooge," John said.

Frank gave his son a murderous look.

"The child is right," Jules said. "But I hope to live up to the Scrooge at the end of the book. And thank you, Mary, for being such a good audience for my ravings in the Jardin des Plantes. I should—and will—do more teaching and less administrating in the future."

"Mama's the Ghost of Christmas," John said after Jules had moved on to another table.

"Mama's something, all right," Frank said, "although I'm not quite sure what."

Although I didn't say so at the time, I felt as if I were partly responsible for Jules's transformation. When I had first met him, he had been a sour man, full of grief and grievances. I think that just talking to me—a neutral, disinterested party—helped him let off steam and realize how foolishly he had been behaving. War, of course, does terrible things to people, and in Jules's case, I think he simply reverted to his prewar self: a learned, gentle man. Of course I'm not a licensed psychiatrist, just a sounding board of note, but I wanted to tell Frank about my theory.

"You know," I said to my husband, "Jules's reformation—"

He held up his hand and said, "Please, I'll spare you my thoughts on the subject if you'll spare me yours. Besides, I think my nervous breakdown is coming on again and I suggest we get out of here before M. Dufin changes back to M. Hyde."

"Let's go home, Mama," John said shrewdly, "in case Père Noël needs help with my presents."

The party was still going strong when we left about three a.m. Stephen was asleep in his stroller and John was flung over Frank's shoulder, out like a light. Merry Christmas to all and to all a good night.

*   *   *

On Christmas Day we did little more than recuperate from Christmas Eve. The boys ripped into their presents, tearing away the wrapping with reckless abandon. Stephen fulfilled my dire prophesies by swallowing one of the little figures from the crèche, then bringing the Christmas tree down on his head. If I could guess people's weight half as accurately as I could guess Stephen's next move, I'd be a rich carnival lady by now.

That night I made roast chicken and mashed potatoes for dinner, followed by a salad and no dessert. We had already eaten our yearly quota of desserts the night before.

I put the boys down early, and each of them insisted on taking his favorite present to bed. John put the fire truck Jules had sent him from Paris under his pillow, and Stephen snuggled up to the little teddy bear my mother had sent from the Virgin Islands.

Frank and I waited for the nightly fire to be extinguished before retiring. I wore my new pink négligee.

"The only good thing about this apartment," Frank said, "is that the champagne is always cold."

He popped the cork and poured us each a glass. Then we lay warm in bed, sampling the caviar and nibbling on bread loaded with pâté. Jules's presents were not going to waste.

"This is us, I'm afraid," Frank said. "Drinking prewar champagne out of postwar plastic cups."

"And beluga right out of the tin, with nary a mother-of-pearl spoon in sight," I added. "But you must admit that this was the most eventful Christmas ever."

"Eventful? Hardly the word I'd use. We almost lost Stephen, and M. Dufin admitted what an SOB he was," Frank said. "Boggling is more like it."

"No," I said. "More of a miracle—right out of *A Christmas Carol*. Wasn't it kind of spooky the way John insisted that the package from Paris was compliments of Mr. Scrooge?" I said.

"The Ghost of Christmas told him so," Frank said. "So there you are. And apropos of nothing, I have something for you."

He reached under the bed and handed me a small package. Inside was a hotel room key and a note that read: *Get Out of Jail Free Card: Good for one night and two meals at the fabulously inexpensive Hotel Montpellier—anytime you feel that the children and I are a burden. Love, Frank.*

"Oh, Frank. This is beyond wonderful," I said.

"It's not much, but I thought you'd like it. Lord knows, I would," he said.

"This makes me very happy," I said.

"Then I propose a toast," Frank said. "To Montpellier."

I'll drink to that, I thought.

"And to another semester at the university," he said.

"We're staying?" I asked.

"To the bitter end. War or no war. I've put in too much time and effort not to get my degree," Frank said with determination. "And I propose another toast: To Messrs. Scrooge and Dufin, the founders of our feast. Merry Christmas!"

Or as John might have said, "God bless me, every one!"

Chapter 14

MISSION TO MARSEILLES. Mary fulfilled a girlhood dream by visiting the Chateau D'If, where her favorite literary hero, the Count of Monte Cristo, was imprisoned.

Mission to Marseilles

January 1951

"I need a few francs for the groceries," I said. "I'm a little short."

My husband looked up from his book and laughed. Then he read aloud:

"'Well, I'm the worst person to come to for advice. I've never been "short," as you painfully call it. And yet what else could you say? Hard up? Penurious? Distressed? Embarrassed? Stony-broke? On the rocks? In Queer Street? Let us say you are in Queer Street and leave it at that.'"

I stared at him, fearing that our financial problems had finally driven Frank around the bend. But all I could utter was an elegant and expressive "Huh?"

"Evelyn Waugh," Frank said, holding up the book he had been reading. "A character in *Brideshead Revisited* precisely summed up our plight. We have moved from Uneasy Street to Queer Street. We did not pass Go and we do not have two hundred francs, let alone two hundred dollars."

"What are we going to do?" I asked, feeling weak in the knees.

"A life of crime is a possibility. We could hold up Mme. Perrin and get away with a few francs from the store. Or we could start a gang and enlist Sophie and her boyfriend, *le terrible* René, to help us. He has a motorcycle and I believe all self-respecting gangs need a motorcycle—for fast getaways."

For all Frank's kidding, we were in desperate straits. The Veterans Administration, after a barrage of telegrams and letters, had suddenly found John's birth certificate, or at least one of the dozen extra copies we had sent to them. At the beginning of the month, they claimed they had sent a check covering August through December payments to Paris. Frank had dutifully made the trip to the capital. No check.

More letters and telegrams followed, more requests for birth certificates were filed, and absolutely nothing happened. A life of crime suddenly seemed a possibility, with one caveat.

"I don't think I'd make a good gun moll," I said. "I haven't got the gams for it."

"Well, as a second choice, how about a trip to Marseilles?" Frank said, reaching into his coat pocket and producing a telegram. "The VA now says they sent our check, care of American Express, to Marseilles," he said. "Someone mixed up Montpellier with Marseilles—all French names sound alike to us'n A-mar-a-kins."

"Can we visit Monte Cristo's prison, the Château d'If?" I asked.

"We may be permanent residents if the check's not there. I called from the Bar d'Oc, but nobody at American Express knows a damn thing. So we're taking a chance."

"What have we got to lose?" I asked.

"Not a lot," he said.

Since Peter and Molly were off to Spain, Frank had talked Peter into lending us the red MG for our trip. We might have been paupers, but we'd certainly be traveling in style—right into debtors' prison, no doubt.

Frank spoke with Elise, and she was delighted to take the boys to her farm for the weekend and assured us she would handle all the details. The mere thought of visiting Marseilles filled me with such excitement, I didn't bother questioning her about the mundane details. Like Paris and London, Marseilles had always seemed to me to be more magical than Camelot or Shangri-la. I grew up longing to see those fabulous cities just to breathe the air and become a part of their long histories. Marseilles especially was synonymous with intrigue, adventure, and mystery.

The day before we left, Elise's husband, Henri, was scheduled to take the boys to the farm. Frank had offered to provide bus fare, but Elise had said that was unnecessary. Henri would take the children, she said. In my mind, I had figured that her husband had a car or at least a horse and wagon. But when the poor man showed up at dusk, he was pushing a large wooden wheelbarrow. It had high sides and a rubber wheel in front.

"He probably made it himself," Frank said. "It makes Stephen's stroller look like a rocket from *Destination Lune.*"

"Frank," I said, "is that old man going to haul the children—what—five miles in a wheelbarrow?"

Frank shook his head in amazement.

Henri was about sixty years old, with grizzled white whiskers and a hawklike nose. He stood ramrod straight and looked sinewy and tough from a life working the soil. He tipped his cap to Frank and me, and we bowed in response.

"For a few cents we could have sent the boys on the bus," Frank said.

"What will we do?" I asked.

"We go with the program," Frank said. "Then we feel guilty later."

I looked at the pile of toys, games, clothes, books, and sundries I had accumulated for the boys' three-day stay and felt guilty immediately—no need for me to wait. So I quietly eliminated most of the items to preserve Henri's health.

We loaded everything in the wheelbarrow, including the boys. Then straining in the traces, Henri shoved off into the setting sun. John waved piteously to us; Stephen was laughing and urging old Henri to go faster. This was a wonderful new ride for him.

They had just about disappeared from view when I suddenly remembered I had forgotten to pack Stephen's toilet seat. Realizing that I was consigning Elise and Henri to a soggy weekend, I grabbed the toilet seat and raced after the retreating figures, waving the toilet seat in the air.

Henri never stopped, but he slowed down long enough for me to catch up and toss the seat into the wheelbarrow. Then, like a well-trained mule, he picked up his previous pace.

"That was ghastly," I said when I returned to the yard of our house. "I feel like some pre-Revolutionary aristocrat exploiting the poor."

"An aristocrat could have afforded a horse," Frank said. "We are simply peasants exploiting other peasants."

That didn't make me feel any better, but the next morning we were definitely aristocrats behind the wheel of Peter's MG.

"Go slowly," I said to Frank. "I want to make sure all the ladies in the neighborhood see us."

I was prepared to wave, in a queenly manner, to my chums, but Frank glowered and punched the gas pedal to the floor, roaring and screeching down the cobblestones. Mme. Perrin, Maman, Sophie, the butcher, and the rest saw only a red blur as we blasted out of town.

"Slow down!" I cried. It seemed to me as if we were doing a hundred miles an hour.

"I'm only doing thirty," Frank shouted over the roar of the engine.

Not believing him, I looked at the speedometer. He was right, but the MG was slung so low to the ground that it seemed as if we were breaking the sound barrier. Any tiny pebble we hit threw us into the air; potholes were like roller-coaster rides. My hair, carefully permed the day before, shot out from under my beret and waved in the air, Medusa-like. I had to hold on for dear life just to keep from being tossed into the street. This was definitely not our old Chevrolet.

Frank had a maniacal glint in his eye as he jockeyed the little red car in and out of traffic, dodging trucks, wagons, and ladies laden with produce. The glint became an insane gleam when we hit the open road and picked up speed.

"I *want* one of these," Frank yelled over to me, steering past a smoke-belching truck.

"I just want to live long enough to see Marseilles," I yelled back.

As we zoomed south that morning, I didn't have a chance to sightsee because I had my eyes shut tight to keep out the dust and grit. The mad pounding of the engine soon gave me a mad pounding headache. But that evaporated when we reached Marseilles. Frank slowed down and pointed over the windshield—and there was the Mediterranean looking as if it had just been painted for the day, so bright and unbelievably blue with the sun glinting gold on the wavelets.

Hundreds of small boats dotted the water—some at anchor, some under sail, and others puffing white clouds of smoke into the crystalline air.

"The Greeks began using this port in 600 B.C.," Frank said, "and it's still going strong."

Off to one side was the Vieux Port, the Old Port, used by fishermen and yachtsmen; nearby was the newer, larger port that handled most of the commercial trade and the passenger ships. The Nazis had blown up the port installations during the war, but everything looked back to normal to me.

We drove up and down the town, every once in a while catching a glimpse of the sea. It was as if the Mediterranean were winking at us. Then at the very top of a large hill, Frank pulled up in front of a beautiful lavender stucco building. A discreet sign out front read: HÔTEL DE LAVANDE.

"Welcome to the Lavender Hotel," Frank said.

"Are we stopping for lunch?" I asked.

"Nope. We're staying here. Peter says it's the best joint in town," Frank said, shutting off the engine.

The silence was deafening. *Had I heard him correctly?*

In our present circumstances any old fleabag would have been all right with me.

"Oh, Frank," I said, looking at the manicured lawns and gently swaying palm trees. "We can't possibly afford this."

"We can't afford another tank of gas," Frank said. "So if we're going to jail, we might as well live it up first."

"But—"

"In for a penny, in for one hundred thousand francs," he said. "Besides, if there's no money at American Express, we can always sell Peter's car on the black market and disappear into the Corsican Mafia."

One thing you can say about Frank: He's an optimist, though not a realist.

A uniformed bellboy raced from the hotel, retrieved our bags, and we were committed. Or should have been.

The desk clerk treated us as valued guests and personally ushered us upstairs. The room was magnificent. So was the other room. And the other room. A three-room suite! Nothing was too good for friends of M. Peter Lord, the desk clerk said, holding out his hand for a huge tip. He was hugely disappointed. Frank told him he'd take care of him when we left.

The walls of the suite were painted Mediterranean blue, and the furniture was startling white, covered with silvery damask. Impressionist paintings decorated the walls, lending color and warmth to the rooms. Everything was so lovely, I was beginning to enjoy the lawless life.

I pulled the curtains aside, and the view almost took my breath away. Stretched out before me was the entire city of Marseilles and the sea beyond.

"Not only can't we afford these rooms," Frank said, looking over my shoulder, "we can't even afford the view."

"If we run right now, we can escape."

"Too late," Frank said. "I've already used an ashtray."

Since we didn't have enough money to dine out, we went downstairs to the dining room and charged a lunch we couldn't pay for to the rooms we couldn't afford. There was a certain un-Puritan thrill to being a deadbeat, I suppose, though when we became prisoners in the Château d'If, we probably could not expect *moules marinière,* lobster salad, and rosé for lunch—every day. I feared it would be swill and grog from then on—if we were lucky.

"Write yourself a liberal tip," Frank told our stunned waiter after our meal.

And why not? This whole preposterous trip had a certain internal logic to it—the kind of logic a madman professes after he has knocked off twenty-two victims.

After lunch we strolled about the sumptuous lobby, absorbing the atmosphere. Well, okay, we gawked. The Lavender Hotel was one of those places where you sink in up to your knees in the carpeting. That was to eliminate those distressing sounds from the guests' shoes, I suppose, so that silence could reign supreme. Everything was cleaned, polished, and shined at least three times a day. If the manager ever saw a cigarette butt in an ashtray, I was sure heads would have rolled.

The staff was friendly, helpful, and hopeful—of a big tip. And they had every right to be. The clientele was a mixed lot—American businessmen, tourists, French aristocrats from the north, a complement of smooth-looking Italians, and even a few gentlemen wearing turbans. But the one thing they had in common was money. Old money or new money, foreign money or French money—it didn't seem to matter as long as it was flowing.

I was disappointed that the guests all seemed perfectly respectable. This was Marseilles, for goodness' sake, and I expected to see Peter Lorre and Humphrey Bogart sneaking around behind the potted palms. And where the heck was Sidney Greenstreet, anyway?

Unable to find any international gangsters or foreign spies, we collected the MG and Frank drove me to the quay where the boats left for the Château d'If.

"Wish me luck," he said, speeding off to the American Express office.

I did and I meant it.

The Château d'If was on the tiny island of If about two miles from shore. It had been built in the sixteenth century to protect the port of Marseilles, but was later used as a prison, mostly for political prisoners. The Château d'If would have remained an obscure penitentiary if it hadn't been for Alexandre Dumas.

Modern youngsters are raised on Dick Tracy and Superman, but back in the dark ages, before such characters existed, I was brought up on the tales of Monte Cristo. I had read or reread the Dumas book at various ages such as seven, nine, eleven, and fifteen. On many a rainy day my brother and I had acted out the escape of Edmund Dantes by tunneling out of one open window in our house and into another room, which we labeled the cell of Abbé Faria. My mother put a stop to the game when my brother threatened to wrap me in a shroud and throw me out of a second-floor window. Perhaps he mistook the rhododendrons for the Mediterranean.

I was musing about the past when I was suddenly besieged by the pilots of the boats tied up at the quay. They had me pegged as tourist material, and I was waved at, yelled at, and jostled by them, each entreating me to select his boat. I chose the least piratical-looking captain, who operated a launch called the *Iles D'Or II*, the *Golden Islands II*, which was gaily decorated with colored pennants.

The ten-minute ride to the island prison cost sixty cents, leaving me with a whopping fifty cents left in my purse. But who cared when I was about to fulfill a girlhood fantasy?

Cristo, I am here, I thought, straining to hear the travelogue given by our captain over the roar of the motor.

The boat docked at the rockiest, most forbidding-looking island possible. As I stared down into the water, I could well imagine Monte Cristo's desperate hope that he would be thrown clear of the rocks while he was tied in the Abbé's shroud.

The steep steps led straight up the side from the water and finally into the prison courtyard, hundreds of feet above the sea. Nothing in my experience had prepared me for the sight of the glimmering sea and Marseilles in the background. The few tourists who had arrived with me were swallowed up by the three-acre island, and I felt as if I were exploring the place by myself.

The huge, round château, built so long ago, was in remarkable repair, and the stone seemed destined to survive many more centuries. I entered the prison with the foolish feeling that I would soon be disappointed and that reality would be death to my romantic ideas. But as I walked around the tiers of cells, each labeled with its most famous occupant's name, I felt the thrill of rediscovering my childhood dreams.

There was the cell of the Man in the Iron Mask, the cells of counts and marquises of lesser fame, and finally the one I had come to see—the cell of the Count of Monte Cristo. How John would have loved this place!

The small stone cubicle was just as Dumas described it, and there was the remarkable hole, just large enough for a lithe man's body to slide through, dug into the two-foot walls. Hoping to reach freedom, Monte Cristo had tunneled instead into the cell of the old Abbé.

The Abbé's room was the smallest and cruelest in the prison, for an average-size man could not stand erect there. As I stood in the dank cell, lighted by a lantern, the whole story came floating back to me. The guide, showing true Gallic sensitivity, left me alone to gaze in wonder and saved his chatter until I returned to the main yard. There he showed me the carvings in the stone done by prisoners to while away the monotonous hours.

I climbed to the top of the stairs, some worn so badly that the center was almost gone, and came out of the dark into the brilliant sunshine. If the prisoners were ever allowed to walk up here, how they must have yearned for their freedom, guarded so well by the sea and rocks below.

As I returned to the courtyard, I heard the insistent honk of *Iles D'Or II* summoning everyone back to the launch and reminding me that there were other wonders yet to see in Marseilles—such was the wonder of a few more francs in my pocketbook.

I squandered the last of my money on a taxi back to the hotel, leaving a crowd of outraged seamen and tour guides damning me for not tipping them.

At the hotel, I rushed up the steps hoping to find Frank, but he hadn't yet returned. I felt a growing lump of fear in my stomach. I tried to read, but I found myself reading the same paragraph over and over, not comprehending a thing; so I put the book away and paced our three beautiful rooms like a fraudulent princess in her castle. *Where was Frank? What had happened?*

Perhaps I should find the local department store, I thought, and steal a pair of black silk stockings to begin planning my gun moll outfit. But that was just a passing thought.

Outside, it grew darker and darker. The lights came on, giving the city a cheery warmth that I couldn't claim for myself. *Why had I ever listened to my madcap husband?* I didn't want to share the Abbé's quarters—especially not after sampling the delights of the Lavender Hotel. I wondered what I could do to help us out of this dire situation. The only thing I could think of was to beg for money. Humiliation was better than incarceration in my book.

So I sat down to compose a telegram to Frank's parents and to my loco mother in the Virgin Islands, asking them for a loan. Those were the hardest twenty-four words I had ever penned. Looking back, I suppose I should have said simply: *Children dying. Need operations immediately. Send as much money as you have. Love, Mary and Frank.*

That probably would have worked, but I was too upset to be devious or to write them the obvious truth: *Frank has gone nuts. French asylums very expensive. Send money at once.*

I was just putting the finishing touches on the telegrams when my wayward husband returned. I could tell instantly that we were in trouble. His face was a thundercloud.

"No luck," I sighed, prepared for the worst.

"You'd better sit," he said.

I sat on the bed, looking up apprehensively.

"I didn't bring the check," he said mournfully.

I started to say something, but he held up his hand to silence me.

"I didn't bring the check," he repeated, "because I brought the cash."

From his suit coat pocket he produced two handfuls of banknotes. I had heard of people who carried wads of cash big enough to choke a horse, but those rolls in Frank's hands could have taken down an elephant.

"I always told you I'd shower you with hundreds," Frank said, tossing the bills in the air. "In this case, francs not dollars, but it's the thought that counts."

I sat there laughing as the bills rained down on me. We were back in the chips, and life was good again.

*   *   *

We spent the next day playing affluent tourists, a delightful change from being destitute vagrants. As we strolled about the city, I was fascinated by its antiquity. Marseilles was already six hundred years old when the Romans conquered it two thousand years ago. Talk about old! In America, anything that happened before the war was regarded as ancient history.

Frank and I wandered through the old town—*Le Panier*—marveling at the little houses all jammed together, leaning on each other like the old folks they were. I was amazed that each *quartier*—Marseilles boasted a hundred or so—had a distinctive flavor to it. Some sections were a thousand years old, some only three hundred, but each one had a church, a square, and a group of old men playing *boules,* a bowlinglike game. These *boules* players gave the big city of Marseilles a very small-town feel.

At noon, overloaded buses, cars, trucks, bicycles, and motorcycles rushed past in a frenzy to get out of town. In true French fashion everyone drove with his horn going full blast. The workers were going home for their two-hour lunch, and no one could stop them—certainly not mere pedestrians. We tried for ten minutes to get across the main street and finally gave up, relaxed, and went with the tide of people leaving the city.

The sidewalk cafés, lined side by side along the waterfront, were accustomed to stationing their prettiest waitresses outside with menus to lure the tourists in. We picked one quickly to avoid being battered by waving menus and assaulted by explosive comments about the cuisine.

Just as the mad rush to return to work began at two o'clock, we headed toward Notre Dame de La Garde, the church whose golden virgin, the patron saint of fishermen, could be seen from any point in Marseilles.

We took the funicular, a hair-raising experience, to get up the hill to the church. The car rose almost straight up into the sky. For thirty cents we got two round-trip tickets. (Who would choose to walk either up or down, I didn't know. There were almost three hundred steps to the top, and even in my gun moll stockings, I didn't think I could have made the climb.)

The church had been built in the nineteenth century in the Romanesque-Byzantine style, and only its location on the hilltop made it spectacular. But if the church was a letdown, the view was well worth the trip. Looking down at the city at one's feet, with the Mediterranean lapping at its shores, brought out my well-concealed poetic yearnings.

I thought of the song that is a national hymn for the French, "The Marseillaise." In 1792 the author of the song sent the words and music from Strasbourg for the soldiers who were preparing to leave for Paris to fight in the Revolution. The soldiers learned the song, and as they went from city to city they sang it. In Paris, the anthem electrified the population when they listened to the southern voices sing it, and the Parisians promptly named the song after the soldiers' city of Marseilles.

I knew from personal experience just how important and sacred *La Marseillaise* was to the French people. Frank had taken me to a sing-along at the Bar d'Oc one evening, and although no one had ever mistaken me for a diva, I loved to sing. Everyone got a chance to choose a song; then the rest would join in. When it came to my turn, I chose the only French song I knew, *La Marseillaise*. I had barely started singing when I noticed a shocked silence and stunned faces surrounding me. Was I that bad? I wondered.

I sang a few more bars; then Frank stopped me and apologized for my ignorance. The French, it seemed, sang their anthem only at official ceremonies or in times of crisis, not at any old ballgame or filling station opening—the fate of "The Star-Spangled Banner." I admired the French policy because a national anthem should be special or it loses its meaning. People simply mouth the words by rote, forgetting their significance.

Footsore and weary, we returned to the hotel for our last night in our magnificent suite. I was perfectly willing to grab a quick bite and hit the hay at an unreasonably early hour. Frank, however, had other plans.

"You know we have to do it," he said.

"What?"

"You know," he said. "What did we eat in New Orleans?"

"Crawfish," I said.

"And Coney Island?"

"Hot dogs."

"Well, in Marseilles, we—"

"Oh, no," I said.

"Bouillabaisse," he said. "We can't leave Marseilles without trying the bouillabaisse."

Yes, we could, in my opinion. I had seen the way they made that fish stew in Montpellier, and I wanted no part of it. In my heart I knew there were octopuses in there, even if I couldn't see them.

"Peter gave me the name of the most authentic place in town, and we're going," Frank said, putting on a tie. "It's de rigueur."

"It's de-sgusting," I said. "Can't we just have a nice meal at the hotel?"

"No. I realize eating bouillabaisse is not pleasant, but we must. It's our duty to go back to America and tell everyone how much we enjoyed it. Then they'll come here and try it, too. The French economy depends on us."

Well, if the economy of France hung on our dinner plans, I supposed I could do my bit, however reluctantly.

We drove through the narrow, twisting streets of the Vieux Port, looking for an obscure street in an obscure part of town. Even the desk clerk at the hotel had never heard of Restaurant Lola. Perhaps Peter made the whole thing up, I hoped.

More than an hour later, I was getting pretty fed up with this enterprise and told my husband to turn around and drive back to the hotel.

"I'll stop and ask for directions," he said.

Frank ask for directions? I knew from experience that he would rather be boiled in oil.

"You're really serious about finding this place, aren't you?" I said, amazed.

"It's a matter of principle now," he growled, pulling over to the side of the street and asking a rough-looking sailor for the rue St.-Charles.

"Lola?" the sailor said. Then he rattled off a complicated list of instructions.

"We can't be too far away," Frank said. "I'll park the car over there and we'll hoof it."

That was easy for him to say—he wasn't wearing heels. The uneven cobblestone streets were death on heels, but from the grim look on Frank's face, I decided it was better to go along than to attempt to inject some sanity into his obsession.

So, tottering up and down hills, my fingers dug into Frank's arm, we stumbled around the dark, dangerous-looking neighborhood, filled with honky-tonk bars and populated by leering prostitutes and drunken sailors.

We skirted two men engaged in a bloody fistfight and finally found the right street. And there was Lola's. Boy, there it was, all right: a dingy, broken-down building that leaned precariously to the left. Through a dirty window I could see a few people sitting around tables; others looked as if they were asleep—or passed out.

Before we could work up the courage to go inside, the door to the restaurant opened and a man in a striped jersey came flying out and landed at our feet. Two waiters dusted off their hands with contempt, then slammed the door in our faces.

"*Bonjour,*" said the man on the ground. Lying flat on his back, he tipped his cap.

"*Bonjour,*" Frank said, stepping over the man's body. I followed suit. We pushed open the creaking wooden door and walked into Lola's.

The smell hit us immediately: a combination of rotting fish, cheap booze, French cigarettes, and unwashed bodies. It wouldn't have surprised me if Julius had been Caesar the last time anyone had swept up in Lola's, let alone washed anything.

Tables were scattered around the room, seemingly at random, and a long wooden bar dominated one wall. Behind the bar hung a painting of a naked woman—Lola perhaps? But it was difficult to make out any details because hundreds of years' worth of smoke and dirt had obscured the naughty parts and made her into a rather androgynous figure.

"So," I said. "This is authentic?"

"Authentically dirty," Frank said, frowning.

I was for running away in horror, but the proprietor had rushed over to capture us. No sense letting tourists escape.

We sat in a booth that was upholstered in green leather, or at least it had originally been green. Now it was greasy and brownish. I could imagine that my dress now looked as if I had sat in a pile of butter. Lola's made my skin crawl, or perhaps there was another reason for that itch—was that a bug I saw?

"Frank—"

"Don't start," he said. "Let's have some wine."

He ordered a bottle of Cassis Blanc-de-Blanc, a local white wine produced only a few miles from Marseilles. The waiter brought it over along with two of the dirtiest glasses I had ever seen outside of my own kitchen.

"Can we drink out of the bottle?" I asked, but Frank was already polishing the glasses with his handkerchief because the napkins were none too clean. I looked around the dark, smoky restaurant, noting that the characters at the tables made our Occitan friends Fricor and Gobert look like Fred Astaire and Cary Grant by comparison. I was sure these seedy men were authentic criminals and would probably kill us sometime between the salad course and dessert—if we lasted that long.

Frank held the glasses up to the dim light and said, "Do you want the one with the lipstick or the one with the unidentified clump?"

"Lipstick, please," I said. *No clumps for me, thank you.*

"Frank," I said. "There's no tablecloth."

"After seeing the napkins and the wineglasses, are you sure you want a tablecloth?" he said.

Upon reflection, I decided that he was right. The fewer things they had to wash around here, the better.

The waiter who came to take our order looked as if he had just ended a shift in the coal mines and hadn't had the time to take a shower. However, his overall appearance seemed to blend in nicely with the rest of the restaurant. Protective coloration, no doubt.

As I sat uncomfortably in the grimy booth, I heard a noise, a tapping noise, coming from underneath the table.

"What's that?" I asked Frank.

"What's what?"

"That noise under the table," I said.

"Oh, that's me," he said. "I'm tap-dancing to the tune of 'Tea for Two.'"

"Why on earth—"

"To keep the rats from biting my ankles," he said, laughing.

I laughed, too, but I checked under the table just to make sure he was kidding.

Frank ordered *bouillabaisse du ravi* instead of *du pêcheur* on the theory that the more expensive the dish, the less likely it was to kill us. A sound theory, I guess, but like all theories not very useful until proven by scientific experimentation.

When the experiment arrived, the theory went out the window.

The waiter staggered over to our table bearing a giant black washtub filled with fish parts: countless different kinds of fish parts.

"Now I know why this place is so dirty," I said. "They use the washtubs for bouillabaisse, not washing."

"This looks . . . interesting," Frank said. "Of course, a squashed squirrel by the side of the road looks interesting, too."

I took the tin ladle and poked among the fish heads and tails, trying to catalogue the contents of this stew. I knew that the French were famous for *fruits de mer*—fruits of the sea—and that at home we have Chicken of the Sea, but this mess of pottage in front of us was definitely refuse of the sea. At this point those innocuous little octopuses at the Bar d'Oc would have been welcomed fare.

"I wouldn't feed this to my cat," I said.

"You don't have a cat," Frank said. "Dish it up."

Reluctantly, I ladled us each a portion of greasy liquid and a piece of red fish, then scrubbed my spoon on my skirt and dug in. Tentatively.

"Not bad," Frank said, tasting his.

And it wasn't. All this fuss over fish stew. I don't know if it was the second bottle of Cassis or not, but I ate another helping of bouillabaisse, this time tasting the exotic North African spices that gave the stew its character.

We didn't make a dent in the enormous washtub of fish, and I'm sure the waiter took it back to the kitchen, added some water, and sold it again. But we had done our duty to the French economy, and I would like to recommend to all Americans that you travel to Marseilles for the bouillabaisse. But order it at your hotel and don't get too authentic.

Frank paid the check and left his usual outrageous tip; we were almost out the door when the waiter stopped us. He asked if we wanted a taxi. Frank said, no, we were parked only a few blocks away.

The waiter turned ashen.

"We'll never get back to the car alive," Frank translated for me. "In fact, he says that it's a miracle, bless the Golden Virgin, that we got here at all."

"Nice places you take me to," I said.

"Armand! Marcel!" the waiter shouted, and two dark, menacing men emerged from the kitchen, wiping their bloodstained hands on their bloodstained aprons. Fish blood, I hoped.

"They will escort you to your car," the waiter said. Then he whispered confidentially to Frank, "It will be all right. They have knives and know how to use them."

Frank tipped the waiter again in gratitude.

We set out for the MG flanked by armed guards. I stumbled along in my heels, thinking that if they slit our throats at least I could say I had seen Marseilles. And that I had gotten a dose of mystery, danger, and intrigue I would never forget.

That I'm alive to tell the tale gives away the ending: We made it back alive. Frank tipped each of the gunsels, who bowed formally and sauntered off into the night.

"Vamoose!" I said.

And we did—with authentic gusto.

*   *   *

We spent a quiet morning enjoying breakfast in bed, followed by a strenuous hour of looking out the window at the city. Checkout time was at noon, so we left at 11:59, making sure we got our money's worth.

Frank drove the MG with his usual panache, which is to say much too fast. For him, I think, the highlight of the trip was driving a sports car. In my opinion those noisy little cars were uncomfortable, unreliable, and unaffordable. They were also cold in the winter, stifling in the summer, and difficult to drive. I couldn't imagine chauffeuring the children to school in an MG, let alone screeching to a halt in front of Gristede's to pick up my order.

I was thinking that a car should be cheap, comfortable, and reliable when I heard a noise. That peculiar noise you hear just before your car suddenly quits on you.

"Oh, no," Frank and I said at once. And sure enough, the loud roar of the engine ceased and all we could hear was the whisper of the wind as the MG rolled quietly to the side of the road.

Frank sat back in the tan leather seat and closed his eyes.

"Aren't you going to check under the hood?" I asked.

"I don't know a damned thing about engines, so looking at one would seem superfluous—don't you think?"

"Oh, I see," I said.

"Peter warned me that the only way to really enjoy an MG is to have a tow truck filled with skilled mechanics follow you everywhere you go," Frank grumbled.

He studied the directions Elise had given him and decided that we were not far from our destination.

"I suppose we'd better walk," Frank said.

Because I was well rested, and wearing my flats, I was agreeable to a stroll in the French countryside. The air was crisp and cold; the earth was brown and lifeless, as if it were hibernating, waiting for spring. But it was the silence that overwhelmed me. I had experienced that utter silence only once before—out on the arid, windblown Texas Panhandle. There was no one about on this lazy Sunday afternoon, but somehow I felt like an intruder.

"This is eerie," Frank said.

"Think about Stephen going on a four-hour crying jag," I said. "And count your blessings."

We walked about a mile, then turned down a dirt road.

"It's hard to believe we're only a few miles from the Oeuf," I said, enjoying myself thoroughly.

"Twenty years from now all this will be suburbs. That's what's happening at home," Frank said. "If Elise and Henri can hold on long enough, their land will be worth a fortune."

But the first sight of the farm elicited thoughts of hard, rural poverty, not fortune.

"Holy mackerel," Frank said. "Tobacco Road."

The weathered, unpainted farmhouse seemed to have gone back to nature, for it was more a part of the surrounding trees than a freestanding building. A fence had once stood around the muddy yard, but it had fallen down years ago and lay tangled and rotting on the ground. Chickens and ducks squawked up and down in front of the house, but I suspected that any self-respecting worm had long since fled this neighborhood.

I said, "This place reminds me of Ma and Pa Kettle's house in the Betty MacDonald book."

Frank laughed and began plunking out "Turkey in the Straw" on an imaginary banjo.

"Let's give Elise a raise," I said, suddenly understanding why she always retrieved almost everything I threw in the garbage. For example, I routinely tossed out the first few layers of leaves on a head of lettuce (it had cost about two cents) and watched in disbelief as Elise carefully wrapped up the discarded leaves to take home—as animal feed, I hoped.

I was pondering the gulf that separated semi-poor from poor when I heard a scream. It was a familiar scream. In fact, it was John's scream.

I looked to my left and saw John come tearing around the side of the house, running for all he was worth. Behind him, and gaining quickly, was a gigantic pig. This was not one of your cute little pink pigs that Walt Disney is so fond of. No, this was an enormous gray creature that could have licked a bear in a fair fight or sent a bull moose fleeing.

We watched helplessly as John dodged to the right and the pig followed, gaining more ground.

"Run!" I yelled uselessly, my heart in my mouth.

Then I caught sight of Henri, pitchfork in hand, jogging behind the pig, shouting, "Solange!"

The lumbering porker slowed its pace for a moment, allowing John to duck into a rickety shed and slam the flimsy door.

Frank and I raced across the muddy field to rescue John.

"It's safe now," Frank said through the slats of the wooden door.

"No, it's not," John said. "Solange will eat me. I'm never coming out."

Frank looked at me helplessly.

"John, this is your mother," I said in my best authoritarian voice. "Come out of that shed at once."

"It's not a shed," he said. "It's *le cabane à lapins.*"

"The rabbits have their own cabana?" I wondered aloud.

"Rabbit hutch," Frank translated.

"Come on out, or your father will break down the door," I said.

"I will?" Frank asked.

We had reached a Mexican, or rather a French, standoff that was broken only by Elise's arrival.

"*Jeannot, viens,*" she said softly. "Come."

The door opened slowly and John peeked out. Not seeing Solange, he ventured all the way out of the rabbit hutch.

He stood in the watery sunshine—covered with blood!

My hand went to my mouth, but my feet remained rooted in the ground.

"Are you hurt?" I finally managed to speak.

He looked down at himself and said, "No. That's rabbit blood. We're eating them for dinner."

I looked inside the dark *cabane* and saw two white rabbits dangling by their unlucky rabbit feet, bleeding from their partially decapitated heads.

After such a tumultuous welcome, we pulled ourselves together long enough to go through the ritual handshaking and bowing expected everywhere in France. In addition to Henri and Elise, we greeted their son, Raoul, and his fiancée, Marguerite. We also formally met Solange, who was now ensconced in her sty with a dozen piglets. Apparently, John had been playing with one of the little pigs when Solange had returned from foraging and had taken a dim view of such meddling. Like any good mother, she had chased the intruder away. Inside the house, Stephen nodded to us casually, as if Frank and I were minor acquaintances, and went back to helping Elise make dinner.

"You know," Frank said, "I don't think Stephen missed us very much."

"I get that feeling, too," I said.

Even John had an "Oh, there you are. Were you away?" attitude to our return. If we had been murdered in Marseilles, I doubted either child would have noticed, so fascinating was farm life, apparently. Not one to dwell on his ungrateful children, Frank soon galvanized the menfolk with the news about the MG. He, Henri, Raoul, and John, dragging boxes of tools, tramped out of the barn and went in search of a car to fix. It has been my experience that when men have tools in their hands, women should leave the vicinity immediately. So I retreated into the kitchen to help Elise (though I knew that I would be about as much help as Stephen).

I watched with shuddering awe as she and Marguerite skinned the rabbits, cut them up, and put the pieces in a battered pot. They added vegetables, potatoes, and even some of the blood that had been drained from the rabbits.

Elise and Marguerite worked smoothly, as if they had been a team all their lives. They didn't say much, but they seemed to know what was needed next and then accomplished the task without fuss or bother. Had I joined them, I believe I would have broken the rhythm. I could picture the two of them thirty years from now, Elise wizened and thin, Marguerite chubby and jolly, making dinner just the way they were doing it now.

The kitchen they worked in wasn't much larger than the galley on a small sailboat. That was typical of French kitchens—small space, wonderful meals. I didn't know how they did it. In America we have opulent, all-electric kitchens that seem to take up an acre of space, yet what comes out of them is often dull and flavorless. All Elise had to work with was a wood-burning stove and a cold-water pump over the sink, but she could cook the pants off any American chef I had ever encountered.

The rest of the house was spare and threadbare, but clean, furnished with odds and ends that must have been in the family for generations. An antiques dealer might have made a killing here, but they were not yet descending upon the impoverished countryside, scouring it for cheap treasures that they could resell in Paris or London or New York at obscenely inflated prices.

On the first floor was the living room, which doubled as a dining room. A small fireplace blazed away brightly, trying its best to cheer up a gloomy space. Upstairs were three tiny bedrooms, one of which the boys were sharing. In all, the house was pretty basic, even by French standards, but people had been living in it—successfully—for hundreds of years.

Elise let me make the salad, a safe bet, and I made sure I selected the outer leaves for Solange. Stephen was happily battering a tomato with a dinner knife, so I lost myself in the domestic routine until I heard the chickens cackling and the ducks squawking in alarm.

I looked out the window, and the little red MG came zooming up the dirt road with Raoul at the wheel, his father in the passenger seat, and Frank and John perched precariously behind them. Raoul had the same maniacal glint in his eye that afflicted Frank every time he drove the MG.

They all piled out of the car like clowns in a circus and spent a good ten minutes slapping each other on the back for fixing a cracked distribulator or something. Henri broke out his private supply of plum brandy, and the party began in earnest.

"Between my husband and my son, there is only half a mechanic," Elise sniffed. But she didn't say anything to the men, who were in the throes of self-congratulations.

"I held the flashlight!" John said exuberantly, wanting to be part of the historic event.

Raoul, who was about twenty, re-created his drive several times, steering the air, making roaring sounds, gear-change sounds, and braking sounds.

"J'ai conduit l'em jay!" he repeated over and over. "I drove the MG!"

It's not love and marriage that go together like a horse and carriage, I thought. *It's men and sports cars.*

We sat down to dinner at eight. That is, Frank and I, the children, Henri and Raoul, sat down. Elise and Marguerite served, dishing up the rabbit stew and four other courses, including my unspectacular salad.

After dinner we wanted to take the boys home in the car, but Elise said she couldn't bear to part with them. They were sleepy and wanted to go to bed, she said. I didn't believe that for one minute, but we arranged to haul all their equipment back with us that night and come get them in the morning.

Before we left, I asked to use the facilities and was shown an actual outhouse out back—a two-holer that made me laugh. I was certainly glad I had chased Henri down the street, waving Stephen's toilet seat. No need for that here. It had never occurred to me that Elise would lack indoor plumbing. But then, I hadn't expected a wood-burning stove or a wheelbarrow either.

At eleven o'clock, after the usual round of handshakes, bows, and kisses, we roared off for home. I had the useless toilet seat between my feet, a box of emergency diapers digging into my ribs, and a storybook scraping my leg. But as we zoomed through the darkness, I couldn't help but reflect that in three short days we had seen the extremes in France, from Elise's dilapidated farm and Lola's ridiculously dirty restaurant to the lavish Lavender Hotel, an oasis of wealth and privilege that we would never have dared enter if we hadn't been dead broke. Like the Count of Monte Cristo we had seen both worlds, but unlike the count, we had found nothing but nice people looking out for our welfare.

That left me feeling very rich, indeed.

Chapter 15

AMERICANS GO HOME! read the sign behind John and Stephen. Many Americans living in France were resented because of their capitalist wealth—a fault that never applied to the Littells.

The Gibson Girls

February 1951

I stared at the raindrops running down the windowpane. It was another dark, dank, dismal day in Montpellier.

"It's been so long since I've seen the sun, I've forgotten what it looks like," I said absently.

John, who had been painting a picture at the kitchen table, looked up at me as if I had suddenly gone mad. "You remember, Mama. Do you want me to paint you a picture?"

"That would be nice," I said. "What we need around here is a little color."

In Montpellier, February was the cruelest month. Spring was so near you could almost taste it, but the skies retained their winter gray; and even if it wasn't cold by St. Louis standards, it certainly seemed that way.

I looked over at John's rendition of the sun—big, yellow, spiky.

"Now I remember!" I said, taping the picture to the window. I hoped that by the process of sympathetic magic, the real sun might soon appear.

"Do you like it?" John asked.

"It's beautiful," I said. "I know what we'll do," I went on, suddenly inspired. "Let's go to the art museum and look at some wonderful pictures."

We dressed in our rain gear, said good-bye to Elise and Stephen, and marched out into the cold and wet, on our way to the Musée Fabre.

Our progress was slow because John insisted on jumping into every puddle on the way, but we eventually arrived at our destination—soaking wet.

The museum was founded and named for François Xavier Fabre, who had been a student of the world-famous artist J. L. David. Old FX decided that he too wanted world fame and moved out of France to the capital of the art world then, Italy. He worked hard during the late eighteenth and early nineteenth centuries, producing a large body of work. The problem was he wasn't much of a painter.

But if Fabre was deficient as an artist, he had an eye for good art and an equally critical eye for the ladies. One lady in particular caught his fancy—the Countess of Albany, the rich, beautiful widow of Bonnie Prince Charlie. They were, how you say, soul mates; and when she died, she left M. Fabre a pile of money and a stack of paintings.

Fabre brought the loot to Montpellier and established what many considered to be the finest provincial art museum in France. If you can abide Fabre's own rather ordinary pictures, you also get to see the works of Veronese, Bernini, Caravaggio, Delacroix, Courbet, Ingres, David, Corot, Gericault, and a host of others.

Although the museum is housed in a former Jesuit college, there was nothing Jesuitical about it. In fact, the Musée Fabre was the least intimidating of art museums. At the Metropolitan Museum of Art in New York, I always felt I should be wearing a ball gown and kid gloves or else the guards would chuck me out in the street. At the Fabre the guard was usually asleep or eating lunch.

John and I squeaked across the rolling wooden floors in our rubber boots, looking at the pictures as we went. There were only a few visitors on that day, which was why a woman's loud voice startled me.

"No, dear. It's not Courbet. It's Corot," the woman said in English.

"But the sign says Courbet," another woman said.

"The sign is wrong and I am right," the first woman said. "It's mismarked."

John and I attempted to skirt the loud voices and escape into another room.

"Bushwa!"

I turned around at the sound of the woman's loud voice, now right behind us.

The speaker was an enormously tall, thin woman I took to be in her sixties. She wore a full-length mink coat and bulky, sensible shoes. Her hat was a confection of lace that featured small birds peeking out from behind a bright red ribbon. She had the chiseled features and high cheekbones of a former beauty. Her two companions, wearing similar mink coats, floated in her wake. If they had stood side by side, they would have formed a stair step.

"You there, child," the tall woman said. "Come here."

John, recognizing the voice of authority, dutifully walked over to the intimidating trio.

"Look at these two paintings and tell me which is the best," she said to John, who had to crane his neck to see her. She was at least six feet tall.

John looked at the two rather second-rate Renoirs and chose the one with the ballet dancer.

"Precisely!" the tall woman roared. "Even a child knows the difference, and in my opinion your opinion, Edna, is total bushwa."

"You're wrong, Cornelia," Edna said. "Look at the brushwork."

"Bushwa to your brushwork," Cornelia said. "Why is it that we have to go to Paris to see a decent painting?"

John, in the meantime, had scooted back over to me and was looking at the ladies with openmouthed awe. He didn't know what to make of them and neither did I.

They stalked down a row of paintings, muttering comments to each other until they came back to me.

"This is not exactly the Louvre," Cornelia said. Then she dismissed the nice Pissarro I was looking at, calling it jejune.

"You there," she bellowed at me. "Is that your child?"

I said he was.

"Smart fellow. Knows his paintings. You must be smart, too.

Come to tea with us on Thursday," Cornelia said. "We'll be discussing American Romantic authors."

Taken aback at such an abrupt invitation, I nodded politely, but
she knew immediately I was dissembling.

"I'm quite serious, my dear," Cornelia said. "We get so lonesome here in Montpellier for new opinions, new faces. American
faces. You must come."

She then introduced herself as Cornelia Edgerton and her
companions as Edna Van Dine and Viola Greenaway. Cornelia, it
seemed, lived in Montpellier year-round, and Edna and Viola came
to visit her periodically. She gave me her card, which listed her address as the Hôtel du Soleil, the Sun Hotel. Before I knew it, I had
accepted her invitation without quite knowing what had hit me.
You had to have an iron will to resist Cornelia.

"Tea and authors? You?" Frank said when I told him the news.
"When was the last time you read Hawthorne or Poe or Washington Irving?"

"I've read them all," I said.

"Yeah, when you were twelve."

"Well, it has been some years," I admitted, "but it might be
fun."

"Bushwa," John piped in.

Despite the opinions of my husband and son, I was really looking forward to some adult conversation and an elegant tea at an elegant hotel. I made inquiries about the Hôtel du Soleil, but nobody
had ever heard of it. That reinforced my notion that the three
ladies, clad in their magnificent mink coats, must live in a hotel so
exclusive that all my peasant friends were ignorant of its existence.

Not that I had many friends left, peasant or otherwise. In fact,
half the population of Montpellier was out to lynch me. You see, a
week ago I had been shopping at the general store, buying up what
was left of the rusted canned goods, when Mme. Perrin's niece, Sophie, cornered me. She asked me several questions about America
and how you got there and whether you needed a visa or not.

Things like that. I told her what I knew, but I suggested that she check with the local passport authority to get the real scoop. I thought she was probably too young to get her own passport without her aunt's signature, but this was France, after all, and who knew what the local regulations were?

I didn't think about that conversation until a few days later when I was confronted by an outraged Mme. Perrin. Sophie and René had taken off together and were heading to Marseilles to be married. Then they were hopping a tramp steamer and going to the United States. And now everything was my fault.

I tried to defend myself as best I could, saying that I didn't know about the elopement or approve of it in any way, but Mme. Perrin didn't believe me. Neither did the butcher, who glowered at me with more than the usual quota of hatred in his eyes, or the lady at Le Bon Lait, who now gave me milk from the bottom of the can. I got suspicious looks from the wine store lady, and even my friend Pascal, the owner of the Bar d'Oc, was unusually cool toward me. I was the talk of the town, the meddling foreigner who had precipitated a misadventure of monstrous proportions.

For days I scrupulously avoided my old haunts while mounting a counterattack through Elise. I told her my side of the story, and bless her, she believed me.

"Sophie was always flighty, even as a child," Elise said. "And René—impossible!"

Like the coward that I am, I let Elise fight my battle while I hid out in the new shopping district and the Musée Fabre. Being on the lam in Montpellier was no fun. I missed my former friends and couldn't stand the thought that they blamed me for Sophie's behavior.

So you can see why I was eager for Cornelia's bright-sounding tea party at the Hôtel du Soleil.

The day of the tea I didn't each lunch, thinking that there would be cakes and sandwiches galore. Getting there, however, was a problem, because it was so far away. I had the address, and with my map of Montpellier I plotted out the best bus route. Waving a cheery, "*Au revoir,*" I plunged into another dark, rainy afternoon. It took more than thirty minutes to get to my stop, then another ten minutes to find my way to the correct street.

I was in a dreary residential neighborhood with long rows of stone houses moldering in the rain. If there was a hotel here—sun or otherwise—I couldn't find it. Dogs barked wildly and cats hissed ferociously at me as I trudged up and down the empty street looking for the address. I stopped and checked Cornelia's card and compared the number to the one posted on a splintery wooden gate: Number 22. That was correct, but what lay behind the gate I couldn't tell. The gate was eight feet high.

Screwing up my limited courage, I rang a rusty bell that was attached to the gate. The sound set the dogs to barking again, and I was ready to call the whole thing off when a face appeared through a grille in the gate.

"Mme. Littell?" a man hissed from behind the grille.

"*Oui,*" I said in my best French, amazed that a hotel employee would know my name. I didn't think I was *that* infamous despite *l'affaire* Sophie.

The man opened up a monk's door to let me in. I stepped over the threshold and into the nineteenth century. The large courtyard, paved with light-colored stones, led to an ornate porte cochere where horse-drawn carriages must once have sought shelter. The hotel itself was an enormous pile of sandstone with mansard roofs and slate shingles. Dormers and cupolas dotted the facade, giving the building a comfortable, quirky look. I could imagine myself holed up on the third floor quietly reading a book or drinking a glass of sherry while looking out at the rain.

"*Magnifique,*" I said.

"Yes, madam," the man said.

"You're English," I said.

"Yes, madam."

Odd that a French hotel would hire an English doorman, I thought. Perhaps they had a lot of English tourists. Rich English tourists, by the look of the place.

I was ushered into a three-story foyer laid with black-and-white marble tiles; overhead was an enormous gilt-and-crystal chandelier. I didn't see a registration desk, just Louis XV tables and chairs. And a grand curving staircase, carpeted in burgundy.

I was led through a ten-foot-high door half covered with black leather and entered a room that was the size of an airplane hangar. The room was punctuated with oases of furniture—a grouping here, a piano and chairs there. At the far end of the room a fire was blazing merrily, but for the life of me I couldn't see anyone. I felt as if I were trapped in a furniture warehouse.

"There you are, my dear," Cornelia yelled from a chair near the fireplace.

No wonder she spoke so loudly. In this vast space a normal tone of voice would be swallowed up by the two-story ceilings and the massive Aubusson carpet that muffled every sound.

I chose a path through the furniture obstacle course and wended my way toward Cornelia's voice like a ship following a foghorn.

The three ladies sat in a circle around an inlaid table, looking at me with such intensity that I hoped all my buttons were buttoned and all my zippers were zipped.

"Welcome to my house," Cornelia boomed.

She owned the hotel?

"What a wonderful place," I said.

"A bit down at the heels," Cornelia sniffed. "Grandfather built it in the 1860s, you know. And once upon a time the Hôtel du Soleil was one of the most famous *hôtels particulier* in Montpellier."

So that was it: This wasn't a commercial hotel at all, but a private residence called a *hôtel particulier,* meaning a mansion. I was glad I hadn't tried to tip the doorman, who of course wasn't the doorman at all, but the butler.

"Edna, Viola, and I were at Wellesley together," Cornelia said after I had joined the group. "In ancient times."

"Mary's not a Wellesley girl," Viola declared. "She's too practical. More like a Smith girl. Am I right?"

"Well, actually—"

"Of course you are," Cornelia said.

If she wanted to pretend I went to Smith College, I could accept that. I've been called a lot worse in my time. Besides, I didn't think my degree from the University of Missouri would mean all that much in this company.

"My father was in wine," Cornelia said. "Or more particularly, in grapes."

"My father was an attorney," I volunteered. "Railroads." Well, more like trolley cars for the city of St. Louis, but I thought railroads sounded much classier.

"Abraham Lincoln was a railroad attorney," Cornelia said. "And look what happened to him."

"Shot," Viola said, nodding her head.

These ladies certainly kept up with the news, but somehow I didn't make the connection.

"Now," Cornelia said, rubbing her hands together, "let's have tea. As it's Thursday, we always start with Gibsons."

I had never heard of a Gibson, but I imagined that it was named for the famous Gibson girl of the last century. I pictured a wasp-waisted glass filled with fruit juice and topped by a little umbrella. But when the butler arrived bearing a silver tray, umbrellas were definitely not included. He had brought two bottles of English gin, a bottle of vermouth, a bucket of ice, and a bowl of little onions. No tea. No hourglass-shaped glasses. No sandwiches.

"Shall I mix, madam?" the butler said.

"Bushwa!" Cornelia said. "Whatever gave you the idea you could mix a decent Gibson, Edwards?"

"Sorry, madam," Edwards said and glided away as if he moved on tracks.

"That's the problem with English butlers: They want to be part of the family," Viola said. "But they're better than the French— don't you think?"

"Butlers will be butlers," I said airily.

I had never employed a butler in my life, and frankly they made me nervous. They were always looking at you, waiting for you to use the wrong fork or drink from the finger bowl or something. Besides, Edwards probably made more money in a month than Frank and I did in a year.

With a practiced hand Cornelia mixed the Gibsons and poured out two glasses. Then she repeated the process and poured two more lethal-looking drinks.

"Cheers!" she said, downing half her glass.

I sipped mine. It burned my tongue and tasted just as it should—a glass of gin with little onions in it. In other words, awful.

Once the ladies had established my bogus lineage to their satisfaction, they began to talk about themselves.

"We're all widows," Cornelia said, "and have been for many years."

"I'm not a widow," Viola said.

"You might as well be," Cornelia said. "For all the good Parker does you—traveling around with that floozy, embarrassing you and himself."

"She's not a floozy," Viola objected. "She's his aide."

"Is that what they call them nowadays?" Cornelia said unkindly.

"Do you have a husband?" Edna asked me.

"Of course she does," Cornelia said. "Smith girls are very domestic as well as practical."

I was glad I had gone to such a respectable college.

"I've had four husbands, all told," Cornelia continued. "Individually, they weren't worth much. But collectively, they left me enough to keep a roof over my head."

Some roof, I thought.

"Husbands are fine, in their way," Cornelia said, "as long as they don't go chasing about with floozies."

"Chasing about with aides, dear," Viola said.

I took another sip of my vile-tasting Gibson, surprised to find that it was half gone or, because I was in a pessimistic state of mind, half full. If only I could have found a potted plant nearby in which to dump the drink.

"Shake up another round," Viola said to Cornelia. "Mary's almost dry."

Viola was the shortest of the three ladies. She had ash-blond hair that had taken someone a lot of time and effort to manufacture; she was trim and fit-looking in her heavy blue linen suit—a suit that probably cost more than a ticket on the *Veendam*. Edna, the middle lady, was wearing a flowered afternoon dress with a white collar that matched her puffy white hair.

Always the most dramatic, Cornelia was dressed in a mauve caftan of some kind. She was so tall and thin, she must have had all her clothes made for her. Come to think of it, none of the ladies had ever battled the crowds at Galeries Lafayette. In my off-the-rack suit, I felt like the maid.

I took a sip of my second drink, which I now found had lost its bitterness.

"You're not from Boston, are you?" Edna asked me.

"Of course she's not," Cornelia boomed. "Otherwise we'd know her."

I told them I was from New York, but I didn't specify where. Naturally, they assumed I was from Manhattan.

"New York is too busy for me," Edna allowed. "We're all from Boston, of course, except Cornelia, who has recently become an expatriate."

"New York is dirty, Boston is dull, and Montpellier is dirty and dull. But I can't sell this house and I can't afford to keep it up—unless I live here. So live here I must," Cornelia said.

Poor dear, I thought, *forced to live in a palace.* I wondered how she would cope with nightly fires and cold baths.

"I'm parched," Edna said, urging Cornelia to whip up another round of drinks. I tried to demur, but they paid no attention to me and filled my glass again.

Viola leaned back in her chair, savoring the drink, and said, "Yesterday, we were talking about the use of dramatic irony in Hawthorne's shorter works."

"The only thing ironic about Hawthorne, dramatic or otherwise, is that he changed his name from Hathorne because his grandfather was one of the judges who convicted the witches in Salem," Cornelia said. "One should keep one's own name—don't you think?"

"What's ironic about that?" Viola asked.

"Well, if you don't know, I'd be the last person in the world to explain it to you, dear," Cornelia said. "Besides, we've done old Nathaniel to death. Let's let Mary choose the topic."

With a little prep from Frank, I was ready for that question.

"Over the holidays my husband read Dickens's *A Christmas Carol* to our son John several times, and I was struck by how Dickens actually invented Christmas as we celebrate it," I said.

"American authors, dear. We're discussing American authors," Edna interrupted. The three ladies looked at me with disdain.

"Ah," I said with an air of sagacity. "But did Dickens make up all his material, or did he have a source or prototype to work from? A precursor, so to speak."

That got 'em.

"In my readings," I continued airily, "I came upon *Bracebridge Hall* and saw immediately that this was a possible forerunner to Dickens's Christmas works. The author, of course, was Washington Irving."

"Ha!" Edna said. "I believe you are absolutely right. Irving skewered the English and made them like it."

Ta-dah! My comments were a hit. Or to be more accurate, Frank's comments were a hit. But I was delighted to have initiated a truly interesting discussion. The three ladies were walking libraries of literature. They knew everything about every book published in the nineteenth century, including the footnotes and bibliographies.

After my opening salvo, I fell back on my training as a journalist: When you haven't got a clue, ask questions. And when confronted by people with specialized knowledge, just prime the pump and stand back as they gush out the information. I've always found that a good listener is invariably considered extremely intelligent by good talkers. So as the ladies held forth on the subject of American Romantics, I sat in rapt attention, biding my time and injecting what I hoped were pertinent questions into the lively conversation.

Now, some people can't walk and chew gum at the same time, but Cornelia could expound on Fenimore Cooper and mix Gibsons simultaneously, never missing a beat. About an hour into our seminar, I realized that I was famished. The little onions at the bottom of my glass were starting to look mighty tasty. I debated reaching into my glass and plucking them out, but decided that it would be more demure to drink the drink and casually swallow the onions. Oddly, the fourth Gibson tasted much better than the first.

The onions, too, were delicious, if not filling, and the only way to get more onions was to have another drink. So I did.

"Or as Poe would have it, the destiny of mankind has already been written," Viola said, causing the ladies to nod their heads vigorously in agreement.

"Fashinating," I said.

Fashinating? I said that?

Fortunately, they weren't listening to me and plunged into an analysis of the narrative structure in *The Scarlet Letter.* While they talked, I ate a few more onions, hoping the butler would bring out a towering tray of finger sandwiches. Soon. I didn't know how many more onions I could eat.

"Mary?" Edna said.

"Oh, I beg your pardon," I said. "I was thinking about Poe," I lied. *A Po' Boy sandwich, New Orleans style perhaps,* I thought.

"I said, would you mind opening the potato chips?" Edna said.

Food!

"Of course," I said, draining my smooth and delicious Gibson, and getting up.

Suddenly, the entire room began spinning. I had to hold on to the edge of my chair to keep from toppling over. I closed my eyes, took a deep breath, and willed the world to stop revolving. When I opened my eyes, I had a difficult time focusing on the bag of Wise potato chips that had mysteriously appeared. Carefully, I took a few steps toward the sideboard, hoping to grab on to it before I keeled over.

With one hand on the beautiful mahogany sideboard and the bag of chips in the other, I pondered how to open it. Teeth. That was the answer, I decided, bringing the bag to my mouth. No, I changed my mind—that wasn't ladylike. So I released my death grip, grasped the bag with both hands, and pulled with all my might.

The bag split in half and a hundred potato chips flew into the air. Then they rained down gently on the priceless Aubusson carpet.

"Oh, I'm sorry," I cried, wondering what to do.

"Think nothing of it," Cornelia said. She rang a silver bell. "Edwards will take care of it."

I spent the next few minutes apologizing for my clumsiness and hoping I hadn't ruined the carpet. Cornelia was dismissive of the whole business, but I felt truly terrible—physically and mentally. I stayed a few minutes watching the room spin; then I made my excuses. If I was going to expire, I didn't want to do it at the Hôtel du Soleil. The carpets would never be the same.

Edwards, the butler, saw my condition at once and took me by the arm to escort me out.

"Smith girls never could hold their liquor," I heard Cornelia say as she mixed another round of drinks.

Edwards put my raincoat on me and offered to escort me to the gate. I accepted readily because I was sure I'd never make the trek across the courtyard. Leaning on Edwards, and using my umbrella as a cane, I successfully completed the journey.

When we got to the gate, Edwards said, "Madam, if you'll pardon the suggestion, I don't believe you should drive."

"Quite right," I muttered. "Would you take me to the bus stop?"

"Of course, madam," he said. "Not many visitors have lasted as long as you did."

Knowing that I wasn't their only victim made me feel a bit better. The three old ladies had drunk twice as much as I, yet they had remained perfectly sober. *They must have wooden legs to store that much booze*, I thought, suddenly realizing that my own legs were pretty wooden at the moment. Every step I took was an adventure. Without Edwards I would have ended up sleeping in a doorway. That made me warm to butlers in general, and regret my earlier uninformed opinion of them.

During the ride home, I forced myself to stay awake, knowing that if I closed my eyes for even a moment, I'd miss my stop and wake up in some spooky bus terminal where the buses spend the night.

By some miracle, I managed to make it back to our house. Frank was reading and the boys were playing quietly when I staggered into the apartment, still using the umbrella as a cane.

Frank looked up and said, "What the hell happened to you?"

"Why, whatever do you mean?" I said, willing myself to stand up straight and speak clearly.

"You're loaded," he said, laughing.

"Loaded with contempt for your accusations," I said with queenly disdain.

"Pardon *me*," Frank said. But he was still laughing.

"I believe I shall make dinner," I said. "Now, let's see . . . where is the kitchen?"

"Stephen, show Mama where the kitchen is," Frank said.

Stephen got up and toddled to the kitchen, which was less than six feet from where I was standing, and said, *"Voilà la cuisine, Maman."*

I knew that.

I decided the first order of business was to light the oven; then I would check to see what was in the house to eat. Fumbling around in my pocketbook, I found a pack of matches, and after several attempts I managed to light one. Holding it carefully, I tried to open the oven door, but the umbrella kept getting in the way. I solved that problem by switching the bothersome bumbershoot to my right hand. Unfortunately, that made me drop the match on the floor.

I hesitated. Should I pick up the burning match from the floor or attempt to light another one? While I was pondering what to do, I noticed that I had attracted an audience. Frank, John, and Stephen were standing in the doorway, staring at me.

"Why, I've matched the drop," I said regally, and bent down to pick it up.

The next thing I knew, I was sitting on the floor, staring at the oven, the umbrella and purse still in my hands,

"*Encore, Maman!*" Stephen shouted, laughing. "*Encore!*"

"What?" I asked, still in a daze. *Perhaps making dinner wasn't such a good idea.*

"You're so funny, Mama," John said, joining his brother and father in laughing at my predicament.

Frank grabbed me under the arms and hauled me to my feet, then propelled me to the bedroom. He aimed me at a chair, but I missed, falling onto the bed.

"But what about dinner?" I asked, closing my eyes.

"If you can't get your derriere in a chair-e-air, I'd suggest you go *au lit,*" he said. I was about to object, but suddenly it seemed much more important to sleep.

The next morning I discovered what a hangover really was. Never in my life had I drunk enough to get one, and with the total sincerity of an ex-rummy, I swore I'd never touch the stuff again. The word *Gibson* was henceforth stricken from my vocabulary and the word *water* was substituted.

My recollections of that awful day were distinctly impressionistic, but I knew with absolute clarity that I had been terribly out of my league with the Gibson girls. I had wanted to keep up with them socially, literarily, and most of all, alcoholically. But I couldn't. I don't know why I even tried. Those three were Ladies of Leisure and I was a Woman of Work. They sat amid the royal splendor in an impressive mansion, exhibiting their considerable knowledge. I was surrounded by dirty dishes and even dirtier diapers, but I had one thing they did not: something to do. They were bored to death and drank to forget they were bored to death. I was too involved in the mundane matters I encountered each day to live as they did and glad of it.

Chapter 16

JOHN'S PARTY GIRLS. John invited the twins, Annette and Anni, to attend his fifth birthday party.

Arrrr!

March 1951

"Not again," Frank groaned.

"But I have to go," John whispered urgently.

"You've already been twice," Frank said.

"Now, Daddy!"

Those were two little words that could galvanize even the most reluctant parent into action, Frank included.

We were sitting in the Cinema Lynx, watching *Treasure Island,* starring that hammiest of hams, Robert Newton. The British actor was in his glory, "Arrr-ing" and "Jim-lad-ing" it up as the pirate Long John Silver. I really got into the spirit of the movie, but unfortunately, John did, too. He got so excited that he had to go to the bathroom three times in ninety minutes.

Normally, that wouldn't have been a problem. But in the tiny Lynx theater Frank had to take John up onto the stage and walk him in front of the screen to get to the facilities. Just as Captain Billy Bones was telling Jim Hawkins about the treasure map, he was interrupted by Frank and John rudely walking into the scene. When Jim was hiding in the apple barrel listening to Long John's mutinous talk, a slouching Frank and a waving John tripped lightly past. And just when things looked blackest for young Jim, trapped in the mast with the evil Israel Hands coming to get him, a loud "Hi, Mama!" erupted from the stage. I expected Jim to flinch, but it was Frank who quivered visibly.

My husband, as I've mentioned, would do almost anything not

to attract attention in public, and he was mortified to be escorting John across the stage at crucial moments in the movie. He swore that, in the unlikely event we ever returned to the Lynx, he was bringing a bucket for John to use.

In my opinion, however, it was all his fault anyway. My husband was the one who had insisted on reading *Treasure Island* to John. I thought the Robert Louis Stevenson adventure was too grown-up for our son, and the three trips to the men's room proved it—as did the constant swordplay at home and John's insistence on playing Jim Hawkins, treasure hunter.

If I found the book to be too violent for a young child, then the movie, I feared, would only make matters worse. But what could I do? Attending *Treasure Island* was a special treat because John's fifth birthday was only two days away.

Birthdays! I could write a book. No, I could write *the* book. I was born on the second worst day of the year—December 24. All my life I had missed out on what other people took for granted— being the center of attention, having a party in my honor, and receiving nice presents. If you were born on June 17, you don't know what I'm talking about; if you were born on Christmas Day, you do.

As a child, I never really had a birthday party. My parents weren't mean—it was just that Christmas Eve at our house was so hectic that there was never enough time. I was given birthday and Christmas presents on December 25, but it wasn't the same. I wanted to get dressed up, invite my friends over, play games, and be the birthday girl. Me. Me. Me. But all I ever received on my natal day was a reminder that I would receive my presents on the morrow. Oh, and a Lady Baltimore cake. Ugh. How I hated it: a white layer cake with white icing and walnuts on top. The mere smell of a white cake with white icing reminded me of all the years I had yearned for a birthday celebration of my own.

In later years, when I worked up the nerve to complain to my mother, she was aghast.

"Why didn't you ever say anything?" she had said. "I always thought you liked Lady Baltimore cakes."

Well, I didn't and I don't. And I still don't know why I didn't say anything at the time. I guess I was too shy. But even if I had spoken up, it probably wouldn't have made a difference. No one wanted to come to a birthday party on Christmas Eve, and no one ever remembered to give me a present. In desperation I once told all my friends that my birthday was officially changed to June 25—as far away from Christmas as possible—but everybody still forgot, including me.

That was why I swore I'd always have birthday parties for my children, make them the center of attention, and spare them my disappointments.

Frank thought I was nuts and he was right. But even in France I wanted John to be the birthday boy. So I had Frank send out invitations to John's classmates, inviting them to the party I was planning. I specified that the parents were also welcome, and because I was ignorant of the children's circumstances, I stated that no presents were necessary.

On the adult side, we invited our landlords, the Sausons, and I got Molly and Peter to attend by bribing them with an ancient bottle of cognac Frank had bought. And we had a surprise guest who invited herself—Cornelia, of all people. She had cornered me at the museum and invited me to tea again. Horrified by that prospect, I had asked her to John's party. To my astonishment, she had accepted. I guess she was lonely, because she told me Viola and Edna had returned to Boston. Frank was on notice to order a barrel of gin and a couple of pearl onions for her.

With Elise as my right hand or, more accurately, with me as Elise's left hand, we set about organizing the party. Everyone was to arrive at eleven, play games, eat a snack, then ice cream, cake, and presents. After that we would all go see the big Mardi Gras parade sponsored by the local businessmen. The plan was simplicity itself.

When the day arrived, I was awakened to the lilting strains of "Spring is sprung, the grass is riz, I wonder where the boidies is?" sung by Frank to the tune of "A Foggy Day."

I opened my eyes to behold golden sunshine pouring into the

bedroom. The scent of fresh flowers and warm earth filled the room with a perfume you couldn't buy in Paris—never mind New York. It was going to be a glorious day in Montpellier for John's birthday.

In the kitchen, I found Frank attempting to teach Stephen how to sing "Happy Birthday" to John.

"Hap birf me," Stephen sang in a lusty voice.

"No, it's John's birthday," I said.

"*Non! Mon anniversaire!* Birfday!"

"I've been trying to convince him that it's not his birthday, but he doesn't believe me," Frank said.

I tried, too, but Stephen didn't believe me either. He was sure it was *his* birthday.

"Heaven help us when the presents come out," Frank said. "He'll throw a fit if he can't open them all."

"And John will explode if he does," I agreed. But that was a bridge we hadn't come to yet, and I had a thousand other things to do.

Elise was in charge of the food, Frank was the master of drinks, and I had assigned Peter and Molly to take care of the parents and Cornelia. That left me free to be social director for the children—with a bit of translation help from any and all.

The menu consisted of hors d'oeuvres for the adults and my world-class tuna salad sandwiches for the children and Frank. Elise had baked a special cake for John and it looked delicious. Unfortunately, I hadn't been able to find little birthday candles anywhere, so I had bought a monstrous votive candle that was almost as big as John. It practically needed guy wires to keep it upright. But it was impressive—even if it looked as if it had been stolen from a cathedral. I had also purchased chocolate and strawberry *glace* by the gallon and Frank had enough liquor on hand to open his own store.

I had decorated the dining room table with birthday place mats and strung red, white, and blue bunting around the room to give it a festive (and patriotic) air. Party hats, noisemakers, and little party favors for the children completed the preparations.

I was admiring my handiwork when the first guests arrived.

"Hi, *Américain*," Marc said, punching John on the shoulder.

"Hi," John said, punching him back.

"*En garde,*" Marc said, drawing an imaginary sword.

"Arrrr, mate," John said, sounding like a soprano Robert Newton. And the duel was on. It was going to be a long day.

Marc's father introduced himself, then headed directly for the bathroom. I thought that was strange until I realized that his name was Le Grand. He was one of the plumbers who had banged on our pipes, and he was just checking his handiwork. Satisfied, he declined our invitation to stay, and arranged to pick Marc up at the parade. I think he was relieved to be free of his overenergetic child for an hour or two.

"*Touché,*" Marc shouted, slamming into my beautifully decorated table and sending a plate to the floor. Fortunately, it was a paper plate, which proved my genius as a birthday party hostess.

Annette and Anni, accompanied by their mother, arrived next. The girls were so cute in their matching white dresses and little pink bows that I was enchanted. They truly looked more like elves than *élèves*. Mme. Valery couldn't have been more than twenty-two, and I could see where the twins got their elfin good looks.

Peter and Molly came next, filled with anticipation, but not for birthday cake.

"Break out the cognac, Frank," Peter said, "and let's have a party."

"*Joyeux anniversaire, Jeannot,*" Molly said, handing John a beautifully wrapped present. "From Peter and me."

I had to wrest the box from John's iron grip, telling him that all presents were to be opened after the ice cream and cake. When it came to birthday party protocol, I had no peers. I kept all presents on a high shelf to discourage Stephen from pillaging and plundering them.

When the rest of the children and the Sausons arrived, I decided it was time to let the games begin. My thought was to play some games in the house, then go outdoors for more fun, and finally come back inside for lunch, ice cream, and cake.

I took out the pin the tail on the donkey poster and told the children gathered around me how to play. After my labored explanation in a mélange of three languages—English, French, and Mary's French— they looked at me as if I had just descended to earth from some other planet.

"Frank!" I called. "Help!" But before he could clarify that they'd be pinning a picture of a donkey, not a *real* donkey, Marc leaped into the air and shouted; Michel, John's friend with the fur coat, gave me a pop-eyed stare; and the twins, Annette and Anni, burst into tears.

This was going well.

"How about musical chairs instead?" Frank suggested. "I'll explain to them what they have to do."

I cranked up the little portable phonograph we had bought at a flea market in town, and Frank lined up the chairs. Then he gave me the signal and Edith Piaf belted out a French song. The five children circled the four chairs warily. When I stopped the music, all the children raced to sit down—and they all did. Anni sat in Annette's lap and nobody was out.

"Not much of a game, Mary," Molly called from the kitchen. "It could go on forever."

After a few more words of instruction from Frank, the children finally grasped the principle of the game, and we successfully narrowed the field down to Marc and John. The last time I silenced Miss Piaf, both boys leaped for the chair, landing simultaneously on the seat. During the titanic struggle that followed, John and Marc hit the floor wrestling and shouting. Taking advantage of the melee, Anni quietly slipped past the fighting boys and sat demurely in the chair.

"*Voilà!*" she said sweetly. "*C'est à moi.*"

"That's not fair!" John cried, disentangling himself from Marc.

"Anni wins," I said. "For ingenuity and for *not* fighting. This is supposed to be a party, not a street brawl. Now behave yourselves, both of you."

John understood my words and Marc my tone of voice, although he looked surprised that I didn't give each of them a clout to the head, French style. They deserved it.

Fearing more outbreaks of violence, I ushered everyone outside for the second part of the party. The Sausons had set out chairs and tables in the backyard, and they were delighted to show off their flower garden, which was just coming into bloom. Frank, Molly, and Peter sat at a table staring at the bottle of vintage cognac like buzzards eyeing a dying antelope, while Mme. Valery and the Sausons held a spirited discussion about the horticultural arts. I got the children organized for a sack race.

Just then a loud, imperious voice boomed across the backyard. "I didn't know children came wrapped these days," Cornelia yelled.

She strode across the yard like a yacht under sail, instantly becoming the center of attention. The children stared wide-eyed at the shimmering form swaying across the lawn. They had never seen the like. Come to think of it, neither had I.

Cornelia was swathed in an ankle-length dress that seemed to be made of silver tinsel. In fact, she resembled a Christmas tree that Frank might have decorated. Around her neck was a fur cape, and her hat was a relic from the 1920s. However, the entire ensemble, draping her six-foot frame, gave Cornelia a dashing, bathtub-gin kind of appearance that left us all breathless.

I told the children to carry on and went over to greet our last guest.

"I brought a cake," Cornelia said.

"Why, thank you," I said. "You needn't have."

"Bushwa. Everybody likes cake."

Unable to deny that general principle, I introduced Cornelia to the other guests. The Sausons stared at her in disbelief; Mme. Valery was shell-shocked, but fortunately Peter turned on the charm and soon persuaded Cornelia to sample the cognac—not that he had to try very hard.

That bottle wouldn't last long, I thought, and I was right. Before I knew it, Frank was rushing upstairs to make a shaker of Manhattans. Molly sat with a petrified smile on her face, and Peter, having discovered that Cornelia was from Boston, began gossiping about mutual acquaintances.

I rescued Molly and had her help me with the children, who were bounding around haphazardly in their sacks.

"If they keep going," Molly said, "maybe they'll calm down."

"Ha!" I said. I knew from experience that their energy was almost supernatural. Just watching the children play made me want to take a nap. Instead, I bribed them to sit down to a quick *menthe* before the treasure hunt.

"Here are the clues," I said to Molly. "Will you translate them for me?" She read the first one in English:

> "To find the gold,
> You must be bold,
> And look for a clue,
> Under the yew."

"That's the worst clue I ever heard," Molly said.

"No, it's not," I said. "Read the next one."

> "Your second clue,
> If you be good,
> Is to be found in something
> Made of wood."

"You're right—that's even worse," she said. "But I'll do my best to translate your doggerel into French doggerel."

Molly gathered the children around.

"Où est le trésor?" John asked. "Where is the treasure?"

"That's for me to know and you to find out," Molly said in both French and English. Then she read them the first clue.

Tentatively, the children wandered around the yard, looking for the right tree. Since there were only four trees, the process of elimination didn't take very long. They whooped with triumph when they found the next clue hanging from a low branch.

"Read it, Molly. Read it!" John shouted.

After she had done so, Marc immediately ran to the woodpile, the other children following him blindly. He rooted through the logs and came up with the next clue: the garden shed.

"La remise?" Anni said. *"La remise de jardin?"*

She knew all about gardening, I guess, because she ran over to the garden shed and found the final clue, which was cleverly hidden on the floor in front of her.

The children were much better at this game than I had anticipated, but I suppose an easy game was better than one they couldn't figure out. They seemed to be having fun, and that was the point.

By now Marc was beside himself. He hopped from one foot to the other, clearly relishing the prospect of treasure. Michel looked winded, and the twins maintained an aloof attitude.

Molly read the final clue to them, and they scattered in all directions, each one having his own idea about where the treasure was stashed. Unfortunately, they were all wrong. The well was at the far end of the yard, and the bucket containing the gold-wrapped chocolate coins was hidden behind it, out of sight. But none of the children were even close. So I took a few minutes away from the game to speak with Elise, who had brought Stephen to the party. Stephen took one look at the children racing around the yard and charged off after them.

I went over to see how Mme. Valery was getting on and said a few halting words to her. She raised an eyebrow at my pidgin French, but at least she didn't burst out laughing, a victory of sorts. Then I turned my attention to Cornelia, who was downing Manhattans with Frank and Peter.

"Sorry I don't have any potato chips," I said to her with a weak smile.

"Think nothing of it," Cornelia boomed. "Potato chips go with Gibsons, never with Manhattans."

You learn something every day.

"And Frank makes a damn good Manhattan," she continued. "Not encumbered by all that vermouth."

Satisfied that my adult guests were enjoying themselves, I went back to Molly.

"Talk about not having a clue," Molly said, surveying the field. "They're totally stumped."

The children had slowed their frantic searching and began to look discouraged.

"Call them back and give them another clue," I said. "Before they all burst into tears."

Anxious to get their hands on the treasure, the children came running when she called. Molly thought for a moment, then gave them directions that would lead them to the well. With renewed hope, they rushed off in the right direction, with Molly and me following to make sure they were successful.

"*Non, Marc, à droite,*" Molly called out, sending the children to the right. The others followed him like a herd of sheep. When they got to the well, they stopped to consider what to do next. Finally, John had the sense to look behind the little stone well. He disappeared from sight; then I heard a roar. Not a roar of triumph, but a roar of outrage.

"Arrrr!" John shouted.

He emerged from behind the well, dragging his protesting little brother by the arm. Stephen's face was smeared with chocolate, and he was yelling, "*Mon anniversaire! Pour moi! Mon chocolat!*"

"Mama, the swab ate all the chocolate," John yelled at me. "Maroon him!"

The other children looked perplexed.

"*Mais où est le trésor?*" Michel asked.

"In Stephen's stomach," Molly said, laughing. "The little devil found the treasure while you lads were poking about."

"You'll walk the plank for this," John threatened. "I'll run you through."

"Just like Ben Gunn in *Treasure Island,*" Molly said. "He found the treasure before Marc Hawkins and Long Jeannot Silver."

My, this was going awfully well.

I managed to rescue what was left of the treasure and distribute the chocolate coins to the children. Then I rescued Stephen from being skewered by his brother and sat them down to cool them off.

"Perhaps we've played enough games for today," I said. "How about some sandwiches and Coca-Cola?"

"Coca-Cola!" Marc shouted, leaping up and leading the merry band of pirates back to the house.

I went into the kitchen and allowed Frank to make me a watery highball. It tasted awful and I put it down. When the ice from the Commune Libre melted, Frank would throw out the drink and make a new one for me. It was a game we played. He pretended to make drinks for me and I pretended to drink them. Thank goodness Cornelia wasn't pouring.

Elise served the children sandwiches and Coke; then I lit the towering candle on the birthday cake. It took two matches to get it started. John tried to blow it out, but no one, especially a child, had the height to reach the stratosphere where the flickering flame hovered, just out of reach—or breath.

"Try standing on your chair," I suggested.

John climbed up on his chair, drew a big breath, and let go with a veritable typhoon of a candle extinguisher. The flame flickered for a moment, but it refused to go out. John huffed and puffed but to no avail; that candle must have been made to survive a drafty church in winter.

"One more time," I ventured.

John reared back and really let the candle have it. The flame went out, all right, but my son tumbled from his chair, his right arm smashing into the cake. Whipped cream spurted out of it like seltzer from a bottle, spattering Marc and Michel. Anni and Annette looked horrified, but the boys laughed and began licking the filling off their hands and rubbing it into their hair.

After I had cleaned the children up, I salvaged what was left of the cake, and gave everybody a piece. Even in its ruined condition, the cake was delicious and we all complimented Elise, who blushed becomingly.

Then we sang happy birthday to John—except Stephen, who

sang it to himself. I dished out the ice cream and everything was going smoothly until I brought out John's presents. Then Stephen went berserk.

"*Cadeaux! Pour moi!*" he shouted, breaking free of Elise and running to the pile of presents he was sure were his. He embraced them and dragged them off the table and onto the floor.

I expected John to be furious, but he just sat in his chair, staring with disdain as Stephen tore into the presents.

I tried to drag Stephen away, but the child screamed bloody murder.

"Oh, let him open them," John said. "He only wants to play with the paper and boxes."

I was impressed.

"That's wonderful of you," I said. "You're acting very grown-up."

"I'm five now," he said nonchalantly.

Boy, was I impressed.

"As long as I get the presents he can have the rest," John said. "Swab."

Well, maybe not that impressed.

With Stephen pacified by a pile of boxes and wrapping paper we were all ready to go to the big parade—all except Michel. His face had suddenly turned the color of his ratty fur coat. I could guess what was coming next and tried to steer him to the bathroom, but I was too late. Coke, tuna salad, ice cream, and cake erupted from him like lava from a volcano.

"Must have been the sandwiches," Molly said unkindly.

"Everybody's a critic," I sighed, trying to calm the poor gagging child.

Fortunately, Elise came to the rescue, cleaned up the mess, and soon had Michel restored to fair health. Like all children, Michel was drawn to Elise, sensing that she was both rock solid in times of distress and a fountain of love that made everything better.

At Elise's insistence, we left Michel in her care and headed off for the parade. She promised to meet us at the Bar d'Oc once Michel had recovered sufficiently.

"Oh, thank you, Elise," I said. "And thank you for baking John such a beautiful cake. I'm sorry he fell on it."

Then I did something that would haunt me. I handed her an envelope with a few francs in it as a bonus for organizing the party. Her twinkly brown eyes suddenly became pools of sorrow. She put the envelope down and took Michel into the boys' bedroom.

What had I done? I wondered. But I didn't have time to figure it out because I could hear Peter tooting the horn for me to hurry.

We took up our station in front of the Bar d'Oc and cheered as the parade passed in review. Frank hoisted Stephen on his shoulders to get a better look at the pretty girls in outlandish costumes and the men dressed as skeletons, devils, and other fantastic creatures.

"*Merci, Maman!*" Stephen shouted to me. "*Mon anniversaire!*" He held his arms out, taking in the entire parade.

"He thinks the parade's his birthday present," Frank said, laughing.

"*Oui, pour moi!*" Stephen shouted with glee.

"Okay, 'Tienne," Frank said. "Let's make this a memorable unbirthday."

Then he jogged down the street, Stephen bouncing on his shoulders, and disappeared from sight. I couldn't imagine what Frank was up to; besides, I was too busy keeping an eye on Marc, who wanted to dart out into the street to get a better look at the floats.

I had just dragged him to safety for the eighth time when I looked up to see a more chilling sight than all the demons in the parade: Mme. Perrin coming for me. "Hide me," I whispered to Molly. "She's going to kill me."

I had been meaning to stop by the general store to clear the air with Mme. Perrin, but I had been so busy . . . well, so cowardly, I hadn't.

Molly knew the whole disgraceful story, and I relied on her to defend me from the enraged shopkeeper. Her advice? "Use Marc as a shield. He could stop a bullet and never even slow down."

Some help.

I had two choices: I could either stand my ground and deal with

Mme. Perrin in an adult, rational way, or I could do what came naturally and run for my life.

I was poised to run when I felt a heavy hand on my arm. Whirling around, I was face-to-face with Mme. Perrin. *Too late,* I thought. I'd swing from the yardarm.

"Bonjour," I squeaked, my throat as parched as Treasure Island.

Then she lit into me, speaking a mile a minute, causing me to lose track of what she was saying. I heard something about Sophie, René, and America, and I cringed.

"What is she saying?" I said, out of the side of my mouth to Molly.

"Shhhh," Molly said. "I'm trying to keep up."

The cascade of words continued on and on, pouring over me, drowning me.

"Ow," Marc complained, and I realized I was digging my fingers into his shoulders. I loosened my death grip on the boy, but not enough to let him escape. It wouldn't do to return a maimed child to M. Le Grand, for if I did, I'd have all seven plumbers and Mme. Perrin after my skin.

The tirade slowly ground to a halt, and Mme. Perrin stood looking at me expectantly. I was so nervous, I hadn't understood one word of what she had said. I pleaded with Molly to help me out.

"You're off the hook, Mary," Molly said. "She's apologizing to you and begs you to forgive her."

I shook Mme. Perrin's hand, glad to be back in her good graces, and assured her I understood.

"She wants to know if you'll come back to the store," Molly said.

"Mais, oui," I said happily. Mme. Perrin probably had a new supply of rusted tin goods for me to buy.

Beaming, Mme. Perrin retreated into the crowd.

"I'm alive," I said wonderingly.

"It seems that Sophie and René are getting married next week, with Mme. Perrin's blessing. She wrangled a job for René with her cousin, who owns a garage. René's to be put to work as a mechanic and they'll live happily ever after."

"But Sophie's only fifteen."

"Yes, but for propriety's sake, they have to get married. You can't run off with a boy for a week, then come back as if nothing happened," Molly said. "At least not if you're petit bourgeois and live in the south."

"I don't mean to be cynical," I said, "but I wonder if Sophie knew precisely what she was doing all along."

"I'm sure of it," Molly said. "That René's an idiot. He never knew what hit him."

Relieved that my reputation was on the mend, I settled back to watch the parade. I didn't have to wait long before the float sponsored by the Bar d'Oc stopped in front of us for all the patrons to admire.

Pascal, as impressed as we all were by a real Hollywood movie—in color!—had put together a moon scene, complete with a rickety rocket ship and pretty girls in bare-midriff space suits. Pascal himself was dressed as an intrepid spaceman, and that was amazing enough, but the real hit of the float was a towheaded child wearing a paper Pernod hat and tossing confetti at the crowd with abandon.

"Hap birf me!" Stephen yelled from atop the float. "*Maman!* Molly! Jeannot! Hap birf me!"

We waved back madly as the float jolted ahead, pulled by an ancient tractor. The rocket ship swayed precariously, the girls clutched each other for support, and Stephen fell down. He looked around to determine if it would be appropriate to cry, but discovered that no one aboard was paying any attention to him, so he jumped to his feet and began throwing confetti again—a blissful look on his face. Frank, I noted, was walking alongside the float yelling, "Good arm."

"How come he gets to ride on the float?" John asked me. "It's my birthday."

Fortunately, Molly fielded that one for me.

"Jeannot, if there's a parade on Etienne's birthday, you can ride the float. Okay?" Molly said.

"Okay," John said. He must have been getting tired. Which reminded me that Elise had not appeared with Michel.

Fearing that poor, sick child had taken a turn for the worse, I enlisted Molly to take charge while I ran back to the house to see what was going on.

At the apartment, I found Elise finishing up the last of the dishes, so I asked about Michel. She told me he was asleep. Then she turned to confront me, a stern look on her face. I shrank into the corner of the kitchen, astounded that this good-natured woman was seething.

Was she quitting? Had I done or said something to offend her?

She dried her hands on her apron and crossed her arms. Slowly, distinctly, and with an emphasis that even I could not miss, she told me that she couldn't take any money for baking a cake for Jeannot. It was a gift, a gift of love, and she had been insulted by the money. Would I please take it back?

I shied away from the proffered envelope as if it were a snake. I hadn't connected the cake with the tip for arranging the party. The two hadn't seemed remotely linked in my mind. In my labored French I tried to explain. And then I explained again. I hated myself for not being able to speak fluently, and I wished that Frank had been there to help me, but perhaps it was better this way. No one can be insincere in a foreign language unless he is better at it than I am in French.

I pointed out that I liked her. She said she liked me, too. I said that I wanted her to stay with us. She said she had no intention of leaving. I explained that since she had gone out of her way to help with the party, I wanted to give her a little gift. She replied that she appreciated that. But, I pleaded, I had not thought about paying her for the cake and had never intended to. I realized that it was her gift to John and had accepted it as such.

Elise looked at me as if inspecting my very soul, and perhaps my distress had shown through my incorrectly tensed verbs and incoherent accent, for she forgave as quickly as she had condemned. She smiled and said she had misunderstood. We would forget it, she said, beaming at me; the twinkle was back in her eyes. Relief washed over me like a waterfall.

The crisis passed, Elise roused little Michel and took him off to the parade, while I collapsed on my bed. What a near miss that had been. I vowed never again to give Elise a tip unless Frank explained it to her first. Her salary was low enough to make us feel bad, but I would do anything—anything!—not to have Elise mad at me. I would rather have a thousand Mme. Perrins despise me than have Elise give me even a frown. I knew now why the children always did just as she said. Who could stand being on her bad side? That was a desperately lonely and terrible place to be.

I reluctantly abandoned my bed and wandered out to the kitchen. I found the pile of unused paper plates and stored them in a cupboard. John's party, I thought, had been a mixed success at best. But I had given my son a party, a real birthday party with all the trimmings, and I would continue to do so until he screamed for me to stop. No child of mine would ever be deprived, as I had been, of a happy birthday party.

Feeling much better, I decided to eat something before returning to the parade. I spotted the beautifully wrapped cake box Cornelia had brought and thought a piece of sinfully rich *gâteau* would be just the thing.

I tore open the foil paper and opened the lid, and there, staring me in the face, was a white cake with white icing and walnuts on top. The dreaded Lady Baltimore had followed me all the way to France, just to make my life miserable again. It wasn't fair, and there was only one thing to say: "Arrrr!"

Chapter 17

GRAND TOUR. John at the ancient Roman arena in Arles. That was just one of the stops the peripatetic Littells made during their last month in France.

George, Abe, and Me

April–May 1951

Spring had sprung many university students from their studies. So with Peter Lord off to North Africa and Molly on her way to Rome, Frank suggested that we do some traveling of our own. Nothing spectacular, just some short journeys that wouldn't over-tax our finances or the goodwill of our baby-sitters.

We toured Sète, down the coast from Palavas, and watched enthralled as boatmen in their gaily colored jerseys jousted like medieval knights—except they did it from their boats. We visited Béziers, a thriving city in Roman times, and enjoyed seeing its famous Cathedral de St.-Nazaire. And we explored Arles, taking John to see the ancient Roman amphitheater there.

Frank and I also took the train to Barcelona, and to my surprise Spain was very much like southern France: No one there could understand my high school Spanish or, indeed, my French. The one big difference between countries, however, was that life in Spain revolved around death. So on a sweltering Sunday we joined the throng headed for death in the afternoon—the bullring.

Tickets in hand, we pushed our way to the assigned seats—and found them occupied by a family of Spaniards who seemed disinclined to move. Frank spoke with the usher and was told to just brush them aside and sit down. But fearing an altercation in the oppressive heat, my husband suggested that we retreat to the nearest café for an aperitif.

I was relieved. I knew that bullfighting was regarded as a sacred tradition, but like bouillabaisse, it was a tradition that I could do without.

One of the hazards of living in a foreign country for an extended period of time is that you begin to lose your national identity. That was Frank's theory, anyway. I suppose he was referring to the children, because I certainly didn't feel very French. If anything, I felt like the perennial outsider: a strange American in a strange land.

Stephen, however, had gone native. He spoke French almost exclusively, and although he could understand English perfectly well (when he cared to), he preferred to make his demands known *en Français*. To give him credit, though, it seemed as if he could say no in at least eleven languages. In fact, no was his favorite word, and it had been since he had learned how to talk. Looking on the bright side, I knew I wouldn't be one of those stunned mothers who suddenly found themselves battling the "Terrible Twos"—that awful age when a sweet, compliant child suddenly became a naysayer of note. After the "Onerous Ones," Stephen's behavior could only improve.

Unlike his brother, John spoke English about half the time. I envied his ability to switch back and forth between languages with skill and ease. He could begin a sentence in French and end it in English and not think it was any big deal. Like his father, he had the knack.

I found it amusing that Frank was often mistaken for a Parisian. The people in Montpellier knew immediately that his accent wasn't local, but it was precise and formal, so they divined that he must be from the capital. He took great pride in that distinction, as well he might, for it was quite an accomplishment.

Still, Frank worried that the boys would forget they were Americans, and he made a point of teaching them how to play baseball and football. He talked to John about our country, and we took our son to too many Hollywood movies for his own good.

Frank had also bought a children's book about famous Americans and made a great show of reading it to the boys. I found that laudable, but I should have known that my husband would put his own stamp on history.

That observation was hammered home to me one lazy May afternoon while I was contemplating a refreshing siesta.

"Mama," John said, "tell me about Colonial days."

"Of course, dear, what would you like to know?"

"What did you do?" he asked.

"What did I do when?"

"Back in Colonial times. What did you play? Did you wear those funny shoes and big wide dresses?"

I realized that all children thought their parents were ancient, but this was ridiculous.

"Look here," I protested, "just how old do you think I am? I didn't live in Colonial days."

"But Daddy said you knew George Washington," John said.

"I cannot tell a lie," I said. "I didn't."

"Oh."

He clammed up after that, and I knew I would have to confront the world's most outrageous teller of historical tales—Frank.

"What are you reading to the boys?" I asked him that night.

"The book about great Americans," he said innocently.

I didn't believe him for a minute, and when I heard gales of laughter from the children's room, my suspicions were confirmed. I knew from experience that there wasn't a single laugh in that book.

There was only one thing to do: spy.

"George Washington had to cross the Delaware," I heard Frank say, "but the river had frozen solid. He had to go quietly because he wanted to surprise the Hessians on the other side."

"Who are Hessians?" John asked.

"Germans fighting for Britain," Frank said.

"I thought Germans fighted against Britain," John said.

"Fought," Frank said. "Wrong war. In history you need a scorecard to find out who's on whose side.

"Anyway, it was Christmastime, and the Hessians were whooping it up, drinking eggnog and eating king's *galette*, and thumbing their noses at poor George Washington, who was stuck on the wrong side of the river. They thought George couldn't possibly attack them. And then . . ." Frank paused dramatically.

"Along came Mama!" he announced triumphantly.

The boys giggled.

"Hooray for Mama!" John said.

"That's right, and she said, 'See here, George. I have this handy-dandy ice pick, and I'll sit in the front of the boat and chop the ice—very quietly—and those nasty old Hessians will never hear a thing.'

"'I don't believe it,' George said.

"'I'm the fastest ice chopper in New Jersey,' Mama said. 'And I'm willing to bet you a dollar I can do it.'

"'Where did you get the money?' George asked.

"'It's the silver dollar you threw across the Potomac,' Mama said, handing him the coin.

"'Well, all right,' George said. 'But I'm going to stand in the back of the boat to make sure you do it right.'"

Frank picked up the book on his lap to show the boys the famous painting of Washington crossing the Delaware.

"There's George Washington standing up," John said. "But where is Mama?"

"Behind that soldier there," Frank said, "taking a nap."

"Mama always takes naps," John said.

"Some things never change," Frank said. "But that day Mama had enough energy to chop up all the ice, and the American soldiers went on to lick the sh—tar out of the Hessians. They were so completely surprised that they choked on their own eggnog."

Frank suddenly clutched his throat and imitated the sound of a corps of Hessians gagging. Soon all three of them were hacking and coughing up eggnog.

"Now, really," I protested when I could be heard above the noise. "An ice pick?" But when I looked at the boys' happy faces, I had to laugh, too.

John and Stephen were hard to quiet down, but after they were asleep, I reproached my husband.

"What a thing to tell them," I said. "Why me?"

"I couldn't stand to read that book to them again," Frank said. "I know I bought the damn thing, but it's deadly dull—like all children's books. So I decided to spice it up a bit. I don't change the facts. I just put you into the picture, so to speak."

I was in the picture, all right. I was in all the pictures. The next story I overheard was about my close friendship with Abraham Lincoln.

"When Lincoln was a young man," Frank confided to the boys, "he built a raft out of logs he had split, filled it with tin cans like Mama buys, and went down the Mississippi River to sell the cans in New Orleans.

"He hadn't gone very far when he ran into—guess who?"

"Mama!" both boys cried.

"Right," Frank said. "She was lolling about on a raft with Tom Sawyer and Huckleberry Finn."

"Who are they?" John asked.

"Refugees from another story," Frank said. "Anyway, Mama said, 'Huck, Tom, jump into the river and swim to that island over there. You can play at being Indians while I'm away with Abe.'

"Now, Mama was the champeen raft paddler in all of Missouri, so naturally Abraham Lincoln was glad of her company. They tied their rafts together and floated down the river until they came to New Orleans."

"Then what happened?" John asked.

"Abe sold all his tin cans to Mama and decided to walk back home to Illinois. He was a big man—six-four, I believe—and he had those long legs, which were perfect for a long walk. Mama wanted to go with him, but with her short legs, she gave up about two miles out of town. 'So long, Abe,' Mama said. Then she returned to New Orleans, which is why she talks so funny today—in bad French and in English."

Hmmm.

I decided that it was best to ignore the whole business, but Frank's version of history had a compelling quality. I heard all about me and my good friend Paul Revere, and when Wilbur and

Orville Wright were trying to get airborne at Kitty Hawk, you know who was holding the rope.

But the story I loved the best was about the horseless carriage.

"One day Mama was walking down the street when she saw this old, old horse. He was groaning and straining and neighing because a lady on the block kept forgetting to take out her garbage and the poor old horse had to back the wagon up to the lady's door once a week. 'I'm sooo tired,' the horse said to Mama."

"Mama talks to horses?" John asked.

"That's the rumor," Frank said. "Though always in English. Even horses don't understand her French. Anyway, Mama was real upset that the old horse had to work so hard, so she decided to do something about the problem."

"What did she do?" John asked.

"She looked up and down the block and saw Henry Ford just sitting on the curb doing nothing. And you know Mama—she can't stand to see a man relax. So she said, 'Henry, you lazybones, why don't you invent the horseless carriage? That way all the horses can retire and be put out to pasture.'

"Mr. Ford thought about it for a while and then he said, 'All right, I will.' And he did.

" 'What are you going to call it?' Mama asked when he showed her his invention. Henry said he hadn't decided, so your mother suggested he call it after himself. Henry agreed, but as it turned out, Mama was very disappointed."

"Why?" John asked.

"Because," Frank said, rushing to the punch line, "she meant for him to call it a Henry!"

John and Stephen didn't get it, but I laughed out loud, betraying my presence outside the bedroom door.

"Gotcha!" Frank said with a wink.

He had, indeed. But I found that all the stories about America and Americans had made me homesick. I didn't say anything to Frank, but after almost a year abroad I was delighted to be leaving. I loved Montpellier, but for me home was not where the hearth was; it was where the United States was. I was proud to be an

American and I had to agree with the French Communists: Go home, Americans! I was all ready to comply when things got complicated.

"Great news," Frank said one day. "My old fraternity brother Bill Southwick and his family are coming to Montpellier. They'll only be in town for two days and they want to get together with us."

I had heard about Bill Southwick for years, but I had never met him. He was two years older than Frank, but they had formed a lasting friendship in college.

"Their son is eight years old," Frank said. "That's hard to imagine."

Not so hard to imagine when you realized that Bill and his wife had married in 1938. According to Frank, the wedding at Bill's father's place outside Philadelphia had been the social event of the season. I was a struggling newspaper reporter in Texas and didn't know much about Main Line society. I still don't, but I gathered that Bill's father, the manufacturer of an internationally known brand of fountain pen, was fabulously wealthy. Bill himself had shunned the family business and had gone to work for the State Department. He had been posted to Switzerland just before the war and had been trapped there for the duration.

"Bill's now in Belgium," Frank said. "And he's coming here by way of Bordeaux. I hope he brings a case or two of Chateau Lafite 1929."

On the appointed day, we met at the same elegant hotel where Jules had hosted his *réveillon*. Bill Southwick turned out to be well over six feet tall and as handsome as a movie star. I could picture him, a tennis sweater tied around his neck, a martini in his hand, lounging by the country club pool. His wife, Christine, was a lovely, fresh-faced girl, dressed with casual elegance. She had lustrous brown hair drawn back in an unflattering bun, but even bald she would have been a striking woman. Frank had told me Christine was the girl next door, but that in Bill's neck of the woods, you needed a small plane to get to the neighboring estate in less than a day.

As a couple, they were smooth, suave, sophisticated—and even nice. I liked them both right away.

After several rounds of drinks (Coke for me), several rounds of secret fraternity handshakes, and several rounds of stories from long ago, we sat down to dinner in the imposing hotel dining room. Frank didn't get his two cases of Bordeaux, but we had two lovely bottles at the table. Then the bombshell exploded.

"Frank, I haven't been entirely truthful with you," Bill said.

"Then you did throw a spitball against Dartmouth," Frank said, laughing. Bill had been a pitcher in college, Frank a second baseman.

"Certainly not," Bill said with mock indignation. "My regular stuff was so good that day, I didn't need it."

"That was the game in which I made my greatest play," Frank said. "There was a man on first and one out. Bill here threw a low curve that the batter bounced up the middle. I ran to my right, leaped ten feet straight up, caught the ball, pivoted in midair, and threw it to the first baseman, getting the runner."

"Three cheers for Frank," Christine said.

"Unfortunately, only one cheer," Bill said. "It was a beautiful play, but Frank was still in the air when he threw the ball to first and never touched second base. The runner went to third on the play and eventually scored."

"We lost the game," Frank said. "And I knew then I'd never play for the Yankees or even the St. Louis Browns."

"That's why I'm here," Bill said.

"To offer me a major league contract?" Frank said, laughing.

"To offer you a job," Bill said. "You can have a contract, too, if you like."

Frank was obviously stunned because he opened his mouth to say something; then he took a sip of wine and remained silent.

"What kind of job?" I asked finally, breaking the silence.

"As you know, my father makes fountain pens," Bill said. "He's looking for someone to learn the business and take over the European operation."

"And he wants me?" Frank managed to say. "I only met him once or twice."

"Ideally, he wants me," Bill said. "But I'm quite satisfied working for State. Three generations of pen makers is enough. But I recommended you."

"But, Bill," Frank protested, "I don't know a damned thing about the pen business. And come to think of it, I don't know a damned thing about business in general."

"I told the old man you were an up-and-coming young executive at Bethlehem Steel before the war," Bill said.

"You know that's a lie," Frank said. "I was only a trainee with a bleak future. I was almost glad I was drafted into the Pennsylvania National Guard in 1941. I got used to living in a tent."

"My father is looking for a linguist," Bill said. "Someone who is intelligent and adaptable. Prior experience in the business may be a handicap. Do you realize we haven't sold a single pen in all of Europe for the past twelve years? We want you."

"That's very flattering," Frank began, but Bill cut him off to tell him how much the job paid. The salary about knocked my socks off. It was five times what Frank had been making back home teaching.

"And that's just to start," Bill continued. "The job also comes with a car, and we can arrange to lease you an apartment in a building we own in Paris. The rent is nominal. You'll have to travel, of course, but you'll have a whopping great expense account."

Expense account? I liked the sound of that.

"So tell me about the expense account," I said, imagining myself buying mink coats and sparkling diamonds at the company's expense. The wife of a young executive had to look the part, I thought, and I would be willing to sacrifice my usual nondescript look for the good of my husband's future.

Bill went into detail about every aspect of the job; then he became serious when Frank asked him about the problems involved.

"The one thing my father is really worried about is the competition from those newfangled ballpoint pens," Bill said.

"Junk," Frank said. "A flash in the pan. Nothing will ever replace the fountain pen."

"I don't know," Bill said. "Father's pretty shrewd."

"Believe me, stick with the tried and true," Frank said. "I convinced our friend Ed Meyers not to take a job with some fly-by-
night outfit in California. Imagine, they claimed they had a camera
that developed its own film, right inside the camera. Now, there's
an idea that will never catch on. I told Ed he'd be a fool to leave a
perfectly good job with the Packard Motor Company."

"You might be right," Bill said. "I'm no expert."

"Of course I'm right," Frank said. "And ballpoints—cheap
plastic crap—can't compare with the fine writing instruments that
your father makes."

We parted on a friendly note, with Frank inviting Bill, Christine,
and their son, Billy, to our house for lunch the following day.

That night Frank and I had one of our marathon discussions.

When I was a girl, my mother had always told me to make a list
of pros and cons when I had an important decision to make. However, there was a serious flaw in that system. Somehow I always
chose "because I want to," over "dirty, dangerous, unhealthy,
criminal, and fattening." But at least Frank and I made a stab at being rational.

"On the positive side, there's the money," Frank said.

"And the whopping great expense account," I put in.

"The car and a cheap apartment in Paris," Frank said. "With
that kind of dough, we could hire a couple to cook and clean, and
we would solve the Elise problem."

The Elise problem had been plaguing us for months. Poor Elise
wanted desperately to accompany us to America. She couldn't
stand the thought of being separated from the boys. In fact, she felt
so strongly about this that she was willing to leave her husband
and son to stay with us for a year or two. I would have been glad
to have her, for she was my friend and the children loved her
dearly, but there were two insurmountable problems. The first was
that Elise spoke no English. She would be terribly isolated in the
U.S. with no one to talk to but our family. As far as I knew, there

were only two kinds of nannies in our village: snooty English ladies in gray uniforms and ancient black women who had been with the same family for a hundred years. What a French countrywoman would make of them, I shuddered to think.

The second problem, of course, was money. On Frank's salary we were lucky to eat regularly, let alone employ live-in help. In America, if we paid Elise what we did here, we would be arrested for white slavery. And if we paid her the prevailing wages, we'd be forced to live in a tar-paper shack.

The job in Paris was the solution to the Elise Problem. If she wanted to come to work for us there, she wouldn't have to experience what I had in Montpellier—the loneliness and isolation.

"And now the cons," Frank said. "We'd become expatriates like Cornelia. We could probably get back home once very couple of years, but no guarantees."

"And the children?" I asked.

"We could send them to the American School in Paris or Zurich," Frank said. "Or to public school in England."

Boarding school! I didn't like the sound of that. I hadn't put in all that time and energy taming my children only to have some anonymous boarding school enjoy the benefits or claim the credit.

"And the biggest con of all," Frank said. "Suppose I fail and get canned? We'd be stuck in Europe with no job, no prospects, and no hope. Remember the Depression? Who knows when there might be another one? At least at home I have a job I know I can do."

I poured us a cup of coffee, and we sat silently for a while. Then Frank said, "What do *you* think we should do?"

"The truth?"

"The truth," he said.

"I was excited about going home," I said. "The Gristede brothers have been sending me billets-doux, trying to entice me back with two cents off on green beans. And truthfully, I think I'd rather live in the U.S. than in Europe."

"Then you don't think I should take the job?" he said.

"I didn't say that," I said. "If you think this is a great opportunity, you know I'll stick by you—for better or for worse, through thick and through thin, through Montpellier and Paris or even Budapest."

"I've got to think about this," Frank said, belaboring the obvious.

The Southwicks arrived the next day, accompanied by their eight-year-old son, Billy. The three of them were dressed as if they were going to a wedding. The way they scrutinized our tiny apartment, I thought perhaps they would write us a relief check on the spot, but they didn't. Frank had wanted me to make tuna salad sandwiches, but I had refused. Bill and Christine were definitely not sandwich people. So I had Pascal at the Bar d'Oc prepare lunch for us. All I had to do was to heat everything up. *His* cooking, of course, was a complete success.

"Wonderful escargots, Mary," Christine said. "You must give me the recipe."

"Sure," I said. "All you do is walk down our street for three blocks, turn right, and ask for Pascal."

She looked at me strangely, but being a diplomat's wife, she only smiled.

After lunch, Frank said, "Come on, Bill. Let's toss a ball around. You can show John your curve."

"It's been ages," Bill said. "I'm rusty."

"Then throw your spitter," Frank said.

The boys trooped out to the backyard. Frank caught, Bill pitched, and John stood bravely at the plate. Stephen and Billy were consigned to be the outfield.

Bill fired one in.

"Ow!" Frank said, dropping the ball. "I've got no hands these days."

"It has been more than fourteen years," Bill said, rubbing his arm.

"Daddy, I didn't even see the ball," John complained. "He throws too fast."

"Hey, Billy," Frank called out. "Why don't you come up here and take a swipe at the ball? Show John how it's done."

Billy, a gangly, dark-haired child, shook his head.

"What's the matter?" Frank said, laughing. "Afraid the old man'll fan you?"

"Frank," Bill said, walking to home plate for a conference, "he doesn't play baseball."

"What? When his father was one of the greatest collegiate hurlers of all time?" Frank said in wonderment.

"Hardly that," Bill said modestly. "I tried to teach him to play, but he told me that even if he learned, there was nobody to play baseball with in Switzerland or Belgium. I'm working all the time."

"I'm sorry," Frank said. "Well, give John another pitch—if your arm can take it."

Bill threw a few easy pitches, and John managed to get hold of one and slam it to Billy. But the eight-year-old just watched as the ball landed at his feet. He picked it up and threw it awkwardly to his father.

The game ended quickly because the adults were out of shape and the three boys soon lost interest.

"You want to play trucks?" John asked Billy.

"No, thank you. Do you play chess?" Billy asked.

"What's that?" John said.

While Billy was explaining the intricacies of chess to an uncomprehending John, Stephen took the opportunity to hurl himself into Mme. Sauson's garden and rip up her roses.

"*Fleurs!*" he cried, snatching them out by the handful and throwing them in the air. One landed on his head and he laughed hysterically. The Southwicks looked as pained as Frank.

I rushed over to stop the plant plundering and dragged a screaming Stephen away from the garden. By the time I got things sorted out, I heard John telling Billy chess was too hard.

"Besides," John said, "I hate chess. It's a dumb game. But I can hit like Joe DiMaggio."

"No, you can't," Billy said.

"Yes, I can," John insisted, and the argument continued until Frank broke it up.

"He can't hit like Joe DiMaggio, can he?" Billy asked Frank.

"Not yet," Frank said.

There was a long pause; then Billy said, "Mr. Littell, who is Joe DiMaggio?"

"Probably the greatest all-around ballplayer who ever lived," Frank said, aghast. "I saw him play at Yankee Stadium."

"Where's that?" Billy asked.

"The Bronx, in New York City," Frank said.

"I've never been there," Billy said. "Only to Pennsylvania to see my grandfather."

"You'd like it," Frank said. "The stadium is huge."

"We're going to India," Billy said. "Next month."

"That's a long way away," Frank said.

Billy shrugged.

Frank assured the child that he would find living in India a fascinating experience, but he had a strange look on his face. I couldn't tell if he felt sorry for Billy or was envious of him.

As the party broke up, Frank made his plans to visit Bill's father in Paris over the weekend. Then, with the inevitable secret fraternity handshake, which by now wasn't so secret, and a lot of fond farewells, the Southwicks departed, on their way to Provence—and beyond.

Frank was gone for only two days, but it seemed like forever. I went about my daily routine completely absorbed in thought. Sometimes I would convince myself that living in Paris would be great fun; sometimes I couldn't stand the idea. The money was wonderful, but I knew myself well enough to realize that I didn't need furs and jewels to be happy.

I wasted a lot of brainpower trying to foresee the future. In five years, would I be a chic Parisienne or a New York housewife? Somehow, I couldn't picture myself as either one. It was odd, but all that mental exercise reminded me of the time I was still single and had visited a gypsy fortune-teller. She had told me—for fifty cents placed across her palm—that I would marry an army officer and die in a pool of blood on the streets of New York. Oh, how we had laughed, my friends and I, at such an outlandish prediction.

That was well before the war, when army officers in Texas were about as scarce as Hungarian noblemen. I didn't know any officers—Army, Navy, Marine, or even police. Then along came the war and Frank with it. Score one point for Madam X, the All-Knowing, All-Seeing.

The second part of her prophecy—delivered with a suspicious-sounding Texas twang—had seemed equally absurd. To die on the streets of New York, you had to go there first. I had never been to New York and hadn't planned to go. But before I knew it, I was living only a few short miles from Gotham. I was still alive and kicking, but if I wanted to avoid a bloody death, perhaps living in Paris was the answer. Not that I believed any of that nonsense. Really.

So it was with feelings as strong and mixed as one of Cornelia's Gibsons that I waited and fretted for Frank to return.

Finally, late on Sunday afternoon, I heard Frank's tread on the stairs and I suddenly felt queasy. I vowed to myself that no matter what his decision, I would be happy for both of us.

"How did it go?" I asked him when he opened the door.

"Very well, indeed," he said.

I smiled bravely, taking a deep breath.

"Mr. Southwick was charming and encouraging, and he even offered to raise my starting salary," he said.

"That's nice," I said. "So?"

"So I thanked him for his kindness," Frank said, making himself a drink. "And I turned him down."

I let my breath out slowly. "What made up your mind?" I asked, feeling much, much better.

"It was something that John said."

"John?"

"After the Southwicks left, he asked me what was wrong with Billy. Nothing, I told him. But then he said, 'He's a boy, but he talks old,'" Frank said.

I laughed. Billy did talk old for a child who was only eight.

"It's not funny," Frank said. "That poor little boy has no idea who he is. He's not Swiss. He's not Belgian. And he'll never be Indian. Billy could host an embassy reception, but he can't throw a baseball. He's on his soccer team at school, but he's never even seen an American football game. He's one of those unfortunate international kids."

"What's an international kid?" I asked.

"You see them all the time," Frank said. "They're the children of American diplomats, oil company executives, and other people who do business abroad. Their children are overly sophisticated, but they belong nowhere. They have no real feeling for any place on earth. To them America is just another country with no more significance in their lives than a tour in Peru or a year in Iraq. To be an American, and to appreciate being an American, you have to live in America—not just read about it in a book."

I was taken aback by the intensity of Frank's words. But he wasn't through.

"I didn't spend five effing years in the Army so that my children could become faux Frenchmen or fake Flamands," he continued. "I served my country because it was and is my country, and I don't want my kids to be international kids. I want them to be Americans.

"We're going home."

The word that came to mind wasn't *Arrrr!* this time. It was *Hallelujah!* My heart leaped with joy: We were going home at last, and I was more than ready to leave.

And speaking as someone who knew both George Washington and Abraham Lincoln intimately, I'd say we made the right move.

Chapter 18

(Left) BON VOYAGE. Stephen, Frank and John about to board the French liner *Liberté* in Le Havre. (Right) SHOCKING! Mary wore the most conservative bathing suit she could find in France. But back in America, her "bikini" caused the outraged members of a country club to ban her from the pool.

One Day Less

September 1951

We had come home to America, but unfortunately it was going to be one of those days. Our Never-Fail alarm clock had failed to wake me up, and even before I got out of bed it was already too late. Breakfast was a hasty gulp, punctuated by barely civil remarks from my husband and older son. They were both going to be late, and I was the villain.

Stephen spilled his milk all over the table, and John staged a real treasure hunt for his shoes, socks, and jacket. "Mama!" John shouted.

"Look in the closet for your jacket. Look in your dresser for socks," I called back to him.

"I've got to go," Frank said, running out the door. "You take John to school."

He had the car, and it was a long, long walk.

Collapsing at the breakfast table, I put my elbow in a blob of grape jelly and looked at the havoc four people could create in a whirlwind fifteen minutes. The table was strewn with crumbs, wadded paper napkins, and pooled with milk. And how could I forget the plate of curdling egg yolks that my husband had delightfully decorated with cigarette ends, ashes, and burned matches? I wanted to scream, but there was no time.

Hurriedly, I found John's shoes and socks; then I threw some clothes on Stephen and myself. We were almost out the door when the bell rang.

"Happiness!" a deep voice intoned.

Oh, how I wish I had some, I thought, but happiness wasn't sold door to door like an encyclopedia. Happiness was only my laundry.

The laundry! I had forgotten to get it ready for Fred, the Happiness driver.

"Can you wait a minute?" I asked. "If I don't get Frank's shirts out, he'll have to go to work bare-chested."

"All the time in the world," Fred said. He was a large, jovial man who had been driving the same route for forty years, and he knew more people in town than I did. Like Giles the garbage man in Montpellier, Fred was used to harried housewives, but he had one big advantage over Giles: His truck never got tired of waiting.

I threw a pile of dirty shirts and sheets in a bag and lugged them to the front door.

"Mama, Mrs. Burnett is going to yell at me if I'm late," John said nervously. "You're not supposed to be late for kindergarten."

"I'll explain things to her," I said.

"She'll be mad," John warned.

"Say, Mrs. Littell," Fred said, "do you want me to take him to school?"

"Oh, I couldn't ask you to do that," I said.

"Nonsense," Fred said. "The company will never know—if we don't tell 'em."

I was dubious about that proposition.

"Pleeeze, Mama," John squealed.

"There aren't any seats in the truck," Fred said. "But you can ride up front with me and hold on to the dashboard. I'll have you to school in no time."

"Can I, Mama?" John said. "Mrs. Burnett is waiting for me."

I looked at my watch. If John left now with Fred, he'd be on time. If I walked him, we'd be a half hour late. Since I was just as scared of Mrs. Burnett as John was, I gave my grudging consent to Fred's wild and dangerous plan, proving—once again—what a bad mother I really was.

"Just drive slowly," I called to Fred as he and John roared off in a cloud of exhaust smoke, my son hanging on for dear life.

Returning to the kitchen, I hoped I had done the right thing. I knew that some children in our town were driven to school in limousines, while others were carted to and fro by their mothers, but I believe this was the first time a child ever arrived at kindergarten in a laundry truck.

As I sat at the table surveying the wreckage of breakfast, Stephen took the opportunity to sidle up to me and test the climate. He watched me warily, debated a second, and then deciding it was worth the gamble, he grabbed the edge of my place mat, spilling the coffee I hadn't had time to drink.

I jumped up, desperately brushing the lukewarm coffee from my lap, while he laughed and clapped his hands as if I were a demented ballet dancer doing a mad pas de deux.

I wondered seriously if military schools accepted two-year-olds. I always liked a man in uniform.

"Why did you do that?" I asked him in my most controlled voice.

"Dance again, Mama!" he said, laughing. "Dance again!"

Dance? Perhaps that was what I had been doing for the past two months. I certainly hadn't had much time to come to grips with our year abroad. Sometimes I would wake up in the middle of the night and wonder just where I was: France or America? It was unsettling; it made me feel lost between two worlds.

I don't know what I was expecting upon our return to the United States, but it certainly wasn't dirty dishes and dirty laundry. Somehow, I had it in my head, that once I was back home, all my troubles would disappear and that life would be a carnival of pure happiness. I don't know why I thought that—my life had never exactly been a Fred and Ginger musical—but I did. I think I was just longing for tranquility and order after a year of uncertainty and disorder.

But as the days progressed, my life seemed to regress into chaos, and I found myself wishing the children were older and needed less attention. Then, I told myself, I would be free to wallow in such luxuries as the occasional trip to the hairdresser and a good night's sleep. My life would be settled and not subject to constant turmoil and distraction. The future beckoned, yet I was still haunted by the past. Not the distant past. The recent past.

Before we left Montpellier for good, Frank and I made a lightning tour of the Riviera—French and Italian. We had a marvelous time in Cannes, but I almost lost Frank to Nice. The moment we stepped off the train, my husband was completely captivated by the city. His reaction might have been due to the brilliant sunshine that greeted us there (after two days of rain), but I think there was something more. It was as if he had suddenly discovered what he wanted to do for the rest of his life: sit in a café and stare at women.

"You take the children back home," he said, sitting at a table overlooking the sandy beach and blue Mediterranean. "I'll just stay here. But don't worry. I'll send money if I get work."

Nice was, well, nice, but I didn't find it heaven on earth as Frank did. Cannes seemed about the same to me, and I liked Monte Carlo, too. I won enough there to buy us a first-class dinner by playing twelve and twenty-four (my benighted birthday) on the roulette wheel at the casino.

But when it came time to leave Nice, Frank wouldn't budge.

"I'm serious," he said. "I'm never leaving this place. Maybe I can get Mr. Southwick to hire me on as the official Nice pen seller."

He had me worried. Frank was such a good actor, I never knew when he was teasing me or when he was being serious. There was only one way to find out. If I got upset and he was kidding, he would relent. If he was serious, something drastic would happen—like a divorce.

"All right," I said, after pleading with him for an hour to get packed. "Stay here and see if I care."

He took a long moment—a very long moment, in my opinion—and said, "We'd better go, then."

That was the right response, but in my heart I think he really would have preferred to stay. Nice had that powerful and uncanny effect on him.

We returned home after five days, and I discovered we had spent more than a hundred dollars. Frank always traveled first-class, which is why we traveled so rarely, I suppose.

The children were in good spirits after their stay at Elise's farm, and John had even made friends with Solange, the monstrous porker who was destined for the larder come fall. Frank, however, was depressed. I didn't know if it was leaving Nice behind or having to take his examinations to earn his degree.

"There's only one thing to do," he told me before the written portion of his finals. "Stay up all night and cram."

He sounded like an eighteen-year-old freshman, not a thirty-year-old man, but he had been a self-confessed Ten O'clock Scholar for the past few months, and I was willing to do anything I could to help.

"Put the children to bed, make me a pot of coffee, then let me alone to study," he said.

That sounded reasonable. So at eight o'clock I left him poring over his books, and a few hours later I went to sleep.

Apparently it worked. Frank passed all his exams, both written and oral, with flying colors, earning a *diplôme d'etudes françaises*. My other student did almost as well, winning a copy of *The Little Prince* for excellence in mathematics and penmanship. Translated, that meant he could write zero to nine in a semilegible fashion, but I was so proud of him. He had arrived in France not speaking a single word of French, and he had not only overcome all obstacles, he had won a prize doing it.

I was also glad that John's friends, Marc, Michel, Annette, and Anni were all promoted—Marc by the skin of his teeth. Mme. Lanval must have decided that a year with Marc was enough.

After the children's graduation ceremony, Frank and I were enjoying a glass of champagne, deciding that a little bubbly should be made a part of the elementary school curriculum in the United States, when Marc ran up to Frank and said proudly, "I passed."

"Me, too," Frank said. "At the university."

"Good," Marc said. "Now you can go to work—like you're supposed to."

"I suppose I must," Frank said wistfully.

On a sad note, Peter and Molly had decided to split up. I had thought that they might get married, but they were both too independent-minded for that. Peter was bound for Washington, D.C., where he had some mysterious government job waiting for him, and Molly had decided that she was going to Scotland to enroll in the University of Edinburgh.

We attended a lavish farewell dinner given by Peter at his hotel. For hors d'oeuvres we had olives, sardines, and tomato salad. Then came the consommé, followed by artichokes with a tangy sauce and asparagus with Hollandaise. A grilled turbot was served next, followed by chicken breast. Dessert was chocolate cake with chocolate sauce and cherry sorbet in brandy. We had vin rosé, vin rouge, and vin blanc, in addition to a bottle of cognac. What a feast—*sensationnelle!*

Our own bon voyage party was hardly as grand. We invited Jules and all our student friends who were still in Montpellier to the Bar d'Oc. Frank was in all his glory as host, buying bottles of wine as if they were about to be rationed. I was in a more subdued mood. As much as I was ready to go home, I really hated to say good-bye to Jules and the rest of our friends.

"I'm going to miss our talks in the botanical gardens," I said to Jules over the noise of the crowded bar.

"And I'll miss you," he said gallantly. "It will be so lonely there by myself."

I was on the verge of tears when John chimed in with, "And I'll miss the ice cream."

"You see," Jules said, reading my mood. "Jeannot is not a sentimentalist. He is a realist, as we all must be."

We promised to write each other, and so far we had been faithful to our word. But it was not the same. Sitting in the cool, aromatic gardens, listening to Jules describe the history of France, was one of the most pleasant experiences of my life. I also liked to think that my uncritical concern for his welfare nudged him toward a new outlook on life. And that my fierce defense of the American role in winning the war made him see his foreign students in a more appreciative light.

Toward the end of the party, Pascal called John up to the bar and let him have two free chances at the peg board.

"Voilà!" Pascal said, reading the first slip of paper. "Grenadine!"

John had won a bottle of grenadine. On his second pick, Pascal, without reading the paper, said, *"Mon Dieu! Menthe!"*

John was ecstatic at his luck, but I wasn't fooled. The two bottles were a present from the owner of the Bar d'Oc, and luck had nothing to do with it.

I was touched, but Frank was almost in shock when, as we left, the two Occitan separatists rose gravely and shook his hand.

"Au revoir," Fricor said.

"Au revoir et bonne chance," Gobert said. "Good-bye and good luck."

There was a stunned silence in the bar. No one had ever heard the two old men speak in French before. Frank considered their doing so a mark of honor, for Fricor and Gobert always spoke Occitan. Always—until the Littells left town.

"Perhaps there's hope for the French state," Frank said later. "What they need is a politician like me to bring together the disparate elements of society."

And speaking of society, we paid a social call on Cornelia that wound up as a contest of wills and whiskey. Frank, although he was outclassed when it came to discussing French realist novels, drank poor Cornelia under the table. Edwards, the butler, had to help her upstairs. But as he was steering Cornelia to her bedroom, the butler leaned over the balcony, a smile on his face, and said to Frank, "Thank you, sir. Thank you very much indeed." Poor Cornelia. Those who live by the bottle die by the bottle. Or at least have to retire early.

I spent our last few days packing and trying to sell all the household items we had accumulated since September. The icebox went first, followed by the dishes, silverware, and linen. Stephen's stroller was a white elephant, so I decided to cart it with us as far as Deauville, where we were going for our final weeks in France.

I shook myself out of my reverie to call in my order to Gristede's. Checking off the list I had written on the back of an envelope, I quickly got that chore over and done with. In France, housewives toted the barge and lifted the bale all the live-long day. They had their own containers for wine, milk, water, and oil. Here everything was disposable, thank goodness, and storage space plentiful, so the incessant trips to the store were unnecessary. It was my theory that the stunningly beautiful French girls of eighteen were soon turned prematurely old at thirty-five because of all that lugging and hauling.

I drank another cup of coffee, which, by the way, was made in my trusty but battered percolator and tasted far superior to any in France. Then I told Stephen that it was too nice a day to stay inside.

"No," he said.

"Come on. Let's go feed the ducks."

"No."

That second no meant yes, I knew from experience, but Stephen just couldn't abide to utter the offending affirmative. The "Terrible Twos" were no worse than the "Onerous Ones"—just as I had predicted.

We grabbed a quarter loaf of stale bread and headed for the duck pond. I took Stephen's new, American-built stroller—one you pushed instead of pulled—but he insisted on pushing it himself instead of riding in it.

It was a magnificent fall day, still warm but the summer heat had lost its fierceness, heralding the cooler weather to come. We ran, skipped, hopped, leaped, jumped, and ambled down to the pond, depending on which gait Stephen favored at the moment. I had found that it was much easier to herd cats than to get a two-year-old to walk in a straight line. But we eventually arrived at the water's edge.

Stephen's former method of feeding the ducks was to eat the

bread himself and throw leaves to the poor hungry mallards. That changed, however, when he tried the same trick on a pair of visiting Canada geese. They took umbrage at his stinginess, bounded out of the water, brushed him aside, and ate the whole bag of bread. Stephen was more circumspect after that and shared at least half the bread with the birds.

Personally, I didn't see why the ducks and geese even wanted to eat American bread. It tasted terrible. The French, although they may have been a hundred years behind us in retailing, were two hundred years ahead of us in baking. There was simply no taste in our soft, spongy bread. Or in our chocolate. To savor a delicious *pain au chocolat,* I had to travel into New York City, shop in specialty stores, and spend a fortune. That had dramatically cut my consumption of both bread and chocolate, and I'm sure my waistline thanked me for it.

But if I missed the food in France, I missed Elise even more. Parting with her had been an ordeal for all of us. Stephen was weepy for weeks afterward, calling out her name piteously. John would constantly correct me, saying, "If Elise was here, she wouldn't do it that way." I don't know which bothered me more: the tears or the taunts.

We gave Elise a farewell present upon leaving—a beautiful leather pocketbook, as she seemed to admire mine so much. I hid a big tip in the purse, hoping she would find it long after we left town. I didn't ever want to go through another cake episode. If she insisted on being mad at me, I wanted to be four thousand miles away.

I was lost without her, but I knew we had made the right decision not to bring Elise with us. The cultural clash would have made us all unhappy. There was just too big a gulf between rural Montpellier and the suburbs of New York. Most of the time *I* felt like a country bumpkin in this prosperous little village. I couldn't imagine loving, trusting, thrifty Elise ever adjusting. She didn't know it, but I think we did her a favor by letting her remain in France. Still, I missed her dreadfully.

*   *   *

After leaving Montpellier, we had spent a week riding the rails, just touring around, which pleased me enormously. There's nothing like a long train ride to lift my spirits. The rhythmic rocking of the carriage also improved Stephen's sleeping habits, which was a blessing for us all. Eventually, we landed in Deauville on the English Channel. The weather was cold and rainy, but we became beach habitués nonetheless. John, however, needed some coaxing that first day.

"But I'll get wet," he said, looking out the window of our hotel at the driving rain and crashing surf.

"Not if you run between the raindrops and jump into the water before you get soaked," I said.

"Oh," he said. And he did.

I unpacked the bikini I had bought in Palavas and found that in Deauville it was more than conservative—it was downright Victorian. The girls on the beach wore practically nothing, and I looked like someone's spinster aunt. However, a month later, as a guest at a country club in New York, I was banned from the pool for being shockingly risqué. *Moi?* I was both exceedingly embarrassed and secretly thrilled that my French bathing costume would cause such a stir in the States. I felt very international. Mortified, but international.

We were treated royally in Deauville by a former Army Air Force friend of Frank's. Claude and his wife, Monique, couldn't have been nicer or more hospitable, and it was with a real sense of sadness that we left for Le Havre and boarded our ship, the *Liberté,* for the journey home.

What a big ship! You probably could have hung the poor, pokey little *Veendam* on the davits of the *Liberté* and used it as a lifeboat. Formerly the German luxury liner *Europa,* the *Liberté* was captured by the Americans in Bremerhaven and used as a troop transport from 1945 to 1946. Then it was handed over to the French by the United Nations in compensation for the loss of the *Normandie.* With their usual style and elegance, the French had refitted the ship using much of what had been salvaged from the *Normandie*. Even in second-class things were first-class.

Some things, however, remained the same. We left France as we had arrived, for I had picked up a painful rash on my poison ivy foot and was forced to wear a hideous pair of white socks with sandals. Then, on the day we sailed, Frank ordered a bottle of bon-voyage champagne that, although it hadn't been made in Montana, was flat and sheep-y tasting. Déjà vu? Who knew? *Au revoir,* France, we said with a limp and a grimace, *au revoir.*

"At least we're still alive," Frank said, standing on the deck. "And that was a near-run thing."

I was prepared with the leash to restrain Stephen, but I found that, amazingly, he would actually sit in a deck chair for long minutes at a time before running off. John, too, had lost his fascination for hanging over the fantail, and he had discovered a passion for shuffleboard. I even had the nerve to bring Stephen to the dining room for meals. What a difference a year made.

The big excitement aboard ship was the appearance of Sugar Ray Robinson, the prizefighter. Frank and John were agog when Mr. Robinson pulled up to the quay in a fuchsia Cadillac convertible. He was dripping with jewels and surrounded by a bevy of beautiful chorus girls. John and Frank went to see him work out in the ship's gym, though I think Frank was more interested in pulchritude than in punching.

"Have you seen Nice?" I caught him saying to one of the showgirls.

We had a rough crossing that rendered Frank, Stephen, and John hors de combat for most of the trip. I, on the other hand, must have had a cast-iron stomach, because the rolling of the ship bothered me not a whit. I was almost the only person in the dining room for two days running. Boy, did I feel like an old salt.

But I felt even older when I took a green-tinged John up on deck to air him out, despite the rolling seas and hammering rainstorm.

"I don't feel good, Mama," John said, holding his stomach.

And indeed, he had turned from charteuse to the color of Sugar Ray's Cadillac.

"You should go get your crayons," I said lightly, "and toss them into the ocean to make it blue again."

He looked at me with a pained expression. "That's not why the sea is blue, Mama," he said. "It's blue because of the refraction—"

"Okay, okay," I said, cutting him off. "I was just kidding."

But I wasn't. John was growing up and I hadn't even noticed.

The *Liberté* docked in Manhattan on a Friday morning, and we were met by the same intrepid people who had chased around the countryside to see us off. Our friend Eleanor drove us home. (*Home!* What a wonderful word.) She had stocked our house with food and made us a casserole so that I wouldn't have to unleash my culinary wizardry on our first night back. Frank thanked her effusively—rather too effusively, if you ask me.

Making the transition from France to the U.S. proved to be more difficult than I had imagined. Stephen, with his lack of English, had a terrible time adjusting. He clung to me like a vine, obviously confused about where he was and why. Worse, he cried for Elise all the time and promptly forgot everything he knew about toilet etiquette. But within a month he was speaking English regularly and had suddenly remembered what that great porcelain thing in the bathroom was for.

John, too, got off to a rocky start. The first day home he went out to play with a group of children who were busily building a mud fort. He came back minutes later, his lower lip quivering.

"They won't play with me," he said, tears forming in his eyes.

"Of course they will," I said. "Did you introduce yourself?"

"Yes," he said. "But they won't talk to me."

"What did you say?" I asked.

"*Bonjour. Je m'appelle Jeannot et—*"

"Hold it," I said. "You spoke to them in French?"

"Yes."

"Well, go back outside and try it again, in English this time," I said, in my optimistic voice.

I watched from the window as he shyly approached the muddy

children. I could see him working up the nerve to talk to them. Finally, he did, and within twenty seconds he was right in the middle of the bunch and twice as dirty as they were.

Sadly, he never again spoke French unless prompted by Frank or me. It was Frank's contention that we should take a hands-off approach when it came to encouraging bilingualism.

"We've probably screwed the boys up so badly that they'll become aphasic," he said. "They can learn French or Spanish or Latvian later, if they're interested."

I thought Frank was wrong, but he was the linguist, so I deferred to him. Still, I thought it would be a shame if they failed to build on their knowledge of French. I would have given anything to understand and to be understood in a foreign country.

Since our return, people had often asked me if I would spend a year in France again, knowing all I know now. That was easy to answer: No. But the question was beside the point. Before we left, I was happily ignorant about all the problems we would encounter, but I was equally ignorant of all the fun we would have and all the people we would meet.

A much wiser person than I once said that every journey is a journey of self-discovery. I found out that, as cowardly as I was, I could take all France could throw at me and live to tell the tale. I might have been intimidated by the local shopkeepers, but I usually got what I wanted. I might have made an exhibition of myself, but I like to think that I provided a little harmless entertainment. After all, it was not every day they got to see a negligee-clad lady rush out of the house, garbage pails in hand.

As I watched Stephen cheat the ducks out of half their breakfast, I wondered what was going on in Montpellier at that moment. It made me sad to think of Jules sitting all alone in the botanical gardens with no one to talk to and no one to buy ice cream for. Pascal, I knew, would miss his best customers and yearn for the days when Frank kept the joint jumping. And what of Sophie and René? Were they enjoying wedded bliss or were they repenting in leisure?

I had had a card from Elise informing me that her son had married and that the wedding had been a grand affair. I read the card to the boys, stunned to discover that they were already beginning to forget who she was. It took some prompting on my part to remind them of their special friend and how much she loved them.

And as silly as it was, I thought of Mme. Perrin and Maman at the general store. The O-la-la ladies had been shocked when I informed them of our departure from Montpellier.

"*Ah, ce n'est pas possible,*" the Madame had exclaimed. And she came around the counter to shake my hand. I felt she was really touched to see me go, for I had become a part of her scenery and no French person suffers change—even for the better—easily. Frank, of course, thought I was being ridiculously sentimental, remarking that Mme. Perrin probably never had it so good and hated to see the better part of her revenue leave town.

However, I prefer to think that she really did miss me, in spite of our occasional contretemps. I thought she enjoyed hearing my stories about the faraway land she would never see. I knew Sophie had, to my chagrin. And this winter, when the winds blow down on southern France and the sun ceases to be their friend and heating plant, I hope Mme. Perrin will put a few extra coals in the potbelly stove, for she and Maman are getting too old now for many more bouts with *la grippe.*

I also liked to think that when the women gathered for their daily shopping and gossiping hour they would find the time for a few smiles remembering "L'Américaine" who spoke such funny French and bought up all Mme. Perrin's old canned goods. They will never see my like again, and they were probably darned glad of it.

Our landlords, the Sausons, I trusted, would miss us, too. They weren't getting any younger either, and fighting fires all winter long must have taken its toll. I hoped they had rented our apartment to some long-suffering tenants like us. And I hoped it wouldn't be too much trouble for Mme. Sauson to say hello to Giles and Bruno, although I knew Bruno would miss his apple or carrot from me, if not the extra work that came with picking up my garbage.

Going to France was an adventure—an adventure not many

people would have risked. I hoped the boys, when they grew up, would appreciate everything we went through and profit from the trip. Living in Montpellier was a once-in-a-lifetime opportunity for all of us, and I'm glad we did it—though a second such adventure would probably do me in.

"Bad duck!" Stephen shouted, fending off an overzealous bird who was pecking at the bread bag.

"G-D duck," he muttered, unfortunately sounding just like his father.

These were the times that I would have preferred that Stephen spoke entirely in French. I never did catch on to French swear words, so I was totally immune to the cussing.

I reprimanded Stephen about his offensive language, a classic case of do as I say, not as your father does. Then we bade the ducks a cheery *au revoir* and pushed back through the village, this time with Stephen hanging on to the side of the stroller. We hadn't gone far when I saw a stranger staring back at me from a store window. She looked about as fashionable as a burlap bag. Worse, she had stringy hair, poor posture, and an air of desperation. Could that really be me? I wondered. What a bad reflection my reflection made on me. Had a life of confusion, bother, and grape jelly on my elbow made me into this hollowed-eyed creature? Oh, how I wished I had even a few hours of peace and quiet for myself.

I tore my gaze away in disgust, hoping I wouldn't run into anyone I knew. I couldn't bear it. Naturally, the next person I saw was my neighbor Anne. I looked at her greedily: Every hair was in place, her figure trim, her clothes the latest in fashion, and she smiled in a relaxed manner. Her children were grown up and visited on holidays. *What a life,* I thought.

"Hi, Anne," I said. "You're all dressed up."

"I'm on my way into town to do a bit of shopping," she said. "Then I'm having lunch with my husband."

"That sounds like heaven," I said, pulling Stephen off my leg.

She asked me about John and Stephen. Well, I couldn't help myself. A long recital of all the problems I had must have made her want to flee. But she was game and she listened to the end, for she had that priceless commodity: time.

When I had blown myself out, she smiled again and answered, "Well, my dear, just remember: Every day is one day less."

I understood what she meant, or thought I did. As each day passed, the children would become less and less dependent on me, and there would come a time when they would both be in school and gone for the day. Babies took more time than three-year-olds, three-year-olds more time than six-year-olds. Then one day the family nest would stop vibrating with constant activity. That sounded dreamy.

I got quite a lift just thinking about those fabulous, leisure-filled days to come. Then the boys would have perfect table manners, and never mislay vital things like shoes and jackets. They would always be clean and sparkling, and even Stephen would feed, dress, and entertain himself, and he would be completely housebroken—all the time.

Eventually, I dreamed they would be in college, earning straight A's in their courses, while I flitted tirelessly about my already spick-and-span house, flicking a dustcloth here and there with a graceful touch. Each day I would look exactly like the ads for a perfect young housewife as I stood in the doorway and welcomed home my adoring family, who would appreciate me fully and admire me extravagantly. I would be young and carefree with never a line of worry to mar my alabaster brow. Life would be one long round of fun-filled days. I would have eons of time to make myself the best-dressed, best-informed, and most charming of creatures in this world of Yet to Be. Why, I would even have a chance to do some serious writing about serious subjects, all accomplished in the serious quiet of my impeccably furnished office.

I was lost in thoughts of sublime tranquility when Stephen fell flat on his face. He was more scared than hurt, but I picked him up and comforted him as best I could. His howls, of course, attracted the usual concerned looks from passersby, but I ignored their stares. He had a little cut above his eyebrow that I stanched with my handkerchief, but he insisted on blotting the cut on my dress. So, bedraggled, bloody, and wailing, we continued our journey back to our equally bedraggled house. *Only one day less of this,* I thought grimly.

Then it occurred to me: Every day was one day less, it was true, but it was also one day less for me. I rolled that thought around in my mind with appalled fascination. I didn't like that idea at all, and I wondered if that was what Anne had meant me to know.

To achieve that golden time I was looking forward to would take years and years. My very best years. And if I were to live in a cocoonlike state until the children were grown, my emergence as a butterfly would look pretty silly. Whoever heard of a wizened, gray-haired butterfly?

Stephen looked up at me and gave me a tentative smile. I hugged him and smiled back, and I really put my heart into it. I didn't want to wish away my life for a quiet old age. Granted, these were the diaper, disorder, and discipline years, but how lonely it would be not to have a child to cuddle. How I would miss not having my boys to watch as they grew tall and strong. What sort of exchange had I been thinking about to leave the hectic madness of my present life for a spotless, lifeless home?

I resolved then and there to stop wishing my life away for a very dull, quiet future. Oh, there would still be days—days like today when everything seemed to go wrong from morning to night, days when I regretted that Frank hadn't taken the job in Paris. A live-in couple and Elise would have made life bliss.

I tried to think of peace and quiet as imported products, like French bread and chocolate, to be savored only occasionally and at terrific expense, but I wouldn't ever wish to trade my life away. I'd hurdle those days as they came, for I knew then that, truly, each day *is* one day less for all of us.

I admit my philosophy isn't all that original or profound, but then, what can you expect from someone who serves swan for Thanksgiving dinner and sends her son to school in a laundry truck?

Acknowledgments

Obviously, this book could never have been written if my mother hadn't had the foresight to record our adventures in France and delight in recounting them to me when I was a child. Her insights and humor made a difficult trip worthwhile. I'm only sorry that she didn't live to see the publication of *French Impressions*. I like to think she would have approved.

My father deserves a share of the credit—or blame. Without his tenuous grasp on reality, the trip to France would have been impossible—indeed, ludicrous. But I have to commend him on not becoming a fountain pen mogul. If I had grown up in Paris, I would now be an aged international kid and not a Yankee fan.

I met my brother, Stephen, for a drink recently and asked him if he would like to be mentioned in the acknowledgments. After all, it was his damp, howling passage through France that provided much of the material for this book. "Frankly," he said, "I'd rather have a hundred dollars." Too late, Steve. Consider yourself mentioned. I need the money for Yankee tickets.

But the driving force behind this book was my sister. And I mean "driving." In the introduction to Montpellier, when I mentioned that the Oeuf (the open pedestrian mall) was closed to traffic, I neglected to say that my sister and brother-in-law, in an amazing feat of automotive tourism or perhaps terrorism, blithely drove across the crowded piazza, oblivious to the local cops chasing them.

On their first pass they marveled at the lack of traffic and waved cheerily to the gendarmes, who were waving back frantically at them. On their second tour of the Oeuf, they drove slowly, looking for a good place to have lunch. The cops got closer but just missed them. Finally, on their third circuit, they began to wonder why several hundred people were shaking their fists at them. The French, they knew, could be cool toward tourists, but this display was downright rude. So they slowed down, allowing the official Montpellier police golf cart to overtake them.

After much shouting, gesticulating, and bad language (both intentional and unintentional), the French fuzz let them off with a stern warning.

That incident led to the genesis of this book, a project that never would have been completed without the help of my sister, Susan Littell Johnpeter.

Although she wasn't born until long after these events, she was my ace researcher, picture editor, and invaluable consultant.

I would also like to thank Kim Easley for her crisp translation of technical materials; Xavier Clairardin for his patient work on the "Little Engine" section; Irene and Laurent Boulu for their hospitality and valuable information about life in Montpellier; and to Audrey LaFehr, the bravest editor in New York—for more reasons than one.

Any errors in the text are mine alone.